MUSIC THERAPY FOR HANDICAPPED CHILDREN

Volume III

Multihandicapped
Orthopedically Handicapped
Other Health Impaired

Wanda B. Lathom
Charles T. Eagle, Jr.
Editors

MUSIC THERAPY FOR HANDICAPPED CHILDREN
Vol. III: Multihandicapped, Orthopedically Handicapped,
Other Health Impaired
Wanda B. Lathom & Charles T. Eagle, Jr., editors

PRINTED IN USA
ISBN: 0-918812-78-X

Library of Congress Catalog Card No: 84:72744
Printers: Rose Printing, Inc., Tallahassee, Florida
2nd printing: June, 1994

For further information and catalogs, contact:

MMB Music, Inc.
Contemporary Arts Building
3526 Washington Avenue
Saint Louis, MO 63103-1019

Phone: (314) 531-9635, (800) 543-3771 (USA/Canada)

CONTENTS

MONOGRAPH 1

MUSIC THERAPY FOR MULTIHANDICAPPED CHILDREN, Sr. Mariam Pfeifer

MONOGRAPH 2

MUSIC THERAPY FOR ORTHOPEDICALLY HANDICAPPED CHILDREN, Mary Toombs Rudenberg

MONOGRAPH 3
MUSIC THERAPY FOR OTHER HEALTH IMPAIRED CHILDREN,
Lenore M. Schwankovsky, Perry T. Guthrie

ILLUSTRATIVE FIGURES

MONOGRAPH 1

MONOGRAPH 2

THE PROJECT MUSIC MONOGRAPH SERIES
Foreword

The monographs in this series were prepared to be used in a "Special Project: A National In-Service Training Model for Educational Personnel Providing Music Education/Therapy for Severely/Profoundly Handicapped Children." This grant (No. G007091336) was made to the National Association for Music Therapy, Inc. and was funded by the Office of Special Education. The workshop trainers were Registered Music Therapists (RMTs) who were selected to attend one of the two National In-Service Training Institutes in Music Therapy held in Denton, Texas in June, 1980 and in 1981.

During the First Institute (1980) and the year following, during which in-service workshops were given, it became apparent that more detailed information was needed concerning music therapy for specific diagnostic categories listed under the general area of "Severely-Profoundly Handicapped Children." Although the Institute participants demonstrated expertise in the area(s) in which they were employed, they needed more information to use in in-service workshops for personnel who worked with children from other diagnostic categories. Thus, some of the participants were asked to write monographs to provide information on this area.

Before the Second Institute (1981), the first draft of each monograph was sent to Wanda Lathom, Project Director, and Charles Eagle, Training Coordinator. They provided editorial comments and asked external reviewers for further suggestions. These led to the second draft, which was presented to the Second Institute.

Participants for the Second Institute were selected to work in modular units: (1) a team leader who was the author of a monograph, (2) a music therapist who had carefully reviewed the music therapy literature of the area, (3) a clinician currently working in the area who could demonstrate techniques, and (4) a clinician currently working in the area who could demonstrate assessment techniques. Each team member made a presentation to the entire Institute and each team carefully reviewed the monograph related to their area. Thus, the entire Institute evaluated each monograph and the contributions of members of the modular team. This peer review was of great value in preparation of the third draft of the monograph, which included suggestions and material submitted by the modular team of other colleagues who could contribute to the contents. These drafts then were submitted to the Project Director and Training Coordinator for editorial review, and individual conferences were held with each author during a grant meeting held in Denver (November, 1981) after the annual conference of the National Association for Music Therapy. The fourth, and final, revisions were submitted by the authors in January, 1982. Thus, each monograph represents extensive work by the primary author and considerable peer review and contributions from music therapists throughout the country.

Each of the monographs presents some of the pertinent music therapy research of the area, although a complete report would have been beyond the scope of some of the monographs. However, each author assumed the responsibility to review an extensive body of literature relevant to the area.[1] Through case histories, examples of techniques, and discussion, each author has made the relevance of this literature evident.

The monographs were initially written to accompany the goals and objectives for inservice training, as stated in *A Manual to Conduct In-Service Training Workshops for Music Educators, Administrators, Parents, and Special Educators*. However, it has become obvious that the monographs will be of use to practicing clinicians, colleagues in related treatment areas, and to students who plan to enter the profession of music therapy. In most areas, it is particularly apparent that additional research is needed. Many suggestions are offered by the authors for researchers who wish to pursue this endeavor.

The challenge for our continued scholarly growth, both while working as students and as practicing music therapists, was stated by E. Thayer Gaston (1964):[3]

> This striving for continued learning, probably by avid reading, after formal education, ought to be a primary activity in the continued growth of music therapists. The constant goal of becoming a scholar should be prominent in every training program. It is an ingredient of the educative process that needs day-by-day emphasis. It should not be left to chance. To leave it out is to insist that students shall not go beyond their teachers.

As music therapists continue to study, to conduct research, and to share information, both within the profession and with others who attend in-service training workshops, the continued growth of the profession and the subsequent improved service to handicapped children will not "be left to chance."

[1]This search was aided by two working drafts of *Music therapy for handicapped children: An annotated and indexed bibliography* by Charles Eagle, which was published as part of the grant project. Other publications emanating from the project were *Music therapy: A behavioral guide for the mentally retarded* by Clifford K. Madsen, *An assessment manual in music therapy* by Donald E. Michel and Michael Rohrbacher, and *The role of music therapy in the education of handicapped children and youth* by Wanda Lathom.

[2]Lathom, W. (Proj. Dir.). *A manual to conduct in-service training workshops in MUSIC THERAPY for music educators, administrators, parents, and special educators* (rev. ed.). Lawrence, KS: National Association for Music Therapy, 1981.

[3]Gaston, E. T. Developments in the training of music therapists. *Journal of Music Therapy,* 1964, *1*(4), 148-150.

THE PROJECT MUSIC MONOGRAPH SERIES
Authors and Editors

MUSIC THERAPY FOR HANDICAPPED CHILDREN:

DEAF—BLIND. **Sr. Lucille Cormier, RMT,** Department of Music, College Misericordia, Dallas, Pennsylvania.

EMOTIONALLY DISTURBED. **Darlene Watson Paul, RMT,** Conservatory of Music, University of Missouri at Kansas City.

HEARING IMPAIRED. **Jean Buechler, RMT,** Broward Exceptional Adult Education, Ft. Lauderdale, Florida.

MENTALLY RETARDED. **Sara A. Carter, RMT,** Sunland Center, Tallahassee, Florida.

MULTI-HANDICAPPED. **Sr. Mariam Pfeifer, RMT,** St Joseph's Center and Marywood College, Scranton, Pennsylvania.

ORTHOPEDICALLY HANDICAPPED. **Mary Toombs Rudenberg, RMT,** Moody School, University of Texas Medical Branch, Galveston.

OTHER HEALTH IMPAIRED. **Lenore M. Schwankovsky, RMT,** and **Perry T. Guthrie,** Department of Music, California University at Long Beach.

SPEECH IMPAIRED. **Susan Gurvich Miller, RMT,** Department of Music Therapy, Southern Methodist University, Dallas, Texas.

VISUALLY IMPAIRED. **Peggy Codding, RMT,** Department of Music, University of Wisconsin at Eau Claire.

AN ANNOTATED AND INDEXED BIBLIOGRAPHY. **Charles T. Eagle, Jr., RMT,** Department of Music Therapy, Southern Methodist University, Dallas, Texas.

EDITORS: Wanda B. Lathom, Ph.D., RMT, Professor of Music Therapy, Conservatory of Music, University of Missouri at Kansas City.
Charles T. Eagle, Jr., Ph.D., RMT, LPC, Division of Music, Southern Methodist University, Dallas, Texas.

PREFACE

Less than two years ago (October, 1982), the 1st Edition of the Project MUSIC Monograph Series was published. This 10-part monograph set, entitled *Music Therapy for Handicapped Children,* was one of several outcomes of a three-year, federally funded grant in music therapy. Over 200 practicing music therapists contributed directly to these monographs. Each of the authors has extensive clinical and academic experience and is expert in working with the handicapped about which s/he writes. The authors have spoken from the heart, candidly describing their professional experiences.

In the monographs, you will find clinical descriptions of the handicapped person, *how* the person can be clinically assessed, and *how* the music therapist works with this person. The monographs also contain research reports and theoretical positions, and outlines of activities and case studies, as well as illustrations, glossaries, and extensive lists of references. Examples are presented of progress notes and IEPs/IHPs. Stated goals, objectives, and techniques are also included.

The response to the monographs has been beyond our expectations. Music therapy clinicians, teachers, and administrators have been enthusiastic in their support of this Project. Other professionals have also been supportive, such as special educators, music educators, arts therapists, and parents of handicapped children.

For the 2nd Edition, we decided to combine the monographs into four volumes. *Volume 1* contains the three monographs on music therapy for hearing impaired, visually impaired, and deaf-blind children; *Volume 2,* music therapy for emotionally disturbed, mentally retarded, and speech impaired children; *Volume 3,* music therapy for multi-handicapped, orthopedically handicapped, and other health impaired children; *Volume 4,* an annotated and indexed bibliography of publications pertaining to music therapy for handicapped children. In all the volumes, the contextual essence of the original, 1st Edition, has been retained. This 2nd Edition has been edited primarily for structural and typographical errors and in some instances, for organizational purposes to allow for more cohesion.

There are many very nice people who have made this 2nd Edition of the monographs a reality. In particular, we extend our grateful appreciation to Dr. Lindsey Merrill, Dean of the Conservatory of Music, Dr. Jack Stephenson, Chairman of the Department of Music Education/Therapy, and Professor George Petrie, all of the University of Missouri at Kansas City; to Dr. Eugene Bonelli, Dean of the Meadows School of the Arts, Dr. Charles Joseph, Chairman of the Division of Music, and Dr. Ann Redmond, Department of Music Therapy, all of Southern Methodist University in Dallas, Texas; and to our graduate assistants at our two universities.

There are six persons who have been especially important and supporting to us as we continued the Project. John and Helen Miniter worked diligently and successfully to fulfill the requests of those who wanted the 1st Edition of the monographs, which was published through the Institute for Therapeutics Research. Steve Meseraull, who printed the 1st Edition and now publishes the 2nd, has been a tower of support. Paul Ackerman has been there from the beginning. Ruth Lathom and Pat Eagle have been concerned, caring, and loving throughout our efforts.

To all these lovely folks, we can only offer our thanks. To the hundreds of significant others, we owe a great deal and wish to express our deep gratitude for your understanding, close attention, and personal commitment to this work.

Kansas City   Wanda Lathom
Dallas   Charles Eagle

August, 1984

MONOGRAPH 1

MUSIC THERAPY FOR MULTIHANDICAPPED CHILDREN

Sr. Mariam Pfeifer

ACKNOWLEDGMENTS

Special gratitude is expressed to:

The principals of the project, Dr. Wanda Lathom, RMT, Project Director, and Dr. Charles Eagle, RMT, Training Coordinator, for providing the opportunity and recommendations necessary for the completion of this work. Co-members of the panel dealing with the multihandicapped at the Second NAMT/OSE National In-Service Training Institute, Denton, Texas 1981, namely: Betty Shirm, RMT; Eileen Kramer, RMT; and Robin Jackman, RMT for their unifying team work.

For continual support, collaboration, and guidance of members of the Congregation of the Sisters, Servants of the Immaculate Heart of Mary, particularly to Sister Marian Denise Walsh, IHM, Administrator of St. Joseph's Center, Scranton, Pennsylvania; Sister Davida Sullivan, IHM for her suggestions, encouragement, and special editing skills; and to Sister Mariel Dougher, IHM for her interest and many hours of typing.

To all the special children at St. Joseph's Center, especially Roxanne, Liza, and Bev, and to the staff members who have given special help: Kathy Norton for her excellent photography and Denise Schaffer, Music Therapy Student/Aide from Marywood College for her continual assistance.

To my teachers at Marywood College and Dr. Richard M. Graham, RMT, University of Georgia who provided me with their high standards of education and a special thanks to Ms. Janet Murphy, RMT, Clinical Training Supervisor at Westchester Developmental Center, Wingdale, New York for her invaluable training that is reflected in this monograph.

INTRODUCTION TO THE DISABILITY

Rationale for Music Therapy

The results of music therapy with the multihandicapped have sometimes been described as "minor miracles," but how can anything be "minor" that helps a child find life more meaningful and channels his emotions into a happier vein? The meaningful and the emotional are intertwined. Just as nonhandicapped people find a vent for their emotions in listening to music or engaging in some sort of artistic activity, so these special people are led by the art of music into various moods—into storm or calm, anxiety or peace, tension or relaxation, sorrow or joy. Music, an expression of mankind throughout the world, speaks to and elicits a response from those to whom no words of any spoken language are yet meaningful. Music therapy helps these multihandicapped children to engage in a world outside themselves, not by beating meaninglessly against it and against themselves, but by using arms, hands, and legs, by using their whole beings to grasp, kick, and vocalize in response to something outside themselves.

Music comes to us with an aura of fun. As Nordoff and Robbins(1971), authors of *Therapy in Music for Handicapped Children*, say:

> Music is a universal experience in the sense that all can share in it; its fundamental elements of melody, harmony and rhythm appeal to, and engage their related psychic functions in each one of us. Its message, the content of its expression, can encompass all heights and depths of human experience, all shades of feeling. Music can lead or accompany the psyche through all conditions of inner experience, whether these be superficial and relatively commonplace or profound and deeply personal. For the child who is intellectually impaired, music and music activities can be vivid, intelligible experiences that require no abstract thought. For the emotionally immature or disturbed child, the experience of the emotional language of music is inviting; the self-subsistence of its melodies and forms provide security for him. Musical activity can motivate the physically disabled child to use his limbs or voice expressively; its rhythmic-melodic structures then support his activity and induce an order in his control that promotes coordination. Music, therefore, becomes a sphere of experience, a means of intercommunication and a basis for activity in which handicapped children can find freedom, in varying degrees, from the malfunctions that restrict their lives. As such, music possesses inherent capacities for effecting a uniquely significant contact with handicapped children. (p. 15-16)

In her publication, *The Role of Music Therapy in the Education of Handicapped Children*, Lathom (1980) answers the question: Why arts programs for the handicapped?

> Children's handicaps can limit their experiences and perceptions of the world. Arts experiences provide an opportunity for children to sort through the bulk of sensory information they receive and allow them to participate actively in their sensory environments. The philosophy of the National Committee, Arts for the Handicapped has stated: "Creative arts experiences can be a powerful vehicle for providing beauty and joy to children burdened by physical, emotional, or mental handicapping conditions. Recent research indicates that increased achievement in sensory, psychomotor, cognitive, and affective skills may be obtained through regular participation in arts activities." (p. 52)

These quotations indicate some of the reasons why music therapy is of vital importance in the treatment of the multihandicapped.

Purpose of this Monograph

The major purpose of this monograph is to express the ways music therapy intervention can help in the development of severely/profoundly handicapped (S/PH). This subdivides into: (1) sharing the philosophy of a facility with a high quality, comprehensive program for S/PH, (2) presenting some general music therapy procedures and techniques used with multihandicapped children, (3) showing how music therapy has served to improve and maintain mental and physical health of the multihandicapped through three specific case studies, (4) showing how music therapy helps to develop basic learning skills—communicative, academic, motor, emotional, and social.

Nicholas and Gilbert (1980) assessed "attitudes toward music therapy research" (p. 209). They found that,

> Despite this generally positive attitude toward research, music therapists surveyed expressed dissatisfaction with the current status of research in the field. For example 75 percent of the subjects claimed that research studies appearing in the literature were not relevant to their daily functioning as music therapists. Similarly, 64 percent felt that current research was not concerned with real-world problems; a chi-square test here revealed significant response differences (p< .01) between clinicians and university teaching personnel, with the clinicians reporting significantly less practicality of research. An even higher overall percentage (18.3%) agreed that more music therapists would be interested in experimental results if researchers concentrated their studies on practical problems. (p. 210)

As most of the content of this monograph consists of "experimental results" and "practical problems" together with techniques aimed at their solutions, perhaps music therapists will find this work "relevant to their daily functioning as music therapists."

Definition of Terms

According to "A Career in Music Therapy" (1980), a brochure of the National Association for Music Therapy, Inc., music therapy is:

> the use of music in the accomplishment of therapeutic aims; the restoration, maintenance and improvement of mental and physical health. It is the systematic application of music, as directed by the music therapist in a therapeutic environment, to bring about desirable changes in behavior. Such changes enable the individual undergoing therapy to experience a greater understanding of himself and the world about him, thereby achieving a more appropriate adjustment to society. (p. 1)

Public Law 94-142 defines multihandicapped as follows:

> Multihandicapped means concomitant impairments (such as mentally retarded-blind, mentally retarded-orthopedically impaired, etc.), the combination of which causes such severe educational problems that they cannot be accommodated in special education programs solely for one of the impairments. The term does not include deaf-blind children. (*Federal Register*, 1977, p. 42478)

Haring and Brown (1976), writing about the mentally retarded, list several of their characteristics. A presentation of these characteristics may help to develop the above definition, since most S/PH are multihandicapped, the list is valuable to those dealing with the population referred to in this monograph. The list of characteristics is as follows:

1. Physical defects are numerous and often severe, i.e., impaired vision, hearing, and mechanisms for motor coordination.
2. May fail to attain an upright and mobile position in space or become ambulatory.
3. May show gross underdevelopment or complete unawareness of the environment.
4. Often display extreme infantile-type behavior.
5. Frequently are unable to interact or communicate with their physical and social environment.
6. Often speech remains undeveloped although sounds are made.
7. Care of bodily functions pose serious problems, i.e., there is absence of feeding and toileting skills.
8. Most often cannot guard themselves against the most common physical dangers. (p. 112)

Because there seems to be some difficulty in distinguishing among the terms *goals, activities, techniques, procedures* and *style,* an explanation of how they are used is given. Maximum maintenance, rehabilitation, happiness, and development of the person are long-term *goals* in working with multihandicapped children. To arrive at these goals, various objectives are utilized for hourly, daily, and monthly intervention, for instance, *activities* that might lead to rehabilitation of the client's use of his hand. Since in the beginning, the client may have little, if any, ability to control the use of his hand, the therapist might work at grasping. This grasping becomes a nearer goal or more immediate goal, or short-term goal, or *objective.* However (and this is where the confusion lies), once the client achieves the goal of grasping effectively, this goal or objective becomes a stepping stone in an activity that may be used to attain other goals. Sometimes these activities are termed *techniques* or *procedures.* However, the technique or procedure is something done by the therapist, not the client; it is the how and the what in which the therapist is engaged while working with the client to help him attain a goal. For instance, the therapist might point to a drumstick to indicate that the client should grasp it; or the therapist might tell him to grasp it, or might pick up the stick himself and bend the fingers of the client around it. The foregoing are performed by the therapist and are his techniques or procedures. So also, whether the therapist uses a gentle voice, a "therapeutic" voice, or a harsh voice is a matter of technique. The way the therapist goes about helping the client achieve goals is also technique. In fact, on another level, this might even be called *style.* In other words, the pianist practices scales, etc., to arrive at orthodox technique but his own personal achievement and use of this technique might be called *style.* Finally, it must be emphasized that goals once achieved may become activities for achieving other goals.

PRINCIPLES, GOALS, AND ASSOCIATED ACTIVITIES

According to Gaston (1968), the three primary principles of music therapy are:

1. The establishment or re-establishment of interpersonal relationships.
2. The bringing about of self-esteem through self-actualization.
3. The utilization of the unique potential of rhythm to energize and bring order. (p.v)

Of course, the establishment of interpersonal relationships can be brought about by a person relating in some pleasant way to the client. The therapist brings to the relationship not only musical skill and therapy technique, but an engaging personality and a tremendous amount of energy. Self-esteem through self-actualization is brought about by a sense of accomplishment, that is, by expressing oneself in some way—indeed by trying to do something and succeeding. Both the therapist and the music must entice the child to action. However, the will to accomplish is only half the battle. One must find the energy and physical ability somewhere and use it meaningfully. Rhythm has moved armies to the sound of the drum. And rhythm is perhaps the most important factor in helping to move some ineffective limbs of children in the directions needed and desired.

In addition to Gaston's three principles, Eagle (1978) has included a fourth primary principle:

4. Cultivating an awareness of, sensitivity to, appreciation for, and satisfaction from beauty through experiential involvement with MUSIC.

Certainly, any sincere music therapist would be inspired to achieve the actualization of this principle, which along with the other three, seems unique among all therapies to music therapy.

If we would consider the above four principles to be ultimate goals of the music therapist, some of the more immediate goals and means of arriving at these include development in the area of auditory, visual, tactile, perceptual, sensorimotor, communication, and academic skills, as well as more appropriate emotional and social skills. It is important to remember that while the therapist may focus on one specific skill area, no one area ever excludes another.

Auditory Training

In the area of *auditory* training the following musical variations may be considered:

- Changing timbre, rhythm, tempo and dynamics to elicit reactions of pleasure or displeasure.
- Imitating changes in pitch and rhythmic beat initiated by the therapist to strengthen auditory recall.
- Imitating rhythm patterns to improve auditory sequencing.

Visual and Tactile Skills

Some musical exercises aimed at *visual* and *tactile* perceptual skills are:

- Playing of resonator bells placed parallel and perpendicular to the child.
- Playing "hello" bells (F and B♭) for the ear, white and black for the eye, and the feel of various sized mallets for the touch, then playing these bells placed together, three inches apart, and then six inches apart.
- Imitating the therapist playing specific tone bars on the metallophone.
- Discriminating various instruments and playing them.

Motor Coordination

Development of *motor* coordination can be divided into skills involving gross and fine motor, diaphragmatic breathing, and visual tracking:

Gross Motor

- Beating of a steady tempo.
- Producing a ringing sound on the resonator bells.
- Reaching for instruments.
- Clapping hands.
- Strumming the Autoharp.

Fine Motor

- Grasping of mallets varying in diameter from 1/4 inch to 1-3/4 inches.
- Using pincer grasp (holding a plectrum) to strum the Autoharp.

Diaphragmatic Breathing

- Allowing the child to feel and imitate the rhythmic pulse of the kalimba or resonator bells played on the chest.
- Producing an 84 decibel tone for one to three seconds on a single reed horn.

Language Development

Communication and *language* (development may be divided into pre-verbal expression, receptive and expressive language):

Pre-Verbal Expression

- Eliciting any kind of vocal play or vocal sound through music stimuli.
- Imitating syllables or specific sounds: *oh, ah, ba, hi, da, de,* etc.
- Beating the syllables of names, or the words *hello, bye, good-bye, good morning,* etc.
- Vocalizing a sequence of several sounds (about five or six).

Receptive Language

- Receiving the word message and responding to it to indicate understanding, i.e., the child follows simple directions with one verbal prompt, such as "Clap your hands," "Liza, beat the drum," "Let's play the cymbal."
- Child pointing to a requested instrument, object, person, body part, color, etc.

Expressive Language

- Singing "hello," "good-bye," "a name," or the name of an instrument.
- Identifying names, objects, colors, or body parts by singing and signing.
- Singing the phrase with feeling, using vowel sounds when articulation is a problem.
- Signing and singing specific songs.

Academic Skills

Academic skills may include working with numbers, vocabulary, and developing other cognitive skills:

Numbers

- Beating the drum one or two times as indicated by therapist.
- Shaking the jingle clogs three times.
- Counting rhythmically numbers 1-10 while beating the drum.

Vocabulary

- Pointing to requested body parts.
- Identifying body parts by name.
- Naming and recalling instruments that are played by blowing, shaking, strumming, beating, etc.
- Identifying colors.
- Identifying musical symbols, such as quarter, half, and whole notes and indicating the concept of each by playing an instrument or clapping.

Emotions Training

Training of the *emotions* is both nonverbal expression in structured situations and development of spontaneity and creativity:

- Demonstrating complete rhythmic freedom by synchronously beating the drum with the therapist between 48 and 204 beats per minute, responding sensitively to tempo and dynamic changes of improvisation of therapist.
- Actively responding to the stimulation of music with physical affect indicating excitement, pleasure, or other emotional responses.
- Developing a musical-dramatic experience by singing or playing the drum as a means of venting one's innermost feelings.

Social Skills

Music is a *social* activity. The group setting is of great value in fostering social skills. These include developing a good self-concept, the ability to get along well with others, a sense of responsibility, and good judgment:

- Acquiring an awareness of self and others through group music activities involving interaction.
- Developing awareness of body image, position in space, laterality, directionality and body parts through movement activities.
- Acquiring responsibility in a group by participating in an instrumental ensemble involving taking turns, following directions, and functioning independently in appropriate music activities.

The foregoing gives some idea of day-to-day goals and some activities that may help the therapist meet them. How the therapist achieves these goals is partly a matter of the personal style of the therapist. The quality and appropriate selection of expressive music for use in accomplishing these goals is paramount.

FUNCTION OF A MUSIC THERAPY DEPARTMENT

In the event that the reader or the future music therapist may have the exciting challenge of establishing a music therapy department, a few words about the functioning of an effective department are in order. Consider in the example below the philosophy of a music therapy department at a treatment and education center for multihandicapped children. Also notice how the individualized education program (IEP) is determined.

Philosophy of the Department

The music therapy department incorporates the basic philosophy of this center for multihandicapped children, that is, "acceptance" and "compassion," seeing beauty in the midst of deformity, hope at the heart of each handicap . . ." The personnel of the department reinforce these ideals by identifying with the basic belief of Nordoff (1976), that in the depths of the child, handicapped or otherwise, there is an individuality that is not deformed and that every child can become a music child regardless of handicap. Through the nonthreatening, stimulating, or relaxing elements music can provide, the child becomes more skillful in his physical, motoric music activities, and/or in uses of his voice. With this mastery comes self-confidence. With self-confidence comes the ability to do still more, and the ability to express more freely this undeformed core within.

Music therapy in this facility is, therefore, believed to be a process whereby a skilled professional is able to create a therapeutic atmosphere or environment and use music to bring about a desirable change in the behavior of the individual client. By "skilled professional," one understands a person who has the ability to select the proper music and use it purposefully; however, the skilled professional must reflect in his personality the humane idea emphasized in the department's philosophy in order that his/her work may be effective in the development of the child.

Development of the IEP

At this treatment and education center for multihandicapped children, the method of arriving at an IEP involves an interdisciplinary team composed of a psychologist who is the chairperson of the group, developmental pediatrician, nurse or direct care assistant, special educator, communication disorders specialist, speech therapist, recreation therapist, social worker, physical therapist, occupational therapist, and music therapist. At meetings of the interdisciplinary team, the facilitator for the individual resident reads the results of the last team meeting concerning a particular child. Then, each member presents an evaluation of the child, stressing his strengths and needs. This data serves to establish the present level of the child's performance, which is stated in the IEP. From these data, the team establishes or re-establishes long-term and short-term goals. Each member of the team determines objectives, procedures for accomplishing them, and assessments for evaluation within his/her own discipline.

Parents are invited and often attend these meetings; however, if they are unable to attend, they receive a copy of the minutes and the proposed IEP for their approval.

CASE STUDIES

All three case studies that follow give credence to the fact that music therapy intervention contributes to the total development of multihandicapped children. However, just as each child is different and each child's problems are different, so too, there are important variations in each study that follows.

Case Study of Roxanne

In the first case study, that of Roxanne, after describing the medical and social background, the therapist has traced progress over a period of four years. This includes base-line data from the initial assessment, program plans, and four annual progress reports.

Basing her report on direct observation, case history and immediate information, the pediatrician analyzed the condition of six-year-old Roxanne as follows: chronic, nonprogressive encephalopathy, possible microcephalia, mental and physical retardation, hypotonia, and autistic-like behavior. What was obvious to all was that Roxanne's eye contact was fleeting, inconsistent, and more often than not, seemingly meaningless. Her day was spent in the self-stimulating behavior of tapping her right hand to her mouth and the left hand to the side of her head. When extremely frustrated, she resorted to hitting her face with both hands, which often resulted in lesions to the face and head. Much of the time, the use of mittens or arm splints was necessary to restrain her from this self-abusive behavior. There seemed to be a consensus based upon the reports (and indeed verified by the music therapist's own observation and report) that the IEP should be directed toward establishing eye contact, vocalizing, grasping, and redirecting Roxanne's inappropriate behavior.

The music therapist's contribution to the IEP consisted of her own report based on observation, attention to the observations of others on the team, and analysis of what music therapy could do to help this child. Observations consisted of the following experimental procedures:

1. The therapist established a base line from which to work by having an aide use a hand tally counter to determine the number of times Roxanne touched her hands to her mouth in a specified period of time.

2. The results of 20-minute sessions calculated in 10-minute blocks were recorded. The division into 10-minute blocks was made in order to determine whether such variables as warm-up time or lack of attention after a given period had any significant bearing upon Roxanne's behavior. The 10-minute periods did not reveal any significant pattern. (See Figure 1.) The initial calculation as indicated on the graph was 358 times in her first 20-minute therapy session. Roxanne's second session showed a decrease of her hand-tapping behavior to 260 times. After ten sessions this behavior was calculated at 150 times in a 20-minute period during the intervention of music therapy. (See Figure 2.)

In addition, a checklist was used which documented Roxanne's responses to musical instruments. These responses included awareness and attention, as well as the ability to grasp, manipulate, and coordinate while performing on each instrument. In working with multihandicapped children, it is important to note whether the above responses have been elicited with full assistance or shaping, minimal assistance or independently. This assessment was also included to determine her present level of performance. This information, necessary to determine Roxanne's strengths and needs, helps the therapist establish goals for the child.

The music therapist's role in writing the IEP and in implementing it included her plan of action appropriate to her own discipline. In this case, it consisted of suggesting music activities that involved increasing eye contact, vocalizing, grasping, occupying the attention of Roxanne, and involving her hands to redirect her undesirable behavior.

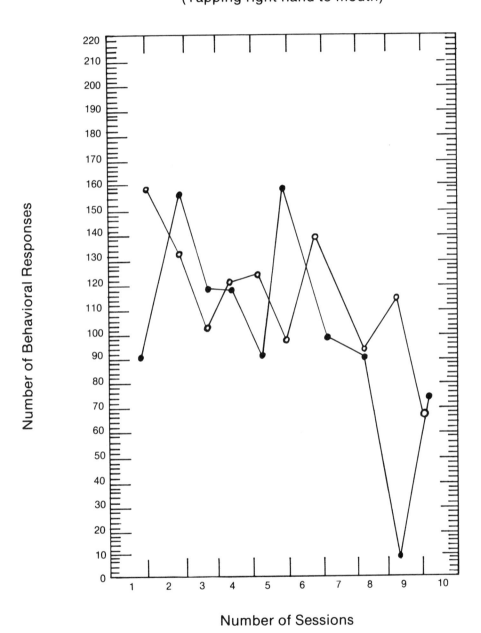

Behavioral Pattern—Roxanne
(Tapping right hand to mouth)

FIGURE 1
Baseline Data in Two 10-Minute Blocks

- ● First 10 minutes of session
- ○ Second 10 minutes of session

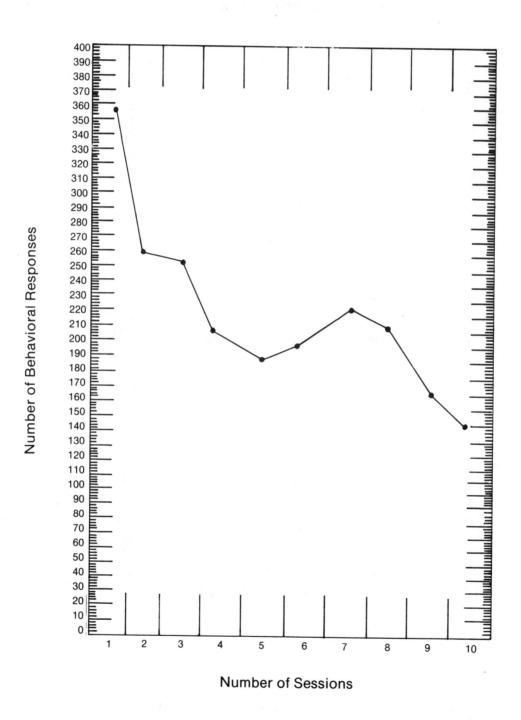

Behavioral Pattern—Roxanne
(Tapping right hand to mouth)

FIGURE 2
Baseline Data in 20-Minute Sessions

The implementation of strategies directed toward these goals was a matter of time and patience, of moving forward a little at a time, and of disappointing regression, although there was a positive general movement in the direction of improvement. An attempt was made to provide a consistent, structured program.

Before music therapy activities were addressed, attention was directed toward improvement brought about when both the music and the music therapist interested and pleased the child. In turn, this provided motivation for eye contact, grasping, socializing, directing of attention toward instruments, music, and people rather than toward inappropriate forms of behavior.

Roxanne's initial music therapy program was planned and the following behavioral objectives were implemented in October, 1977 and were met on the dates indicated:

1. Roxanne will make eye contact with the therapist 10 times per 20-minute session with 100 percent accuracy in 10 trials. (Objective met 3-2-78.)
2. Roxanne will "play" the piano using both hands three times during the "Hello" and "Good-bye" songs with 100 percent accuracy in 10 trials. (Objective met 4-2-78.)
3. Roxanne will play the tambourine on her left hand for six consecutive beats with 80 percent accuracy in 10 trials. (Objective met 3-2-78.)

April, 1978, Roxanne received individual music therapy twice a week and participated in group music/recreation activity twice a month. Although Roxanne received a few music therapy sessions during July, 1977, her regularly scheduled assessment sessions began in mid-September, 1977. Not only did Roxanne's eye-contact improve, but she responded readily to her name, giggled, and began to make some vocal sounds.

On several occasions, Roxanne attended to the entire "Hello" and "Good-bye" songs without resorting to her usual hand-tapping-to-head-and-mouth behavior, but rather played the piano keys in cluster chords, looked at the therapist, or placed her hands on the therapist's hands and helped to make music.

Roxanne played the "Tambourine Song" with her hand for a full verse (16 measures), playing up to 34 consecutive beats with her left hand independently without resorting to putting her right hand toward her mouth, or played up to three or four beats with both hands. Overall, it seemed that music therapy was the key opening the door to a new world of awareness for Roxanne—a positive and enjoyable experience.

Keeping the same long-term goals, redirecting hand-tapping behavior, encouraging vocalization, and improving grasping, the therapist recommended new objectives as follows:

1. Given music stimuli, Roxanne will vocalize three times per session with 100 percent accuracy in five trials.
2. Given a mallet, Roxanne will grasp it independently for 10 seconds while participating in drum activity with 75 percent accuracy in five trials.
3. In song context, Roxanne will play the tambourine with her right hand for four consecutive beats with 100 percent accuracy in five trials.

During the first 10 months of Roxanne's involvement in music therapy, a monthly random calculation of her hand-tapping behavior was recorded. These follow-up posttests were done to show whether or not music intervention helped in diminishing Roxanne's self-stimulating behavior of tapping her right hand to her mouth. Since base-line information in Figure 1 indicated no significant pattern whether recorded in a 10- or in a 20-minute period, the number was tallied during 10-minute periods. (See Figure 3.)

While the power of music and the personality of the therapist have together effected these results, it must be remembered that we are working with human beings who are physically different and with moods that fluctuate from one day to the next, inevitably

Post-Test of Roxanne's Behavior Pattern
(Tapping right hand to mouth)

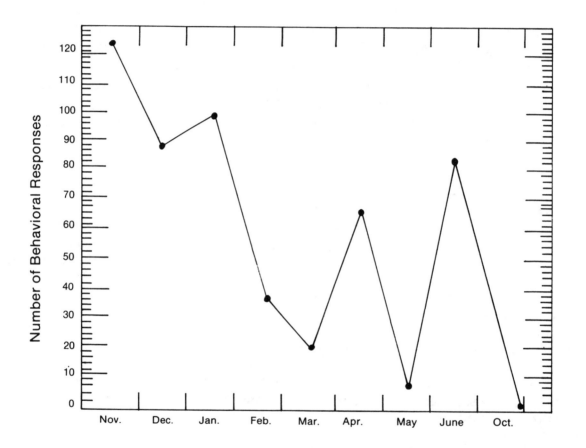

Monthly Calculation

FIGURE 3
Monthly Random Post-Test of Hand-Tapping Behavior

influencing their behavior. The results definitely indicate the effectiveness of music therapy intervention and one of the rewards we, as therapists, experience is the knowledge that we have helped to bring about positive change.

March, 1979. Roxanne's progress report stated that her eye contact was excellent. She responded to her name and often smiled in response to the therapist's smile, indicating visual recognition with auditory stimulation. At times, the music therapist encouraged interaction with other children. Roxanne seemed aware of others and indicated this awareness by touching them or holding hands for a short time. Her awareness of objects placed near her had improved. Also, she watched the "Muppet Show," and sometimes giggled. She also indicated joy by giggling during the group music therapy activities while playing instruments and moving with others.

Roxanne's music therapy objectives as of April, 1978 (mentioned above), were met on the following dates: Objective 1—November 1978; Objective 2—January 1979; Objective 3—March 1979. Furthermore, random calculation of hand-tapping behavior in February, 1979 totaled 23 times in 10 minutes; this indicated that this behavior did diminish when Roxanne was occupied in positive music activities.

New objectives for Roxanne as of March, 1979, with a target date for completion of June, 1979, were:

1. Given a song, Roxanne will play the tambourine with her right hand for two consecutive beats independently with 100 percent accuracy in 10 trials.

2. Given a mallet, Roxanne will beat independently two consecutive beats on the drum with 100 percent accuracy in five trials.

February, 1980. Roxanne received individual music therapy twice a week regularly, except for the month of January. During this time, because of additional staff made possible by a placement from a nearby college music therapy program, she received half-hour individual therapy four times a week. She also participated in half-hour group music therapy sessions twice a month.

Roxanne's new long-range goal became: To increase personal interaction, to redirect hand-tapping behavior to positive activities, and to develop motor skills. Her music therapy objectives were:

1. Given music stimuli, Roxanne will vocalize six times in 20 minutes with 100 percent accuracy in 10 trials. (While Roxanne successfully completed 10 trials, the music therapist believed, for the sake of reinforcement, that this objective should be continued with a target date of April, 1980, some four months hence.)

2. Given a mallet, Roxanne will grasp the mallet with minimal assistance and play the drum for 10 seconds with 80 percent accuracy. Objective was met January, 1980.

3. In song context, Roxanne will play the tambourine on her right hand for three beats in 10 trials. (After trying to meet this objective for several weeks, it seemed to be unrealistic. On September 5, 1979, it was revised to read: In song context, Roxanne will play the tambourine with her right hand for the entire song with assistance, and beat one beat independently. Roxanne met both the original and revised objective January 30, 1980.)

Roxanne showed development in the area of personal interaction. She made excellent eye contact with the therapist and also with several volunteers. She began to relate better with peers, particularly with Jason. Roxanne's hand-tapping behavior decreased significantly while engaged in music activities. (On January 15, 1980 a random calculation indicated that, while engaged in music therapy, Roxanne did not touch her mouth for 15 minutes.)

On February 4, 1980, Roxanne initiated activities with her right hand independently, although she usually used her left hand first. Roxanne also vocalized much more during each session. In observing Roxanne over the past few months, however, the therapist noticed that she had sporadic episodes of coughing almost breathlessly for short periods, stiffening and showing a strange, starey look in her eyes for short periods of time. She displayed nervousness and frustration more frequently by resorting to slapping or rubbing her face before music therapy sessions. A selection of relaxing music was chosen on these specific occasions. This development of seizure activity was discussed with the direct care staff and nursing supervisor, along with several members of the interdisciplinary treatment team. It seemed that Roxanne was reaching a plateau and was headed for some regression because of her seizures.

In the Fall of 1980, Roxanne graduated from her preschool program and was placed in a special class for S/PH in the public school system.

January, 1981. Roxanne received individual music therapy twice a week and group music therapy/recreation twice a month. She seemed to have reached a plateau, and in some respects, to have regressed. The causes may be somewhat complex, i.e., seizure disorder was unknown before in her case, the adjustment to prescribed medication to control seizure activity, her chronic respiratory problems, and the transition of being transported out to school each day. Now after a semester, she is beginning to show more awareness and is responding more positively during her music therapy sessions.

Roxanne's music therapy goals since her last interdisciplinary team meeting were to increase relaxation, to redirect hand-tapping behavior to positive music activities, to encourage vocalization and interaction with peers, and to improve gross motor skills. Because of Roxanne's apparent regression, her music therapy objectives were revised as follows:

1. Given music stimuli, Roxanne will make vocal sounds four times per session with 100 percent accuracy in 10 trials. (To date, Roxanne has met 50 percent of this objective, which will be continued for further reinforcement and completion with a target date of 6/81.)

2. Given a mallet/instrument, Roxanne will grasp with minimal assistance for 15 seconds eight out of ten trials. (This objective will be continued with target date of 6/81.)

3. Given the tambourine, Roxanne will play eight beats independently with her right hand for eight out of 10 trials. (This objective seemed realistic in September, 1980; however, it is unrealistic at this time because of her temporary regression. It is recommended that objectives 1 and 2 be continued with a target date of June, 1981. Objective 3 will be revised to read: Given the tambourine, Roxanne will play four beats independently with her right hand per song for 10 trials with June, 1981, as target date for completion.)

February, 1981. It was heart-warming and hopeful to see Roxanne once again responding positively to music. She was vocalizing to music stimulation, seeming to express herself emotionally in her own way, and was once again making good eye contact. She giggled happily as she played the piano with both hands. Roxanne seemed to receive great joy in experiencing music-making on several instruments of different timbre. She tracked sound well and her ability to grasp was improving. Her hand-tapping behavior was not totally extinguished but, while engaged in music therapy activities, occurred only once or twice in 15- to 20-minute periods. Roxanne was becoming much more aware of her environment and, most importantly, of her peers as well as staff. The following pictures reflect this.

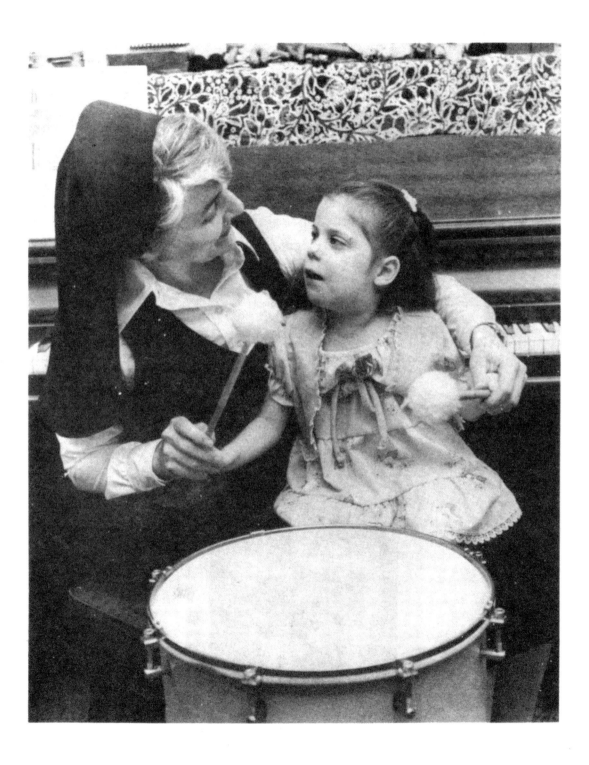

While Roxanne is engaged in music therapy, her hand-tapping behavior is diminished. As the picture indicates, her eye contact also has improved.

Playing the metallophone helps Roxanne improve her
grasping and eye hand coordination.

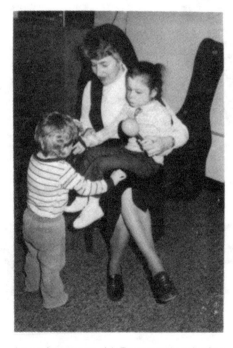

Jason interacts with Roxanne by placing
the maraca in her hand.

Case Study of Liza

Unlike the report of Roxanne's case, Liza's gives emphasis to the close bearing of physical condition upon the mental functioning of the individual. A comparison of a 1977 daily log concerning Liza's responses with a 1981 log shows the relationship with other disciplines and stresses how music therapy serves as an adjunctive or support service as well as a direct intervention. It also shows that definite progress had taken place.

Liza was born July 6, 1974. Newborn examination revealed multiple fractures of the left femur and right tibia and fibula, bilateral club feet, micrognathia (receded chin), and multiple nerve deficits including left lateral rectus paralysis (eye). Liza had poor muscle tone, flaccid paralysis of the lower limbs with absent reflexes, left wrist drop, left-sided facial weakness, and tightness of joints of hips and knees. A diagnosis was given of arthrogryposis multiplex congenita, secondary to neurological myopathy of undetermined etiology.

Liza was discharged to the care of her parents on July 29, 1974, with her left wrist and both legs in casts. On August 7, she was readmitted in critical condition caused by aspiration pneumonia. A further evaluation stated, "biopsy studies of the lower extremities did not reveal the presence of any muscle fibers." Liza's parents also spoke to a professor of pediatrics and were counseled extensively. It was noted that "the problem was related to loss of anterior horn cells and that muscle function and structure were normal." A diagnosis of "spinal muscular atrophy" was given to the parents with a "prognosis of progressive wasting and eventual death." They were also informed that "retardation was definitely present."

When this therapist first met Liza, she was a little girl of three with blonde hair and blue eyes. Like other children of her age, she approached each day with enthusiasm and a zest for life. But in many ways Liza was different, for, as mentioned above, she was born with multiple handicaps. An institution for severely/profoundly medically complex children became her home and world at the age of six months. As an infant, she had been tube fed because her facial muscles were paralyzed and she could not suck a nipple or drink from a bottle. For Liza, it meant that when she got a cold she required oxygen. Her chest muscles were not strong, a defect which resulted in breathing difficulties. Arthrogryposis especially means that the leg muscles are too weak and undeveloped for support. Braces were needed to provide strength for walking, if indeed, walking would ever become a reality.

Liza couldn't walk or talk. She couldn't push a doll carriage, ride a tricycle or do many other things that make up the active world of a child. "If this is true," I could have said, "Why bother? What can I do for a child who really can't compete physically or mentally with her peers?"

Maslow (1971), in discussing a humanistic philosophy of education, says:

> The function of education, the goal of education—the human goal, the goal so far as human beings are concerned—is ultimately the "self-actualization" of a person, the becoming fully human, the development of the fullest height that the human species can stand up to or that the particular individual can come to. In a less technical way, it is helping the person to become the best that he is able to become. (pp. 162-163)

At this facility, we care for and love children like Liza. Despite handicaps, Liza received total nursing care, physical therapy, stimulation in all areas from special education teachers, speech therapists, physical therapists, as well as music therapists. These people work together to help children like Liza reach their potential. When Liza was four, this approach enabled her to roll over, sit independently, feed herself, say her name, sing "la, la, la," and develop more socially appropriate behavior. Regardless of her severe physical disability involving extremely limited muscle development, she made progress in the areas of increased muscle tone in her arms, in listening and attending skills, and in responding to and identifying body parts.

The accompanying pictures illustrate the interest Liza showed in music and how it served as a motivating force, not only in her enjoyment, but in her total development.

By the age of six, Liza had undergone much surgery to correct her club feet and a palatal deformity. About the age of eight, Liza began to improve physically and to make steady progress. She is currently attending a class for physically handicapped, retarded children functioning in the educable and trainable range; and Liza is a child whose prognosis was once "progressive wasting and eventual death."

On January 16, 1981, the psychologist summarized Liza's condition as follows:

Liza is a multiply handicapped six-year-old. She is currently nonambulatory but moves about independently with use of a wheelchair. She has a serious speech problem and often communicates through the use of sign language. Intelligence testing indicates that Liza is functioning in the moderate range of mental retardation, obtaining a full-scale score of 44 on the Stanford-Binet and a 51 on the Arthur Adaptation of the Leiter. Taking Liza's speech into account, it might be expected that she would score higher on the nonverbal Leiter and it is felt that this score more accurately reflects her current level of functioning. Assessment of adaptive behavior indicates that Liza eats independently and is fully bladder controlled during the day. Dressing skills are difficult to assess at present because of the cast on Liza's leg, but she can dress and undress with minimal assistance.

In conjunction with the above, it might be well to quote from *Reaching the Special Learner Through Music* by Nocera (1979):

It is therefore unwise for a teacher to consider the IQ score as an absolute measure of a child's ability or potential. The idea that intelligence is fixed is now obsolete. A classic study, still in progress, has shown preliminary data in which the IQ scores of mildly retarded infants were raised 30 points in four years as a result of educational experiences. (pp. 233-234)

At the conclusion of an Educational/Recreation Program for Preschoolers, the summary statement of Liza's progress in music therapy read:

Liza has been in the music therapy program for three years and has shown probably more marked progress than most children served under the grant. Music therapy has played a large role in bringing this progress about. For Liza, music served to calm a crying, upset baby; and it served to help build muscle tone at the outset of the project. At present, music stimulates vocalization and serves to develop higher cognitive skills. Liza responds appropriately to many verbal cues throughout a session, which demonstrates an increase in receptive language. She is beginning, to some degree, to respond with expressive language.

Her imitative skills are improving; her attention span is longer; her rhythmic response is more controlled and accurate. The drum activity provides Liza with an opportunity to demonstrate a concept of tempo change from slower to faster and a return to the original tempo.

Liza also loves playing the Autoharp and "singing." She also enjoys playing several other musical instruments. When participating with another child or in a group session, she assumes responsibility for collecting the instruments and returning them to the therapist at the conclusion of each activity. Her social interaction is excellent. Music therapy is one more positive program contributing to Liza's total development.

Progress can definitely be seen if one compares a statement from the music therapist's log (9-12-77) with a statement from a more recent log (1-6-81):

Using an adaptive mallet, Liza develops better eye-hand coordination as she plays the "Hello" song on the resonator bells. The "Hello" song from the Nordoff and Robbins' *Children's Play Songs* (1962), begins each therapy session.

Liza improves her grasping and increases muscle tone in her arms while playing the jingle bells.

Drum beating has helped to strengthen Liza's arm muscles, which were once too weak for this activity, and to improve her ability to grasp.

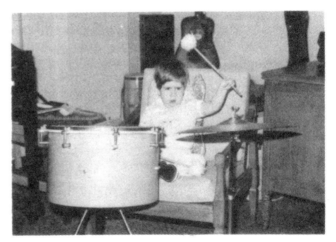

Liza punctuates the "Drum Song" with a crash on the cymbal.

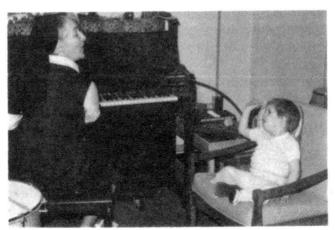

At the end of the period, Liza waves good-bye as the therapist concludes the session with the "Good-bye Song."

September 12, 1977. Liza responded with four smiles during the "Hello" song (Nordoff and Robbins, 1962). She reached for the resonator bell mallet when presented by the therapist and imitated the therapist by playing "hel-lo" (F, B^b) independently using her left hand. When given the drum mallet, she took it with her right hand and beat the drum rather softly with an unsteady beat to 16 measures of "To the Music I" from *Learning Through Music* by Levin & Safer (1975). Liza tracked sound both horizontally (to her left and right) and vertically (up and down), both visually and auditorially. It was recommended that Liza work on increasing muscle tone for grasping and eye/hand coordination through drum activities.

January 6, 1981. Liza interacted well with Aimee and served as a good model for her. She sang all the words to the "Hello" song. She clapped hands to the music and stopped on verbal/musical cue. She discriminated by identifying six different instruments on verbal cue in song context and played each for the duration of the song. Liza sang the whole section of "la-la-la's" from "Sing," sheet music, by Raposo. In the drum activity, Liza demonstrated the concepts "fast," "slow," "loud," "soft," by taking the verbal cues and also the musical cues from the piano improvisation. She was able to imitate 1-, 2-, and 3-beat patterns from like and unlike timbres. Liza imitated three notes in succession on the bass xylophone. She strummed the Autoharp and wanted to help depress the chord buttons as well. Liza signed and sang "My Father's House" with the music therapist. She also followed well the signs for "I Can Sing." The significant happening in this session (significant because of her mouth structure) was that Liza produced five sounds using the single reed horn. It may be interesting to note that during a session prior to this one, Liza displayed some very so-called "normal" behavior by refusing to strum the Autoharp when she did not get her own way. She also refused to beat the drum with Aimee!

Music Therapy Summary

The following describes further how Liza's individual music therapy program served to reinforce and helped meet these goals or needs addressed in her IEP for the school year 1980-1981:

Liza will complete a 5-10 piece puzzle, color within a frame, draw a straight line; Liza will learn her primary and secondary colors and will perform matching activities independently; Liza will count to 10 by rote and will count 1-5 objects and identify the numbers; Liza will verbally identify several pictures and objects independently; Liza will put on and take off her coat independently. She will comb her hair, brush her teeth and wash her hands and face independently; Liza will increase her language development and use of signs. Range of motion will be maintained to increase arm and trunk strength for better mobility.

Music therapy can provide an exciting, stimulating force in the accomplishment of goals in the areas of communications, academics, motor skills, emotionality, and sociability (CAMES). We can see how true this was in Liza's case. Liza's ability to identify colors and match them was one of her music therapy objectives, which was met. The song activity added fun to the learning process. Liza signed the color, while attempting to say it, then held it up or matched it according to the direction given by the therapist. The skills of listening and ability to follow verbal cues are involved in this activity as well. "Listen to the Drum and Now Beat _____" is a song used to reinforce identification and concept of numbers. At the dash, the therapist holds up a number to be played by the child. The child then identifies the number and counts while playing that number of beats on the drum. This not only indicates an understanding of the number concept, and the ability to identify a given number, but also the ability to coordinate two activities—beating and verbally sequencing the number simultaneously.

Liza also performed music activities that demanded visual discrimination and, at the same time, developed auditory discrimination using instruments. This activity reinforced Liza's ability to respond to the therapist's verbal cue in song context and to choose the particular instrument indicated by the therapist. The pleasure of playing each instrument to piano improvisation was rewarding. Liza also recognized and played the names of her peers independently on the drum. Language development and improvement in her use of signs continued to be reinforced in music therapy as you will see in the pictures that follow.

Liza sang and signed such songs as "My Father's House." Improvement in articulation was also encouraged throughout each session from the singing of all the words of the "Hello Song" and the "Good-bye Song" as well as the songs presented in between. Liza mastered blowing the single-reed horn which could be helpful in her total speech development. Motor skills were being developed by strumming the Autoharp, beating the drum, and manipulating various instruments. Eye-hand coordination improved as she played specific instruments. Actually, music was not only a motivating force in the teaching of CAMES, but served also as the teacher.

Pictures are worth a thousand words, so in the following pages, meet Liza in music therapy as she strives to fulfill objectives designed to play a large role in her total development.

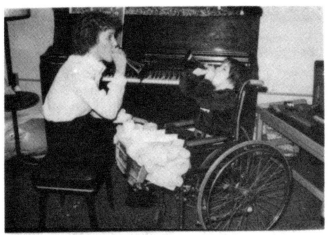

Denise (a music therapy student) and Liza blowing horn. Horn playing demands breath control and the ability to inhale and exhale air. This is helpful in pre-speech programs.

Liza attends to Denise as she signs "House" during the song "My Father's House."

Singing "love, love, love."

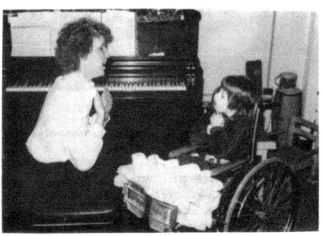

Liza signs "peace" with the therapy student.

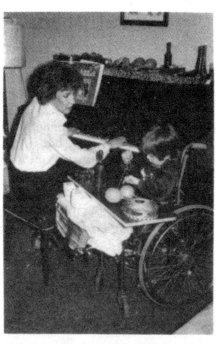

Liza selects the correct instrument on verbal cue from five different instruments and enjoys making music on each one.

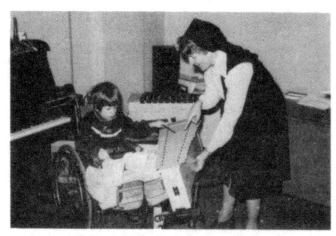

Liza develops eye-hand coordination when playing the specific tone bar pointed to by the music therapist.

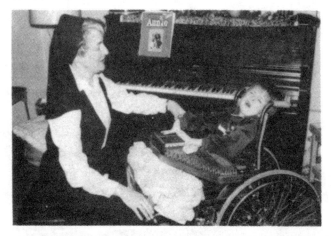

Liza shows independence in her own adapted manner of pushing the Autoharp button with her thumb (other fingers are too weak), strums and expresses her deepest feelings in song.

"Goodbye"

This little girl had baffled doctors, direct care personnel, special educators, parents, therapists of every discipline as she demonstrated her determination and desire to overcome all obstacles in her development. Liza's total program, including music therapy, played a major role as a motivation and stimulation for growth. She is using her talents to the fullest—and after all, isn't that what success is all about?

Case Study of Beverly

The presentation of this case is less detailed than the two foregoing cases. Literature does not often report cases that relate to clients requiring maintenance rather than development because of physical deterioration. In reality, however, this is often the case when working with the multihandicapped, and the beginning music therapist should realize that this also can be rewarding. Such cases demand on the part of the therapist a high level of motivation and often the "steeling" of one's emotions. Bev's case describes briefly this type of circumstance.

Beverly proved that all stories cannot be accounts of progress. Bev was a 13-year-old, multihandicapped child. Her diagnosis indicated hydrocephaly, psychomotor retardation, seizure disorder, and right hemiparesis secondary to a stroke. Recently, she had been declared blind and there were indications that her hearing was also becoming impaired.

Bev enjoyed interacting with both staff and her peers and was known throughout the Center for her pleasant disposition. Regardless of her many handicaps, she enjoyed life in general. Bev's receptive language was good, and her contagious laughter indicated a sense of humor. Prior to a debilitating stroke some six years before, she had communicated expressively using fairly good articulation.

The long-term music therapy goals set for Bev were improvement of articulation, development of a wider vocabulary, improvement in auditory acuity, a greater use of the right arm, and in general, the maintenance of her current level of functioning.

For a long time, Bev was the joy of the first floor where she lived, but since her blindness and her apparent hearing impairment and general physical regression, she seemed to have lost her former emotional resilience and sociability. This is a reality that we must deal with in therapy, not only the success stories, but experiences with children that involve mere maintenance and even regression. These are the more challenging situations that a therapist must face. This is reality!

Although it took longer and a little more "steeling of the emotions" on the therapist's part, music therapy sessions helped to lift Bev's spirit and restore the joy that once seemed to be hers. In this case and in many similar ones, it is truly worth the added effort and energy it takes to share the joy of music that is ours.

The procedures in these three case studies provide examples of how the music therapist addresses the special education problems and how music serves as a powerful aid in the development of the nonmusical skills needed in all learning.

GROUP MUSIC THERAPY/RECREATION PROGRAM

In addition to the individual music therapy sessions, group music therapy/recreation programs take place weekly at this facility. The children are encouraged to socialize or interact with their personal volunteer and other children in game songs, songs demanding body gestures, experiencing the use of rhythm band instruments and participating in wheelchair folk dances. Group activities are golden opportunities for therapy. The imitation of others in the group incites the child to greater physical activity as well as social interaction.

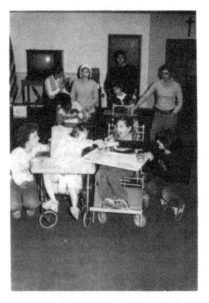

Concluding the "Virginia Reel," we "cast off." Chris and Frankie enjoy holding hands.

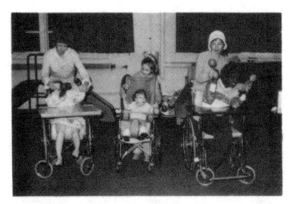

Adapting to the situation is important, for example, "dancing" the "Alley Cat" with your hands.

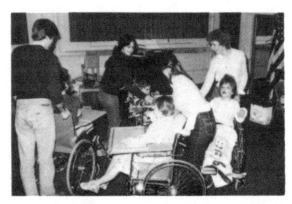

The Music Therapy students enjoy the "Texas Star" square dance as much as the children do.

CONCLUDING REMARKS

This monograph gives some idea of the characteristics of the multihandicapped and of what music therapy can do for this population. It describes many of the goals, activities, and procedures of this work with the multihandicapped and presents some case studies illustrating these. Once again, the wording of Nordoff and Robbins (1971) inspire us by reminding us of that which is crucial for a music therapist who chooses to serve in this challenging, exciting human service:

> In individual therapy and in group activities, the therapist must believe in the intrinsic importance of each life with which he is working. He must respect the inward experiences of that life and feel reverence—and enthusiasm—for the freshness of emotional experience that his work can bring to birth in each child. The music therapist/teacher who has these feelings for the children and the work he does with them, will find his love for music fired anew. These are the well-springs in which his inspirations arise, the inspirations that become—through the children's activities and his—therapy (p. 144).

These are not the kinds of things learned only from a textbook. They come from actual contact with the children and youth served. Knowledge about multihandicapped children and music skills in working with them are necessary, but belief in the intrinsic importance of each child's life in the great healing power that music brings are indispensable.

GLOSSARY*

Arthrogryposis multiplex congenita: Multiple severe joint contractures including club feet, dislocated hips, or involvement of elbows, normal trunk limb proportions, absence of skin creases at joints.

Athetoid: Pertaining to or affedcted by athetosis.

Athetosis: A type of cerebral palsy characterized by continuous, extraneous, involuntary movements that increase when voluntary muscle function is attempted.

Autism: A form of psychosis characterized by an avoidance of human contact, by stereotyped behavior and lack of speech.

Behavior modification: Approach in which positive or negative reinforcers are used to effect desired changes.

Cerebral palsy: A persisting qualitative motor disorder appearing before the age of three years, due to a non-progressive damage of the brain.

Decibel: A unit and measure of difference in the intensity of sound.

Encephalopathy: Related to encephalitis. Any degenerative disease of the brain.

Hemiparesis: Muscular weakness affecting one side of the body.

Hydrocephalic: Pertaining to a condition in which an abnormal accumulation of fluid within the brain frequently causes an enlargement of the skull.

Hypotonic: Lack of muscle tone resulting in floppy rag doll movements.

Microcephaly: Having an abnormally small head.

Orthopedically impaired: Severe orthopedic impairment caused by congenital anomaly, disease, etc.

Paralytic stroke: Sudden loss of muscular power from lesion of the brain or spinal cord.

Perseveration: Persistent meaningless repetition of words or some activity.

Psychomotor: Of or relating to voluntary, conscious movements; development of muscular action and neuromuscular coordination necessary for skilled behavior such as musical performance.

Spastic: Pertaining to a state of sustained muscular contraction of tension frequently associated with impairment of voluntary control.

---

*Definitions of the words in this Glossary are modifications of defined terms found in the following sources:

American Psychological Association. *A Psychiatric Glossary,* 1980.
Dorland's Illustrated Medical Dictionary, 1968.
Parashar, O. D. *Dictionary of Special Education,* 1977.
Taber's Cyclopedic Medical Dictionary, 1977.

REFERENCES

A Career in Music Therapy. Lawrence, KS: National Association for Music Therapy, 1980.

Eagle, C. T., Jr. Personal communication, June, 1978.

Federal Register, August 23, 1977.

Gaston, E. T. "Foreword." In E. T. Gaston (Ed.), *Music in therapy.* New York: Macmillan, 1968.

Haring, N.G. & Brown, L. J. *Teaching the severely handicapped.* New York: Grune & Stratton, 1976.

Lathom, W. *The role of music therapy in the education of handicapped children and youth.* Lawrence, KS: National Association for Music Therapy, 1980.

Levin, G. M., Levin, H. D. & Safer, N. D. *Learning through music.* Hengham, MA: Teaching Resources Corporation, 1975.

Maslow, A. H. *The farther reaches of human nature.* New York: Penguin Books, 1971.

Nicholas, M. J. & Gilbert, J. P. Research in music therapy: A survey of music therapists' attitudes and knowledge." *Journal of Music Therapy,* 1980, *4,* 207-213.

Nocera, S. D. *Reaching the special learner through music.* Morristown, NJ: Silver Burdett, 1979.

Nordoff, P. In D. A. Perry (film producer), *The music child.* Cambridge, MA: David Perry Production, 1976.

Nordoff, P. & C. Robbins. *First book of children's play songs.* Byrn Mawr, PA: Theodore Presser, 1962.

Nordoff, P. & C. Robbins. *Therapy in music for handicapped children.* New York: St. Martin Press, 1971.

BIBLIOGRAPHY
Music Therapy Services for Multihandicapped Children

This related literature was prepared and presented by Betty Shirm, RMT, at the Second In-Service Training Institute in Music Therapy in Denton, Texas on June 23, 1981.

This compilation was prepared to assist educators who are mainstreaming severely/ profoundly handicapped children in compliance with Public Law 94-142. Music therapy is one of the related services which has proven beneficial in this endeavor. The literature is especially relevant regarding music therapy services for multihandicapped children, therefore, some material dealing with one specific disability has not been included.

Selected Readings in Law, Education, Implementation

Abeson, A. & Bolick, N. *A continuing summary of pending and completed litigation regarding the education of handicapped children.* Reston, VA: Council for Exceptional Children, 1974.

Aiello, B. Teachers ask about handicapped children and the new laws. *Education Unlimited,* 1979, *1*(1), 33-36.

Alley, J. M. Education for the severely handicapped: The role of music therapy. *Journal of Music Therapy,* 14(2), 1977, 50-59.

Alley, J. M. Music in the IEP: Therapy/education. *Journal of Music Therapy, 16*(3), 1979, 111-127.

Appell, M. J. *An overview: Arts in the education for the handicapped.* Washington: The National Committee, Arts for the Handicapped, 1977, 13-17.

Biggs, J. L. & O'Donnell, P. A. *Teaching individuals with physical and multiple disabilities.* Columbus, OH: Charles E. Merrill, 1976.

Dykes, M. (Ed.). *Programming for the severely impaired multiple handicapped child with emphasis on the physically involved.* Gainesville, FL: Florida Educational Research and Development Council, 1977.

Feury, J. T. *Legislation—how to deal with it.* Voice of the Lakes, *25*(1), 1976, 2-8.

Gilbert, J. P. Mainstreaming in your classroom: What to expect. *Music Educators Journal,* February 1977, *63*(6), 64-68.

Hudson, F. & Graham, S. An approach to operationalizing the IEP. *Learning Disabilities Quarterly,* 1978, *1*(1), 13.

Kaufman, J. J., Gottlieb, J., Agard, J. A. & Kukic, M. D. Mainstreaming: Toward an explication of the construct. In E. L. Meyen, G. A. Vergason & R. J. Whelan (Eds.), *Alternatives for teaching exceptional children.* Denver: Love Publishing, 1975.

Kukuk, J. W. & Sjolund, J. A. Arts for the handicapped: A national direction. *National Elementary Principal,* January/February 1976, *55,* 86-88.

Nebe, H. J. Music therapy: Its function in supporting the rehabilitation of the handicapped. *Journal of Music Therapy, 8*(1), 1971, 3-11.

Smith, D. *Motor-academic-perceptual curriculum guide for the early childhood education of the multiply handicapped.* Washington, DC: Bureau of Education for the Handicapped, Department of Health, Education & Welfare, 1973.

Turnbull, R. & Turnbull, A. *Free appropriate education: Law and implementation.* Denver: Love Publishing, 1978.

Weintraub, F. J., Abeson, A., Ballard, J. & LaVor, M. L. (Eds.). *Public policy and the education of exceptional children.* Reston, VA: Council for Exceptional Children, 1976.

Articles on Music

Austen, M. P. The effects of music on the learning of random shapes and syllables with institutionalized severely mentally retarded adolescents. *Contributions of Music Education, 5,* 1977, 54-69.

Alvin, J. Music therapy and the cerebral palsied child. *Cerebral Palsy Bulletin,* June 1961, *3,* 255-262.

Benenzon, R. Music therapy in infantile autism. *British Journal of Music Therapy,* Summer 1976, *7*(2), 10-16.

Bertel, M. et al. Music as a facilitator for visual motor sequencing tasks in children with cerebral palsy. *Developmental Medicine and Child Neurology,* 1971, *13,* 335-342.

Cassity, M. D. Nontraditional guitar techniques for the educable and trainable mentally retarded residents in music therapy activities. *Journal of Music Therapy, 1977, 14*(1), 39-42.

Cassity, M. D. Social development of TMRs involved in performing and nonperforming groups. *Journal of Music Therapy, 1978, 15*(2), 100-105.

Darrow, L. G. Conditioning music and approval as new reinforcers for imitative behavior with the severely retarded. *Journal of Music Therapy,* 1975, *12*(1), 30-39.

Dileo, C. L. The use of a token economy program with mentally retarded persons in a music therapy setting. *Journal of Music Therapy,* 1975, *12*(3), 154-159.

Fahey, J. D. & Birkenshaw, L. Bypassing the ear: The perception of music by feeling and touch. *Music Educators Journal,* April, 1972, *58*(8).

Herron, C. J. Some effects of instrumental music training on cerebral palsied children. *Journal of Music Therapy,* 1970, *7*(2), 55-58.

Holloway, M. S. A comparison of passive and active music reinforcement to increase preacademic and motor skills in severely retarded children and adolescents. *Journal of Music Therapy,* 1980, *17*(2), 58-69.

Josepha, Sr. M. Therapeutic values of instrumental performance for severely handicapped children. *Journal of Music Therapy,* 1964, *1*(3), 73-79.

Lathom, W. The use of music with cerebral palsied children during activities involving physical control. *Bulletin of the National Association for Music Therapy,* 1961, *10*(3), 10-16.

Lathom, W. Application of Kodaly concepts in music therapy. *Journal of Music Therapy,* 1974, *11*(1), 61-66.

Lutwak, E. A new mouthstick prosthesis for handicapped patients. *Journal of Prosthetic Dentistry,* 1977, *37*(1), 61-66.

Metzler, R. The use of music as a reinforcer to increase imitative behavior in severely and profoundly retarded residents. *Journal of Music Therapy,* 1974, *11*(2), 97-110.

Meyers, A. *Music as a therapeutic agent in the rehabilitation of physically handicapped children with special references to cerebral palsy and a survey of music education and music therapy for facilities for the education of physically handicapped children.* Unpublished doctoral dissertation, State University of Iowa, 1954.

Ricketts, L. Music and handicapped children. *Royal College of General Practitioners Journal,* 1976, *26*(169), 585-587.

Robinson, M. J. et al. Music therapy activities devised for use with severely and profoundly retarded adults. *Voice of the Lakes,* 1977, 77(2), 8-17.

Ross, D. M. et al. Rhythm training for educable mentally retarded children. *Mental Retardation,* 1973, *11,* 20-23.

Saperston, B. The use of music in establishing communication with an autistic mentally retarded child. *Journal of Music Therapy,* 1973, *10*(4), 184-188.

Saperston, B., Chan, R., Morphew, C. & Banks, K. Music listening versus juice as a reinforcement for learning in profoundly mentally retarded individuals. *Journal of Music Therapy,* 1980, *27*(4), 174-183.

Sato, C. Musical aptitude of cerebral palsied children. *Cerebral Palsy Review,* 1960, *21*(6), 3-8.

Sato, C. A study of rhythm patterns of cerebral palsied children. *Cerebral Palsy Review,* 1962, *23*(5), 7-11.

Schmidt, J. A special challenge: The profoundly retarded multiply handicapped. *Voice of the Lakes,* 1981, *25*(2), 23-25.

Schomer, M. A perceptual development program for the music therapist. *Journal of Music Therapy,* 1973, *10*(3), 95-109.

Schneider, E. H. Music for the cerebral palsied child. *Proceedings of the National Association for Music Therapy,* 1961, *10,* 97-100.

Steele, A. L. Programmed use of music to alter uncooperative problem behavior. *Journal of Music Therapy,* 1968, *5*(4), 103-107.

Steele, A. L. & Jorgenson, H. A. Music therapy: An effective solution to problems in related disciplines. 1. Contingent socio-music listening periods in a pre-school setting. 2. Effects of contingent preferred music in reducing two stereotyped behaviors of a profoundly retarded child. *Journal of Music Therapy,* 1971, *8*(4):131-145.

Weber, R. D. An approach to the use of musical instruments in the education of the trainable mentally retarded. *Council for Research in Music Education,* 1971, *25,* 79-88.

Wolfe, D. E. The effect of automated interrupted music on head posturing of cerebral palsied individuals. *Journal of Music Therapy,* 1980, *27*(4), 184-206.

Books on Music Therapy and Music Education

Alvin, J. *Music therapy for the autistic child.* London: Oxford University Press, 1978.

Aronoff, F. *Music and young children.* New York: Holt, Rinehart & Winston, 1969.

Edwards, E. *Music education for the deaf.* South Waterford, ME: Merriam-Eddy, 1974.

Gaston, E. T. (Ed.). *Music in therapy.* New York: The Macmillan Company, 1968.

Graham, R. & Beer, A. *Teaching music to the exceptional child: A handbook for mainstreaming.* Englewood Cliffs, NJ: Prentice-Hall, 1980.

Greenberg, M. *Your children need music.* Englewood Cliffs, NJ: Prentice-Hall, 1979.

Madsen, C. K. *Music therapy: A behavioral guide for the mentally retarded.* Lawrence, KS: National Association for Music Therapy, 1981.

Madsen, C. K. & Huhn, T. L. *Contemporary music education.* Arlington Heights, IL: AHM Publishing, 1978.

Marion, R. *Educators, parents, and exceptional children.* London: Oxford University Press, 1973.

Michel, D. E. *Music therapy: An introduction to therapy and special education through music.* Springfield, IL: Charles C Thomas, 1976.

Nordoff, P. & Robbins, C. *Music therapy in special education.* New York: John Day, 1971.

Nowicki, A. & Trevisan, L. *Beyond the sound: A technical and philsophical approach to music therapy* (2nd ed.). Available from authors, Box 1694, Porterville, CA, 1978.

Wood, M. *Developmental music therapy.* Athens, GA: Rutland Center, 1974.

Resource Books on Music Activities, Techniques, and Methods

Abramson, R. M. *Rhythmic games for perception and cognition.* New York: Music and Movement Press, 1973.

Bailey, P. *They can make music.* London: Oxford University Press, 1973.

Batcheller, J. & Monsour, S. *Music in recreation and leisure.* Dubuque, IA: Wm. C. Brown, 1972.

Birkenshaw, L. *Music for fun, music for learning* (2nd ed.). Toronto: Holt, Rinehart & Winston, 1977.

Bitcon, C. *Alike and different: Clinical and educational use of Orff-Schulwerk.* Santa Ana, CA: Rosha Press, 1976.

Boorman, J. *Creative dance in the first three grades.* Don Mills, Ontario: Longman's, 1969.

Bradford, L. L. *Sing it yourself: 220 pentatonic folk songs.* Sherman Oaks, CA: Alfred Publishing, 1978.

Burnett, M. *Melody, movement and language.* San Francisco: R and E Research Associates, 1973.

Canner, N. & Kelbanoff, H. *And a time to dance: A sensitive exposition of the use of creative movement with retarded children.* Boston: Beacon Press, 1968.

Cardarelli, A. *Twenty-one ways to use music in teaching the language arts.* Evansville: Indiana State University Press, 1979.

Cesaretti, R. *Piano method for the special child* (Vol. 1). West Babylon, NY: Harold Branch Publishing, 1978.

Deaver, M. J. *Sound and silence.* Pikeville, NY: Curriculum Development and Research, 1975.

Evans, D. *Sharing sounds.* New York: Longman, 1978.

Foster, B. *Training songs for special people.* Boulder, CO: Myklas Music Press, 1979.

Ginglend, D. & Stiles, W. *Music activities for retarded children.* Nashville, TN: Abingdon Press, 1965.

Janiak, W. *Songs for music therapy.* Long Branch, NJ: Kimbo Educational, 1978.

Levin, G., Levin, H. & Safer, N. *Learning through songs.* Boston: Teaching Resources, 1977.

Moore, K. *NOTE.* Stevensville, MI: Educational Service, 1973.

Music for Children: Orff-Schulwerk (American edition, Vol. 2, Primary). London: Scott Music, 1977.

Nash, G. C. *Creative approaches to child development with music, language and movement.* Sherman Oaks, CA: Alfred Publishing, 1974.

Norcera, S. *Reaching the special learner through music.* Dallas: Silver Burdett, 1979.

Nordoff, P. & Robbins, C. *Creative music therapy.* New York: John Day, 1977.

Orlick, T. *The cooperative sports and games book.* New York: Pentheon Books, 1978.

Purvis J. & Samet, S. *Music in developmental therapy.* Baltimore: University Park Press, 1976.

Reichard, C. & Blackburn, D. *Music based instruction for the exceptional child.* Denver: Love Publishing, 1973.

Robins, F. & Robins, J. *Educational rhythmics for mentally and physically handicapped children.* New York: Association Press, 1968.

Sinclaire, C. *Movement of the young child—Ages two to six.* Columbus, OH: Charles E. Merrill, 1973.

Wachhaus, G. & Kuhn, T. L. *Fundamental classroom music skills: Theory and performing techniques.* New York: Holt, Rinehart & Winston, 1979.

Report of Institutes

Improving music experiences for emotionally handicapped children: Proceedings of the institute. Albany, NY: The University of the State of New York. State Education Department, Division for Handicapped Children, Division of the Humanities and the Arts.

The role of music in the special education of handicapped children. Albany, NY: The University of the State of New York. State Education Department, Division of the Humanities and the Arts.

Sourcebooks, Indexes, and Bibliographies

Eagle, C. (Ed.). *Music therapy index.* Lawrence, KS: National Association for Music Therapy, 1976.

Eagle, C. (Ed.). *Music psychology index.* Denton, TX: Institute for Therapeutics Research, 1978.

Galloway, H. F. A comprehensive bibliography of music referential to communicative development, processing, disorders and remediation. *Journal of Music Therapy,* Winter, 1975, *12*(4).

Geddes, D. & Summerfield, L. *Physical education and recreation for individuals with multiple handicapping conditions: References and resources.* Washington: American Alliance for Health, Physical Education and Recreation, 1978.

Johnson, F. Music therapy for the multiply handicapped: A guide to references and resources. *Voice of the Lakes,* 1981, *25*(2), 20-22.

Schulberg, C. *The music therapy sourcebook: A collection of activities categorized and analyzed.* New York: Human Science Press, 1981.

Selected Recordings

Barlin, P. & Barlin, A. *Dance-a-story* (record albums with books). RCA Records, Educational Department, 1133 Avenue of Americas, New York, NY 10036.

Basic songs for exceptional children (Concept Records nos. 1, 2, 3). Children's Music Center, 5375 Pico Boulevard, Los Angeles, CA 90010.

Brazelton, A. E. & Desantio, G. *Get fit while you sit.* Educational Activities, Inc., Freeport, NY 11520.

Capon, J. & Hallum, R. *Perceptual motor rhythm games.* Educational Activities, Inc., Freeport, NY 11520.

Fundamental rhythms for the younger set. Kimbo Educational Box 477, Long Branch, NJ 07740.

Glass, H. & Hallum, R. *Individualization in movement and music* (LP or cassette and manual). Good Apple, Inc.

Janiak, W. *Carnival in motion. Everyday skills. Nice 'n easy. Songs about me.* Kimbo Educational, Box 477, Long Branch, NJ 07740.

Johnson, L. *Simplified lummi stick activities* (LP and sticks). Kimbo Educational Box 477, Long Branch, NY 07704.

Lewandawski, I. & Baldassarce, M. *Limb learning: Music and movement to reinforce learning concepts.* Good Apple, Inc.

Lucky, S. *Four-foot feelings.* Melody House Publishing Company, 819 N.W. 92nd, Oklahoma City, OK 73114.

Ortman, K. *Music for movement* (no. 1 & 2). Children's Music Center, 5375 Pico Boulevard, Los Angeles, CA 90010.

Play-a-long songs (Vol. 1, Grades k-2, Participating in Music: Games, Movement, Improvisation). Educational Resources, Pleasantville, NY 10570.

Palmer, H. *Creative movement and rhythmic expression. Easy does it. Getting to know myself. Learning basic skills through music. Movin'. Pretend. The feel of music.* Educational Activities, Inc., Freeport, NY 11520.

Prudden, S. & Stussman, J. *Creative fitness for children.* Kimbo Educational, Box 477, Long Branch, NJ 07740.

Robins, F. & Robins, J. *Educational rhythmics.* Russell Records, Ventura, CA 93001.

Sounds I can hear (4 albums with graphics). Scott, Foresman & Company, 1900 East Lake Avenue, Glenview IL 60025.

MONOGRAPH 2

MUSIC THERAPY FOR
ORTHOPEDICALLY HANDICAPPED CHILDREN

Mary Toombs Rudenberg

ACKNOWLEDGMENTS

I gratefully acknowledge the contribution of Charles T. Eagle and Richard M. Graham for the final editing of this monograph and to the Orthopedically Handicapped Module team of the National Inservice Training Institute in Music Therapy for their most helpful critiques and contributions: Frances Curley, Laurie A. Farnan, Joy Fisher, and Joseph J. Moreno.

Special thanks go to Faith L. Johnson, Joanna Pasquinelli, and Lee Anna Rasar for the vast amount of information sent to me and for their continued support of this writing.

My warm thanks also go to the following persons for their contributions:

Michael Rohrbacher for consultation and considerable information towards this monograph.

Laurie A. Farnan and Jeannie D. Weiss for photographs.

David Weiss for the drawings.

Patsy A. Eagle and Paulette Haas for their typing.

Melinda L. Boyd, Anne Buvinger, Sheryl Matthews, Linda F. Smith, and Jeannie D. Weiss for case studies shared, and Dellinda Henry for demonstration lessons.

Music therapy interns from Children's Hospital, New Orleans and Moody State School, Galveston, for their papers and ideas.

DEDICATION

This effort is dedicated to my husband,

F. Hermann Rudenberg,

who has patiently supported me in my pursuit of this topic,

and to Jeannie D. Weiss

for her endless patience, encouragement, editing, and typing.

INTRODUCTION TO THE DISABILITY

Much has been written about the Homeric Greeks' belief in the healing power of music, but further study of ancient history will reveal also that severely handicapped people were denied the benefits of this thinking. Babies born crippled were exterminated in keeping with the accepted belief that only those healthy and "perfectly" formed had the *right* to survive and, apparently, any chance of benefiting from the curative effects of music or other of the culture's means of healing ministrations. Paintings, icons, and other art works from the Middle Ages suggest only slightly better fates for severely crippled people who were often pictured cranking out mendicant airs on hurdy-gurdies or otherwise using music to beg for their very existences. We have come a long way since those periods in history to a point where our democratic society now considers that any individual, no matter how handicapped, has *equal rights* with the nonhandicapped. This premise assumes that crippled, or orthopedically handicapped, persons in our society will be provided opportunities for music experiences which are commensurate with their abilities and talents. One means of providing these experiences for the aesthetic and physical well-being of orthopedically handicapped children and youth is through the special set of interventions known as music therapy.

The term, "music therapy," refers to the use of music and music-related activities under the supervision of professionally trained individuals (i.e., music therapists) to assist a client or patient in attaining a prescribed therapeutic goal. When the client is orthopedically handicapped, the music therapist uses music in such a manner as to assist in bringing about increased mobility, greater muscle strength, smoothness of movement, and other physical and emotional improvements. Examples of how this is done will be presented in this monograph in the form of case studies and guidelines for clinical techniques utilizing music. Prior to that, however, there will be some discussion of the nature of that condition known as an "orthopedic handicap," and of the individual described as "orthopedically handicapped."

EXPLANATION OF ESSENTIAL TERMS AND CONCEPTS

Impairment, Disability, and Handicap

According to Stevens (1962), the term "impairment" refers to the actual condition of tissue, e.g., a club foot, diabetes, spina bifida. The term "disability" differs from impairment in that the former deals with lack of ability to do. Finally, a "handicap" reflects the extent to which a disability or an impairment impedes the individual's efforts to lead a normal life. While these distinctions appear to make a good deal of sense, there is the tendency to interchange the terms in general, and occasionally formal, correspondence. The writings which comprise this monograph reflect the attitudes and records of several music therapists, but the distinctions just presented are not always made. The decision was made to adhere to the integrity of the contributing reports rather than being extensively concerned with or attempting to change this particular terminology when it occurs. This should cause no difficulty for the reader, however, because the information presented by the contributing music therapist is clear, relevant, and useful.

Orthopedic Handicaps

Orthopedic handicaps are those conditions which primarily limit a child's physical functioning abilities. Such handicaps are usually quite visible, either due to awkward or uncontrollable movements or to the adaptive equipment this child uses, such as braces, wheelchairs, splints, or artificial limbs. Through learning more about the problem and some of the methods or techniques that have been successful in working with a child with an orthopedic handicap, one can learn to see beyond the visible handicaps which may elicit feelings of discomfort or helplessness. (There are recommended films on orthopedic handicaps listed on page 100.) The music therapist can then begin to work with the *whole* child to help him to realize a wide range of life experiences. The music therapist must first relate to the whole child and give consideration for his limitations resulting from his orthopedic handicap. The point is that, to work effectively with this child, the music therapist must try to help him lead a life which is as normal and as satisfying as possible. This includes providing opportunities for each child to express his personality as well as to meet his physiological, aesthetic, and emotional needs. As will be shown in the present monograph, these needs *can* be met in music therapy.

Orthopedic handicaps have been defined *categorically* to facilitate legislative reports or *functionally* to describe a child's strengths and weaknesses. Public Law 94-142, *Education for All Handicapped Children Act (Federal Register, 1977)* defines the condition functionally in a categorical context:

> "Orthopedically impaired" means a severe orthopedic impairment which adversely affects a child's educational performance. The term includes impairments caused by congenital anomaly (e.g., clubfoot, absence of some member), impairments caused by disease (e.g., poliomyelitis, bone tuberculosis), and impairments from other causes (e.g., cerebral palsy, amputations, and fractures or burns which cause contractures) (p. 42478).

As cited by Kieran, Connor, von Hippel, and Jones (1978), Project Head Start reflects essentially the same point of view toward orthopedic handicaps but offers a slightly different definition:

> A child shall be reported as crippled or with an orthopedic handicap who has a condition which prohibits or impedes normal development or gross or fine motor abilities. Such functioning is impaired as a result of conditions associated with congenital anomalies, accidents, or diseases; these conditions include, for example, spina bifida, loss of or deformed limbs, burns which cause contractures, cerebral palsy (p. 35).

Some of the key terms which appear in these definitions are explained in Handbook VI of the U.S. Office of Education's "State Educational Records and Reports Series" (1970). The important terms from the several accepted definitions for individuals discussed in the present monograph are defined as follows:

Crippled: Individuals with a physical impairment of a type which might restrict normal opportunity for education or self-support. This term is generally considered to include individuals having impairments caused by a congenital anomaly (e.g., cleft palate, clubfoot, absence of some member), impairments caused by disease (e.g., poliomyelitis, bone tuberculosis, encephalitis, and other neurological involvements which may result in conditions such as cerebral palsy or epilepsy), and impairments caused by accidents (e.g., fractures or burns which cause contractures) (p. 319).

The striking similarities and overlap of these definitions reveal how much various agencies and organizations concerned with the orthopedically handicapped, physically impaired individual do agree. What is important to the music therapist, however, is some degree of agreement—a fundamental consensus—among the various therapeutic practitioners as to clinical goals, procedure, and specific techniques. Once established, such basic agreement within the music therapy profession will make it much easier to communicate with other professionals (practitioners) who work with the orthopedically handicapped. One of the purposes of the present monograph is to establish a basis for such agreement, especially with respect to music therapy with orthopedically handicapped children.

Of the many orthopedically handicapping conditions which one may find in public or special school settings (see Appendix A), the following are likely to be seen most often:[1]

Cerebral palsy: A nonprogressive disorder of movement or posture due to a brain lesion; considered congenital if the result of disease or disturbances during pregnancy or at time of birth; considered acquired if the result of injuries during late childhood.

Spinal cord damage:
Spina bifida: cleft spine; congenital condition of open defects in the child's vertebral column resulting from abnormal fetal development.
Paraplegia: paralysis of both legs, or lower limbs, due to injuries below the first thoracic vertebra.
Quadriplegia: paralysis of both legs and both arms, all four limbs, due to injuries above the thoracic vertebra.

Severe burns: Deep second and third degree burns which may produce permanent or temporary orthopedic handicaps due to contractures (permanently tight muscles and joints) or loss of body parts or limitation of body movement due to treatment for the burns.

Head trauma: Severe injury resulting from sudden mechanical force to the head (brain); may be life-threatening or may result in severe residual dysfunctions.

Juvenile rheumatoid arthritis: An "autoimmune" disease of abnormal antibodies attacking normal body materials; usually in remission after ten years of active disease but can leave functional limitations; causes discomfort, limited range of motion, contractures, and subluxations (dislocations of joints); usually severely affects five or more joints of the child.

Amputations:
Congenital: born without a part or a total limb (limbs); result of failure of limb bud development of the fetus.
Acquired: removal of a part of a total limb (limbs) due to an accident or surgery.

Muscular dystrophy: A progressive, diffuse disease affecting the child's muscles (in the present monograph, refers to Duchenne's type of muscular dystrophy); at this date, a terminal disease, usually between ages of 15 and 35 years.

Arthrogryposis: A congenital disease diagnosed at birth due to deformities from stiff joints and weak muscles.

Poliomyelitis: A viral infection which affects the anterior horn cells of the spinal cord, the motor cells; can be life-threatening and can cause permanent paralysis, affects more boys than girls, and lower limbs more than upper limbs or trunk.

Most of the orthopedic disabilities listed above are fairly distinct from one another and can be readily diagnosed. For this reason, the music therapist and other specialists must be aware of the on-going diagnoses and evaluations which are required of children considered to be handicapped, regardless of the suspected condition. Whatever the diagnostic category, the earlier the child is correctly diagnosed, the earlier he can be placed in an appropriate treatment program, and hence, the better the prognosis. Once properly diagnosed, the orthopedically handicapped child qualifies for education and related services, such as music therapy, under the provisions of Public Law 94-142, an important aspect of which is the concept of the "least restrictive environment."

Least Restrictive Environment

According to the federal law, Public Law 94-142 *(Federal Register,* 1977), each state was to have established policies and procedures "which insure that all handicapped children have the right to a free appropriate public education..." (p. 42481) in an environment that is commensurate with, and least restrictive to, their needs. Therefore, children are entitled to "related services," such as occupational therapy (OT), physical therapy (PT), or music therapy (MT) as deemed appropriate. This educational environment for orthopedically handicapped children is determined in large measure by the severity of their handicaps. Despite the severity, however, the child would qualify for the related service of music therapy if his handicapping condition was such as to prevent "normal" learning, i.e., learning in a classroom of his nonhandicapped peers.

If a child is *mildly* orthopedically handicapped, he may attend a regular class in the public school, receive no "regular" therapy, and require no hospitalization for his orthopedic problems. However, another *mildly* handicapped child may be in a regular class part of the day, in a resource room part of the day, and then receive the benefit of related services including music therapy.

If the child is *moderately* handicapped, the determination of the least restrictive environment may vary throughout his life. He may begin in a day treatment center, then attend a public school, spend some time in a hospital or special school, and return to a public school. His placement will depend upon the severity of his handicaps—physical, mental, and emotional; the quality of his maintenance program which includes regular therapy and home follow-up, positioning and activity during his school day; and the cooperation and motivation of the child.

In some cities, usually in larger school districts, there may be a special school which has several classes of children with moderate to severe orthopedic handicaps. In such a situation, there may be several Registered Music Therapists (RMTs) providing music therapy only for these children.

In smaller communities, or in the case of a more severely handicapped child, the child may be in a homebound program where he receives a few hours of formal education per week from a special education teacher and possibly some therapy from a Licensed-Registered Physical Therapist (LPT-RPT), Registered Occupational Therapist (OTR), Registered Nurse (RN), or a Licensed Vocational-Practical Nurse (LVN-LPN).

When *severely* orthopedically handicapped children are served in the public school setting, they may receive music therapy as a related service from a music therapy consultant who may work with a music educator, special educator, and/or classroom teacher. An example of this type of consulting activity is presented in Appendix B, which contains samples of two demonstration lessons presented to the teacher and aide of a self-contained special education class for orthopedically handicapped children by a music therapy consultant from one of the Education Service Centers in Texas.[2] In Appendix C, samples are given of music in a special school. The IEP's (individual educational plans) present music therapy goals, educational tasks, and evaluation procedures.[3]

Parents may prefer to place their children in a special, private, or state school for the orthopedically handicapped. Such schools often provide more intensive therapy and less formal education. These schools are often residential and may be part of a hospital or medical school. Frequently, children are referred to such placements to receive orthopedic surgery and/or daily physical and occupational therapy which would not be available in their home community.

It may be that the degree of an associated or secondary handicap is so great that residential, twenty-four hour care is the most suitable, least restrictive environment. Thus, the child with an orthopedic handicap may be placed in a state school for the mentally retarded or the emotionally disturbed for his secondary handicap, rather than for his primary one of a specific orthopedic problem.

The role of the music therapist will vary in these different environments. In the present monograph, an attempt is made to give samplings of cases, methods, and activities found in such environments. As will be seen, many similarities exist in the goals, objectives, methods, and activities used in music therapy with different types and levels of orthopedic impairments in children.

NEED FOR MUSICAL EXPRESSION

The Need for Aesthetic Expression

A music therapy program for orthopedically handicapped children will have certain elements in it which meet the basic needs of all children. Fundamental among these are experiences to meet the aesthetic needs of the child. All children need opportunities to experience beauty and the efforts involved in producing the beautiful; the orthopedically impaired child has a particular need to experience symmetry, contrast, and unity as these occur as part of every musical endeavor. It is beyond the scope of this monograph to quote the significant amount of research which substantiates the positive effects that aesthetic experiences have on all human beings. Suffice it to say that orthopedically handicapped children, as all children, need the kinds of experiences which come from singing, playing musical instruments, creating, and listening to music.

The Need for Independence of Expression

Music therapists who work with orthopedically handicapped children recognize that, as a result of their disabilities, these children do have needs beyond those of non-handicapped children. Frequently noticed among these children are ingrained dependency patterns developed from overprotection in the home and in the community. It is most important to begin in the home with infant stimulation as described in the home program in Appendix D.[4] The music therapy experience must concentrate upon development of the child rather than upon protection. Activities should be designed to give the child opportunities to respond through vocalization, movement, or playing simple instruments. Initially, the child may be responding primarily to the structure of the music, and then he may respond more freely and uniquely. In general, the more the child moves from total structure in his music responses toward creativity and originality, the better.

The Need for Development of Talent

A major principle to be applied in music therapy with all handicapped children is that of constructing a program based upon the child's strengths rather than his weaknesses, his potential rather than his handicap. For most orthopedically handicapped children, there will be some music behaviors that the child simply cannot accomplish. However, those behaviors which the child is completely capable of performing will be equally obvious. It is upon these strengths and capabilities that the music therapist must build a beneficial program. As a general rule, *the music therapist who seeks out the child's talents and, whenever possible, attempts to minimize his disabilities will do the most good for the orthopedically handicapped child.*

The Need for an Interdisciplinary Approach to Music Therapy

The physical therapist, occupational therapist, and speech pathologist will determine much of what is done for and with the orthopedically handicapped child. To be effective in working with the handicapped child, the music therapist must be more than just acquainted with these therapies; he needs to know specifically what is being done with the children receiving physical, occupational, and speech therapy. Likewise, these therapists should understand what the music therapist is doing to reinforce their therapeutic efforts. The relationships between music therapists and other therapists would improve if each would make an effort to share important insights and understandings gained from his particular vantage point. To the extent that such sharing is accomplished, the child will benefit with meaningful movement activities and efficient muscle strengthening experiences from playing certain instruments or from singing. By knowing what has been prescribed in related therapies, the music therapist is better able to plan music therapy activities which will help the child to obtain his/her goals. The cooperation needed between the music therapist, occupational therapist, and speech pathologist should also exist between the music therapist and other specialists in order to strengthen the interdisciplinary or multidisciplinary approach to education and therapy of the orthopedically handicapped child.

The interdisciplinary team consists of professionals and paraprofessionals who have direct contact with the child and would be found in a special school or hospital setting with a small patient or student population. For the orthopedically handicapped child, this team might well include clinicians from the disciplines of physical therapy, occupational therapy, speech pathology, nursing, medicine, special education, music therapy, recreation therapy, social service, psychology, diatetics, and especially the parents. The interdisciplinary team shares and discusses, on a face-to-face basis, the information they have obtained from their assessments of the child. From this information, the team members then identify the developmental needs of the child and devise ways to meet these needs without assigning particular developmental areas to specific disciplines. As a result, diagnosis, evaluation, and individual program planning for the child becomes a unified, integrated team product.

If the multidisciplinary team approach is utilized, some procedural differences occur. For example, the team may consist of representatives of the same disciplines and the child's parents, but the professional team members may not be the child's actual therapists or teachers. Each representative of a particular discipline reports the findings of the child's assessment only from a perspective assigned to his discipline or program. In this mode, the long- and short-term goals which he recommends may be independent of the findings or recommendations reported by other team members. The total program plan for the child is then made, based on the accumulated knowledge of several team participants. This type of team process is typically found in public school districts where hundreds of children are being served.

In the multidisciplinary approach, the music therapist would likely receive referrals from the team members for music therapy services. The music therapist would not necessarily (but could) be a regular member of such a team. However, he usually would be expected to create long-term and short-term goals after assessing the child referred for music therapy.

The music therapist has a unique contribution to make to the interdisciplinary team by evaluating the total child and assessing cognitive, affective, motor, and social skills. Music therapy provides the child with an opportunity to work toward developmental goals while developing musical skills and/or expressing his emotions through his unique responses to music. For example, handicapped children have a strong need for a feeling of security and independence; the structure of music itself provides the child with security, predictability and order, while his spontaneous participation in music, either vocally, through movement or playing a simple instrument, provides him with a needed realization of independence.

The use of music with the orthopedically handicapped child can decrease distractability, repressed emotions, tension, and hypersensitivity. In addition, the child can become motivated to interact with his peers, reinforce his muscle exercises, or control his positioning. Self-esteem can be enhanced through the joyful experience of interacting with appropriate instruments and singing. These uses of music will be exemplified in the case studies and discussion of special techniques and materials presented in this monograph.

CHILDREN WITH CEREBRAL PALSY, PART 1

While the symptoms and etiology of cerebral palsy will be presented on pages 55-56, a section on techniques for use with severely handicapped children with cerebral palsy is useful at this point. Since therapists and educators are working with many such severely handicapped children in public schools today, it is important to have some guidelines for maximizing the children's participation in music therapy. Since inexperienced therapists and educators may be frightened of programming for these children, it is important to discuss the challenge of music therapy with the severely handicapped. Additionally, the reader is urged to refer to the Glossary for definitions of key terms used below.

Positioning the Child

When serving severely physically handicapped children with cerebral palsy, the music therapist needs to work very closely with trained physical and occupational therapists to learn how to program for early motor responses during music therapy sessions. Frequent consultations should be made and programming developed from the recommendation of these experts regarding:

1. Positioning and moving a child to (a) normalize his muscle tone, (b) inhibit his abnormal reflex patterns, and (c) facilitate normal, controlled movement.

2. Observing for associated reactions in the child's body by watching undesirable movements in one part of the body as an attempt is made to move another part purposefully.

3. Aligning the body so that head and trunk are symmetrical without extremities twisted or turned abnormally.

4. Encouraging smooth, steady movements rather than quick, jerking movements.

5. Avoiding force to change a position or release a tight muscle.

6. Guiding the child's body into desired positions through flexion and/or support at key points on the trunk, such as the pelvis, shoulder girdle, and neck, thus facilitating normalization of muscle tone.

7. Moving extremities as muscles relax (adapted from Johnson, 1980).

Johnson (1980) states that head control is the first major milestone in gross-motor development. This "ability to stabilize the head in space . . . [is] associated with midline alignment of the head with the trunk, without excessive flexion forward or extension backward" (p. 8). Trunk control—necessary for sitting, crawling, transferring, standing, or walking—is dependent upon adequate trunk rotation. While a music therapist should not attempt to substitute for the developmental therapist, occupational therapist, or physical therapist, he still should be as aware as possible of the techniques used to facilitate normal movement. Certainly one should not position a child incorrectly in music therapy, reinforcing bad habits in the child and, therefore, strengthening primitive reflexes. Again, one must keep in mind the needs of the *total* child, and with the severely physically handicapped child, all therapists must be very alert to proper positioning and handling.

A child who retains primitive reflexes will exhibit patterns of abnormal flexion and extension which then inhibit normal body posture and function. The normal youngster will develop selective patterns of countermovements when his center of gravity is displaced. As his motor patterns are refined, he is able to move one part of his body independently of the others. For example, the severely handicapped child with cerebral palsy will have one or more of the following primitive reflexes present (as seen in Figure 1).

FIGURE 1
Primitive Reflexes

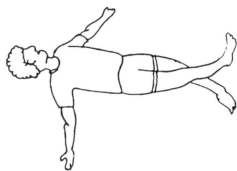

A. Prone Flexion Response

B. Supine Extension Response

A&B. Tonic Labyrinthine Reflex (TLR)

C. Assymmetric Tonic Neck Reflex (ATNR)

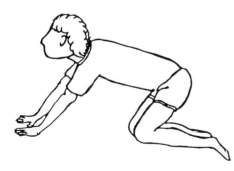

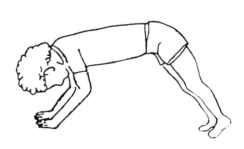

D. Dorsiflexed Head

E. Ventroflexed Head

D&E. Symmetrical Tonic Neck Reflex (STNR)

Tonic labyrinthine reflex (TLR). Increased flexor tone when child is in prone position with hands fisted; hips, knees, and elbows bent close to body (Figure 1A). Increased extensor tone in supine position with head thrown back; mouth open; back, hips, and knees rigidly straight; arms turned outward; less scissored (Figure 1B). Overall, greatly limits visual, manual (hand) exploration of environment.

Assymetric tonic neck reflex (ATNR). Arm extended (outstretched) to one side, face turned to that side, other arm flexed (bent) at elbow, hand near back of skull with same pattern observed in legs ipsilaterally (same side). Leg extended on same side as arm extended, flexed on same side as arm flexed. Overall, greatly limits eye-hand coordination and using hands together (Figure 1C).

Symmetrical tonic neck reflex (STNR). Proprioceptive reflex when head is raised, maximal extension of arms and flexion of legs (Figure 1D). When head is lowered, maximal extension of the legs and flexion of the arms (Figure 1E). Overall, greatly limits child initiating locomotion on four-point, hands and knees (adapted from Baken, 1980).

It is possible to minimize the effects of the abnormal reflex activity through selected positioning. By following the system of Bobath and Bobath (1975) of controlling "key points" located proximally (head, neck, shoulders, and hips), abnormal tone in a child's extremities is reduced. Generally, by placing the child in prone, sidelying, or correct sitting, it is possible to reduce his excessive muscle tone and to help him use his arms and hands.

Some important guidelines to follow are:

1. Handle the child slowly to give him time to react. Often a child may be tactually defensive and withdraw from touch.
2. Avoid pulling or stretching a spastic limb since this increases spasticity.
3. Massage a key area, such as a knee, elbow, shoulder, or hip, or rock the torso to reduce spasticity and help him to move.
4. Keep the child's head in midline and present all stimuli there to coordinate eyes and hands.
5. Change the child's position "every 15-20 minutes" (Baken, 1980, p. 5).
6. Place the child in a prone (on abdomen) position, on slant board, wedge, or bolster to inhibit tonic labrinthine and tonic neck reflexes, facilitating alignment of head and chest and use of hands and eyes in coordination at midline.
7. Place the child in prone position with arms forward to inhibit child pressing back with head and shoulders (extensor thrust).
8. Place the child in flexed side-lying position to inhibit strong ATNR, a marked extensor pattern of entire body, or a TLR, facilitating bilateral use of hands in midline position, visual tracking, and eye-hand coordination.
9. Use adapted equipment such as bolsters to seat the child, with hip flexion, and feet securely on the floor.
10. Use working surface slightly raised for the child to lift arms up, rotate arms in, bring shoulders forward to control extension patterns.
11. Have the child play a musical instrument on a table at nipple height to decrease trunk flexion.
12. Have the child grasp a peg on a nipple-height table with one hand for forearm supination, elbow extension, and external shoulder rotation, while using the other hand to play a musical instrument.
13. Place the athetoid child on the floor in sitting position with legs straight out for the most comfort and control.

14. Place the spastic child in flexed position, side-sitting on floor or supported in a flexed position to inhibit spastic responses.

15. Make sure the child sits on his buttocks and not on his lower spine.

Since it is so important to help a severely handicapped, "nonmoving" child to experience changes in postural position, these changes in position should be used as positive social encounters with a caring human. Prepare the child for the next position by talking to him, placing him in proper position in your arms, asking for his assistance, and waiting for his response. Be gentle in lifting a child but do not accept passivity if he can help. Establish eye contact, allow time for him to respond, and praise his efforts to help you.

(CAUTION: Avoid injuring yourself by bending your knees, keeping your back straight, lifting directly from in front, in back, or to the side of child. ALWAYS lift a heavy child with another person's help. In carrying a child, pause, adjust your position and his, and keep his body close to yours.)

The severely handicapped child with average or above average intelligence is often frustrated by his inability to express himself. Given the opportunity to participate in music therapy, such a child can benefit from "making" his own music. At times, it is most helpful to provide him a means of quick success so that he can readily play or sing with a "normal" family member who may not read or play music by conventional methods.

Case Study: Tom[5]

The following case study is an example of a severely handicapped teenager eager to play the organ with his mother or brother.

Tom was a 12-year-old boy severely involved with cerebral palsy, dyskinetic tension athetosis with some spasticity. He also had mild mental retardation, severe dyskinetic dysarthria, functional scoliosis, and myopia corrected with glasses. His speech was very labored and difficult to understand. He wore long-leg braces and was strapped into a motorized wheelchair through his waking day, except for a few hours of work on mats within his therapy areas. Tom used a headpointer for much of his academic work, such as typing on an electric typewriter, manipulating teaching machines, and using computers. He was an alert, cooperative boy who worked very hard to learn and was functioning on a second-to-third grade level academically.

Tom was seen individually two or three hours a week in music therapy. He had indicated a desire to play the chord organ and to sing. Long-term goals were to provide him a means of self-expression during his leisure time and to help him increase his breathing capacity. Activities included vocalizing and learning to play the chord organ with his headpointer to provide him a means of interacting with his brother or a peer.

Tom quickly learned to play the chords by matching first the letter symbols and then by memorizing the chord changes for simple songs. He also learned to play melodies by matching the numerals on printed music to the numerals above the keyboard of the organ. It was determined that he should learn from this simplified method so that he could play with a peer who could match numerals but not actually read music. Tom soon was picking out scales to show his music therapist that he knew how a scale was built. Then, he began trying to vocalize the scale as he played it. This structured form of music was very meaningful to him, and he began each of his sessions with playing and singing his scales. Soon thereafter, he learned to play the appropriate scale in response to its name, such as the key scale of F or D, having been taught these scales primarily by rote and demonstration.

Prior to discharge from the school, Tom was playing songs in his leisure time with one of the boys from his dorm and with his mother or brother on the weekends. It was possible to send a small chord organ with him to his next school placement, another residential school for children with orthopedic handicaps. A home program for music therapy was sent along with his discharge summary to that school.

Assessing the Child

To program properly the severely handicapped child, one must determine his strengths as well as weaknesses. It is important for the music therapist to evaluate the child prior to establishing long-term and short-term goals. As part of their clinical training, music therapy interns (MTIs)[6] are supervised in evaluating severely orthopedically handicapped children in special schools or clinical settings. The process of assessment can best be explained in the following example of one such evaluation made by a music therapy intern while supervised by a Registered Music Therapist (RMT).[7] The intern had observed and consulted with the occupational therapy and physical therapy staff prior to initiating the individual music therapy evaluation. She had also reviewed the child's medical treatment chart for other pertinent information.

Case Study: Bob[8]

The following case study is an example of an initial assessment report of an orthopedically handicapped boy. Results are shown of the assessment of his response to music and his motor, communication, cognitive, and social/emotional skills.

Music Responses and Skills. Reception: Bob is aware of music sounds. Although, when presented music of different qualities, intensities, and frequencies, Bob does not turn his body toward the source of the sound; he does move his eyes in the direction of the sound.

Perception: When using identical instruments, Bob can identify which is played more loudly by pointing. He cannot identify the order in which instruments are played if more than two instruments are used. If he hears an instrument without seeing it, he cannot identify it. Bob displays both vertical and horizontal tracking of instruments. He cannot associate music with written symbols.

Conception: Bob does not display any preference for different types of music.

Motor Skills. Gross Motor: Bob exhibits primitive reflexes which are unrelated to music as a stimulus. He cannot lie prone on his elbows and shows little lateral head control. When sitting, his head and arm positions are not symmetrical. He can sit independent of supports for short periods of time. Bob can lie down on his stomach from a sitting position and can move himself to a sitting position from lying on his stomach. He cannot cross midline with either arm and cannot creep freely on all fours.

Fine Motor: Bob exhibits very few fine motor skills. His left hand is usually clenched. He can hold maracas, sticks, or bell clusters in both hands when placed there by the therapist, but he has limited ability to reach for and grasp an instrument. He does not have purposeful eye movement from his hand to an instrument. Bob can feel instruments by moving his fingers and hands around the instruments. He cannot transfer instruments from hand to hand.

Bob can perform tone clusters on the keyboard with his left hand closed, moving his arm and hand as a single unit, although it requires much effort for Bob to reach out far enough to touch the keyboard. He cannot bring his hands together to clap.

Bob can shake a maraca only by moving his whole body. He cannot bang a stick on the floor. Bob will reach for the drum, but he cannot successfully produce a clear sound. Even after a crude attempt to release an instrument is made, Bob will retain the instrument in his hands.

Communication. Attending: When Bob responds to a stimulus, his body generally stiffens. When touched, he generally produces some vocal responses and smiles. In response to environmental stimuli, he will hold his head up during an activity, respond to familiar people and objects, and smile in response to verbalizations. He will respond to his own name by a change in facial expression and a few vocalizations. Bob can establish eye contact and maintain it for about four seconds. He identifies the location of sound by turning his head to the right or to the left. Bob will attend to a task for a short period of time by following directions and making eye contact.

Receptive: Bob will respond to verbal praise by smiling and continuing his behavior. He can identify common objects by pointing. His imitation skills are minor because of his physical limitations. He can follow one-step commands like "come," "sit," or "play the drum." He has not been able to follow one-step/two-object, or two-step commands.

Expressive: Bob occasionally produces vocal sounds for no apparent reasons. He will give an audible response to a disagreeable stimulus and an audible response when pleased. Upon occasion, he will laugh out loud.

Cognitive Skills. Spatial Relationships: Bob exhibits body awareness by identifying his head, arms, legs, hands, and feet. He can identify his shirt, pants, and shoes. He is also aware of "front," "back," "right," and "left" concepts. Bob can identify and match circles and squares. He recognizes numbers 1 through 9, and can match and find most colors. Bob recognizes his name in manuscript and he can place his first and last names in order.

Social/Emotional Skills. Self-Awareness: Bob will smile at himself when he looks in the mirror. He can establish self-identity in a musical activity by grossly pointing to himself. He is also aware of his own sex. Bob is willing to try new activities and participates independently.

Awareness of an Interaction with Others: Bob reacts to personal attention by smiling and responding to his own name. Sometimes he will show excitability by increasing his movement. He recognizes familiar people by greeting them nonverbally through smiling and increased movement. Bob accepts physical contact from therapists and peers. He does not seek personal attention and does not generally react to being left out or excluded. He shows awareness of peers in a group setting by watching others when they are helped by the therapist and when they perform. He accepts unfamiliar activities and people. He does not initiate interactions with peers, but nonverbally responds to interaction from them.

Play and Participation: Bob can entertain himself by playing with a musical toy or instrument. He anticipates music activities with pleasure.

Creativity and Expression: During music sessions, Bob exhibits enthusiasm, excitement, happiness, and some relaxation. Maladaptive behaviors that he exhibits include restlessness and frustration.

Recommendations. It appears that Bob will benefit from music therapy sessions because he enjoys music. Hopefully, music will be a motivating tool in helping Bob to utilize his arms through playing instruments such as the drum and tambourine. He can work on improvement of breath control by blowing on the harmonica and kazoo. Rocking and swaying to relaxing music might also be beneficial in relaxing his muscles and extending his arms. Through successful experiences in music sessions, Bob can work through some of his feelings of frustration and can develop a more positive self-image.

Documenting the Program

Documentation is a necessary part of a music therapy program plan. Through such documentation the music therapist is able to justify continuing an existing individual music therapy program plan or altering it as needed every three months.

Case Study: Matt[9]

Matt had been diagnosed as having cerebral palsy with moderate-to-severe quadriparesis, microcephaly, severe mental retardation, and a severe hearing impairment (bilateral sensorineural loss). The etiology of Matt's problems had not been specified in available records. He had increased muscle tone in all four extremities with the left side showing more involvement. He demonstrated a thrusting pattern which initiated from the jaw and head and pulled to the right. When supine, Matt showed total thrusting patterns; he could not lift his head but was able to roll from side to side; muscle tone in the shoulder girdle was especially increased. Range of functioning on the *Bayley Scales of Infant Development* (Bayley, 1969)[10] was from the two- to five-month level. Matt responded to relatively loud stimuli and would turn his head toward the sounds. Visually, he looked at various objects, but because of his delayed response, these needed to be presented slowly. Results of assessments indicated Matt was currently functioning in the severely retarded range.

Given Matt's inconsistent responses to sounds, he was assessed for possible treatment by the music therapist. Results of this assessment indicated the need for individual therapy, with a program plan including the following goals and objectives:

1. Provide auditory stimulation with voices, music, and drum.

    a. Reward eye contact with clapping, smiling.
    b. Reward any vocal responses with mimicking.
    c. Use auditory vibrations to encourage and sustain trunk, head control, and reaching responses.

2. Stimulate vocalization from the child.

    a. Stimulate chest and back with use of large stereo speaker and bass drum in close proximity to these bodily areas.
    b. Use music with definite rhythmic pulse.
    c. Place Matt in various positions: tailor and puppy sits, tall kneel, and stand-by facilitating appropriate positions, using body rhythms.
    d. Facilitate side-to-side movement while imitating vocalizations.

3. Provide for development of localization and consistent response to sound.

    a. Allow response time (up to 30 seconds).
    b. Reward with smiling, clapping.
    c. Inhibit abnormal responses (ATNR, other reflexes).

Following implementation of this program plan for a period of one year, Matt was reevaluated and the following results were noted: He was more consistent in his responses to sounds and had, therefore, made significant progress in all areas to achieve the above objectives. Matt now responded to sounds from the drum by batting at the drum surface, reaching for the stick, and maintaining an appropriate sitting, standing, or kneeling position 25% more often than on the initial assessment. He vocalized in response to auditory stimuli by cooing and giggling, and in at least one point in each session, Matt attempted imitation/mimicking of vocal sounds initiated by the drum, stereo speaker, or music therapist. Given his improvement in all goal areas, the interdisciplinary team recommended that Matt continue in a similar music therapy program with emphasis on the goal areas previously mentioned.

Sample IEP for Matt. Long-Range Goal: Matt will develop consistent responses to auditory stimuli on a continuum.

One-Year Objectives:

a. Matt will localize the source of a sound by turning his head toward the source 6 of 10 times. *Procedure:* A large drum and a stereo speaker will be played, and his name will be called. All distractions will be removed from the area, including visual and other auditory distractions.

b. Matt will be allowed up to 30 seconds to respond and responses will be rewarded with smiling and clapping.

c. Matt will maintain an appropriate standing position for a minimum of 60 seconds following facilitation by the music therapist, with support at one key point (shoulders or hips).

d. Matt will bear weight on his extended or flexed arms on the surface of the 26-inch base drum. *Procedure* (for b, c, and d): The music therapist will fix all points of support on the child. The sound of the drum will be the motivator. The pommel will be placed between Matt's feet. The music therapist will maintain Matt's weight on his heels while inhibiting his abnormal reflex patterns.

Measurement of Objectives: Observation will be made by the music therapist and evaluation repeated at 3-month intervals.

Using Special Techniques

Four special techniques useful in dealing with severely orthopedically handicapped clients are herewith presented. The neurodevelopmental treatment (NDT) and sensory (sensorimotor) integration are used throughout the USA, primarily in the areas of physical and occupational therapy. The controlled sensory stimulation is a multisensory technique often used in special education and occupational therapy, but also used in speech and physical therapy. Bliss symbolization is a specific method of alternate means of communication used most frequently by speech therapists or special educators.

1. *Neurodevelopmental treatment* (NDT) is a specialized program of specific handling, positioning, facilitation, and inhibition techniques which promote the normalization of muscle tone, the integration of abnormal reflex patterns, and the development of normal responses to the environment.

2. *Sensory (sensorimotor) integration* is the process by which sensory information is received and coordinated in the central nervous system; information comes via the senses of vision, hearing, touch, gustation, and olfaction, as well as through the kinesthetic, vestibular, and proprioceptive systems.

3. *Controlled sensory stimulation* is a multisensory approach to treatment in the various disability areas which requires monitoring sensory input and responses constantly. Consequently, reevaluation must take place periodically. Children need not have a deficiency in a sensory area for this technique to be useful. In fact, most physically/multiply handicapped children require multisensory activities in their program plans to facilitate learning and development.

4. *Bliss symbolization* is an organized set of graphic/verbal symbols to be used by nonverbal clients with a baseline level of receptive language skills. This is done by having clients select symbols with a finger point, gross hand point, eye contact, and electronic scanner, or by other methods. The client communicates basic needs, responses to social situations, conversations, information, etc., through using isolated symbols or combinations of symbols to form complete thoughts. Each board in the series of Bliss boards is increasingly more complex.

To utilize these and other specific techniques, music therapists are encouraged to seek continuing education courses. Information about such courses may be obtained from colleagues, particularly in physical and occupational therapy, speech therapy, or special education and/or by checking with universities or schools of allied health sciences.

One music therapist[11] has described a three-year plan in which she was involved with older students using Bliss boards in a variety of settings. During the first year, she used music activities to reinforce the actual learning of the Bliss symbols, promote accuracy and speed, and allow the students to make a variety of responses during the time frame of a song. During the second year, the speech pathologist met the Bliss class as a language group, and the music therapist met them for more sophisticated use of the Bliss symbols within the music therapy group. Here, the students applied the Bliss symbols in a nonlanguage setting and made responses in alternative, or nonverbal, language (e.g., "Name That Tune"). Also, the symbols were used while involved in perceptual/motor/rhythmic activities via music. During the third year, the nonverbal Bliss students and a group of peers who did not use the symbols were placed together in a music therapy group. All were encouraged to communicate with non-Bliss users through their symbols, and the non-Bliss users became familiar with this means of communication.

Adapting Musical Instruments

Traditional musical instruments are often inappropriate for the severely handicapped child. Instruments must be adapted for the child with missing limbs, involuntary neurological impulses, or limited motor skills.

An excellent sourcebook for adapting instruments for the orthopedically handicapped child is *Clinically Adapted Instruments for the Multiply Handicapped* by Clark and Chadwick (1979). Throughout their book, they emphasize the need for frequent consultation with an occupational therapist in making adaptations of instruments with the severely handicapped child. With such consultation, the music therapist then can reinforce desired kinds of movement through strumming motions, such as supination and pronation, elbow flexion and extension, radial and ulnar, abduction and adduction, and range of motion with the wrist. Also, grasp and release or types of degrees of prehensions can be developed through the use of various adapted picks.[12]

Included in the Clark and Chadwick text are suggestions for adapting picks, beaters or mallets, shakers, bells, simple wind instruments (single-reed horns, bird whistles, melodicas, harmonicas, etc.), stringed instruments, and percussive instruments. Adaptations can be made through building up handles, using straps, gloves, and cuffs or making adjustable frames and stands. Examples of some of these can be seen in the photographs in Appendix E.

While positioning of the body of the child and the instrument is of primary importance, the positioning of the hands or the type of hand grasp is especially important. Various types of hand grasps are explained in the Glossary.

Appendices F, G, and H contain excellent material regarding fine motor skills in music and adapting instruments, samples of materials and instruments used in making adaptations, and ranking of common instruments in terms of difficulty to produce sound.[13]

It is important for the music therapist to consult with the speech pathologist before adapting a wind instrument for a child. It may be that he is not a suitable candidate for therapy with musical instruments that need to be inserted into his mouth or pressed against his lips due to an exaggerated gag reflex, sensitivity around his lips, or inability to have lip closure. Likewise, Clark and Chadwick (1979) caution that the use of straps, cuffs, or gloves in helping small children with poor or no palmer prehension to hold and manipulate beaters and instruments must be cleared with the Human Rights Committee of the institution or school. This is a very valid statement since such use could be interpreted as restraining devices.

Other suggestions for adapting equipment and musical instruments include:
- rubber spatula or reinforced rubber doorstop to strum Autoharp;
- large adapted rhythm instruments (wheelchair sandpaper blocks);
- supported crossbars (five different heights) from which rhythm instruments and other props can be suspended; crossbars allow for width of even an electric wheelchair;

- large 26-inch bass drum, with foam padding around all rims; smaller children can lie on drum (side lying or supine); several children can kneel around drum; drum can be played by several children at once; vibrations permeate floor, chairs, etc.;
- large print music, both published and home devised;
- song sheets with words color-coded to indicate chord changes;
- removable velcro strips for keyboards with color, numeral, or letter codes.

Moving with the Child

Critical for the orthopedically handicapped child is the opportunity to move. The music therapist should program carefully to include movement and dance for even the most severely handicapped. The desire to dance and to move rhythmically seems to be innate in all human beings; even the most severely handicapped child has the right to experience the joy of moving to music.

The music therapist working with a severely handicapped child will need much patience in helping this individual to express himself through movement. However, to make it most meaningful and therapeutic, the music therapist should take the time and energy to position the child in such a way that he is able to move. Initially, encourage the child to move as he is positioned in his wheelchair or on a stretcher or bed. This may mean that he can only move his head slightly or an arm or a leg minimally. However, after conferring with the physical and/or occupational therapist or a specially trained dance therapist, the music therapist should help the child to be positioned on a mat, if appropriate, for greater freedom of movement. While this will mean much one-to-one physical handling of the child, this needs to be done whenever it is not specifically contraindicated.

Through movement or dance, the child will be awakened to his own total body in a nonthreatening manner. Through the pleasure of moving to music, he will reach out to discover and explore his own kinesphere (space around his body). If he has been denied a limb or part of his body, he may gradually discover it again through volitionally moving more freely to music.

While the child will gain from being passively moved to music, the therapist should encourage spontaneous, independent movement. In some instances, the child may be so weak or so rigid that he cannot initiate movement, so for some time, the therapist will need to help him move by isolating his body parts. (**CAUTION:** Since the music therapist is now placing himself in a "hands on" position, he must be certain that he has consulted with the physical and/or occupational therapist as to the limitations or contraindications for each child.)

Gradually, the music therapist needs to give the child an opportunity to initiate his own movement. Then, the therapist should mirror this movement and try to expand, extend, or vary his movement. It is recommended that the child be encouraged to move freely to instrumental or vocal music without structured lyrics such as "shake your head, raise your right hand." Perhaps he will be responsive to simple humming, whistling, or a glissando on a piano or xylophone. The primary goal at this stage is to allow and encourage the child to move at will.

If a severely handicapped child can move his head or hands only slightly when requested to move or to dance, the therapist should give him verbal and tactile reinforcement for his movements, and should then help him to experience more movement. Just as we meet the severely handicapped child on his own level of singing—perhaps from the low pre-singing level of vocalizing—and then program to help him move upward, movement programs should begin with the child's most basic moves and seek to expand and increase performance.

The severely handicapped child often is very fearful of movement, even changes in positioning. We can help decrease these fears by assisting him to explore his space through movement to music. Often the music serves as a needed distractor or reinforcer as he attempts new positions or extends a limb in an unfamiliar direction.

Further discussion of movement and dance will be included as each specific orthopedic handicap is addressed in this monograph. Techniques for encouraging vocalization, speech, and singing will be included under the topics of cerebral palsy and closed head injuries.

CHILDREN WITH CEREBRAL PALSY, PART 2

Of each 100,000 births, six are estimated to be children born with cerebral palsy each year. One will see two children with cerebral palsy per 1,000 school-aged children. Cerebral palsy is a nonprogressive disorder of movement or posture due to a brain lesion. Congenital cerebral palsy is the result of diseases or disturbances during pregnancy or at the time of birth (86% of the cases); acquired cerebral palsy is the result of injuries during late childhood (14% of the cases) (Bleck, 1975c).

Types and Characteristics of the Problem

According to Salter (1970), three main types of cerebral palsy comprise 90% of the total cases:

1. Spastic type, 65%: pyramidal system lesion in the cerebral motor cortex.
2. Athetoid type, 20%: extrapyramidal system lesion in the basal ganglia.
3. Ataxic type, 5%: cerebellar and brain stem lesion (p. 240).

The remaining 10% consist of tremor, rigidity, mixed, and atonic types. Even though the spastic, athetoid, or ataxic movement patterns predominate, there is considerable evidence that great diffusion of brain malfunction exists in cerebral palsy. Also, one will not see a "pure" case of a spastic type, athetoid type, nor ataxic type in any child.

Some characteristics of the three main types of cerebral palsy are:

1. *Spastic*
   - spastic muscle imbalance causing flexion, adduction, and internal rotation probably involving different limbs: monoplegia—one limb; hemiplegia—upper and lower limb of one side; diplegia, or paraplegia—both lower limbs; and quadriplegia, tetraplegia, or bilateral hemiplegia—all four limbs;
   - increased muscle tone, paralysis of voluntary movement patterns, strong contraction of muscles with attempted movement or stretching, increased deep tendon reflexes, clonus (repetitive muscle contractions);
   - swallowing may be affected; slow labored speech.

2. *Athetoid*
   - involuntary, uncontrollable movements in muscle groups of all four limbs and face; deep tendon reflexes usually normal; twisting, writing contortions in limbs, meaningless grimaces in face;
   - difficulty in swallowing, jerky speech;
   - involuntary movements increase under emotional tension or attempts at voluntary movements, excess movement absent during sleep.

3. *Ataxic*
   - disturbed coordination of muscle groups, poor equilibrium or balance, unsteady gait;
   - tremulous, quavering voice;
   - intelligence usually unaffected.

Etiology of the Problem

The etiology, or causes, of cerebral palsy are grouped according to onset: prenatal (before birth); perinatal (around the time of birth); and postnatal (after birth) (Bleck, 1975e). Prenatal causes include the following seven determinants:

1. *Prematurity.* Birth weight less than five pounds and less than 40 weeks gestation (in the womb). Accounts for 33-60% of all cases of cerebral palsy.
2. *Unknown causes.* Estimated 30% of prenatal cerebral palsy.
3. *Infections* in mother during pregnancy. Rubella in first trimester of pregnancy, viral or parasitic infection.

4. *Fetal anoxia* (lack of oxygen to the fetal brain). Knotting of umbilical cord, hemorrhage in mother, separation of placenta.
5. *Metabolic disorders.* Toxemia of pregnancy in last trimester due to diabetes in mother.
6. *Blood incompatibility* of fetus and mother. RH factor preventable in most cases with immunization of mother and/or early exchange transfusion in infant.
7. *Inherited.* Rare, but seen in familial spastic paraplegia.

Perinatal causes include at least two reasons for cerebral palsy:

1. *Fetal asphyxia, anoxia, or hypoxia.* Lack of oxygen which may be due to lung collapse, pneumonia, or pain-relieving or sedating medications depressing respiratory centers of fetal brain.
2. *Birth injury.* Use of forceps, breech birth (feet first), prolonged labor, excessive birth weight.

Postnatal causes are at least five in number:

1. *Encephalopathies* (brain infections and toxic conditions). Meningitis, encephalitis and lead poisoning account for 57% of all postnatal cerebral palsy.
2. *Head injuries.* Falling from heights, automobile accidents, or battered children account for 18%.
3. *Cerebral embolism or thrombosis* (clot or hemorrhage). Usually produce spastic hemiplegics.
4. *Cerebral anoxia.* Lack of oxygen due to near drowning, carbon monoxide poisoning.
5. *Brain tumor.*

Handicaps associated with the described motor disorders of cerebral palsy include:

1. *Mental retardation.* 50% seriously mentally retarded, 25% educably retarded.
2. *Speech or language defect.* 48%.
3. *Hearing defects.* Athetoids often, but only 2% of spastics.
4. *Visual problem.* Hyperopia (far-sightedness), esotropia (crossed eyes), or failure of upward gaze.
5. *Cognitive disorders.* 86% of spastics, 12% of athetoids, and 55% of spastic hemoplegics (from acquired cerebral palsy).
6. *Perceptual and visual/motor disorders.* More common in spastics, especially spastic hemiplegics.
7. *Oral-dental problems.* Drooling and difficulty in swallowing.
8. *Astereognosis.* Loss of shape and texture sensation of hand found in spastic hemiplegics.
9. *Labile temperament and short attention span.* Frequently seen (adapted from Bleck, 1975c).

Treatment of the Child

Treatment for the child with cerebral palsy often includes physical therapy, orthotics (bracing), orthopedic surgery, nursing, occupational therapy, speech therapy, special education, and sometimes drug therapy. When available, the child may also receive music therapy, recreation therapy and/or adapted physical education, counseling, dance therapy, and play therapy. Throughout the child's life, social service plays an important role in helping the family become involved with therapists in treatment.

There are numerous special techniques that are used in working with the child with cerebral palsy. Often the same technique may be used by the physical, occupational, and speech therapists, but to different degrees of concentration or to different areas of the child's body. The various therapists need to have close communication, and when possible, treat the child together as a team. While the mastery of these special techniques requires considerable training, the music therapist working with orthopedically handicapped children should become familiar with techniques being used with these children by other therapists. This can be achieved through observing and consulting with those therapists, reading about the techniques, and participating in special courses in these techniques.

Two of the most popular techniques used today are neurodevelopmental treatment (NDT) and sensory (sensorimotor) integration. Another technique of interest to music therapists is the facilitation technique of Margaret Rood, in which muscles are activated through sensations of heat, cold, and brushing. If the occupational therapists are using this latter technique around the oral area, the music therapist should observe and discuss it with these therapists prior to introducing even simple wind instruments to the children.

When a child is treated in a special school for children with cerebral palsy, it is possible to reinforce the interdisciplinary team goals in addition to musical goals. This is seen in the following progress note in SOAP form.

Documentation through SOAP

A method of documentation used in many hospitals today is the Problem Oriented Report (POR) method through which the patient's progress is written directly in a master chart. The therapist writes Subjective (S) observations, Objective (O) statements, Assessment (A) interpretations of the O statements, and a Plan (P) of what will be done as a result of these observations. This method of documenting is called SOAPing and the Objective and Assessment statements should refer to specific problems compiled by the team.

Case Study: Melanie[14]

The following case study presents an example of SOAP documentation. (The problem list was not yet available in the chart so there is no reference to the numbered problems.)

S — "Are we going to play the piano today?"

O — "The patient is working on keyboard activities. She moves her fingers independently with her left hand and is working to gain independence with her fingers of her right hand. She can identify "quarter," "eighth," "half," and "whole" notes. She can clap rhythms with these notes and can play keys on the piano in correct rhythm. The patient walked to the music therapy cottage two times on a paved walk using a metal walker and long-leg braces; it takes approximately 20-30 minutes. She returns to the school in her wheelchair. The patient has been doing movements to music which require use of her right upper extremity such as raising her hand, touching her toes, and stretching her arm to the side.

A — The patient is making progress in keyboard activities which incorporate different rhythmic patterns. She seems to enjoy her success; and it is a motivating activity for the patient to use her right hand. She seems to learn new songs quickly and retain the concepts from session to session. She does well walking to the cottage and seems to enjoy singing as she walks. It appears to be a challenge for her to walk that distance so the success she has had is motivating. The patient's range of motion seems to have improved through movement to music. In this respect, she tends to compete well with her peers which results in a greater range of motion than was observed in the past.

P — Continue keyboard activities. Make a possible adaptation for her right hand. Walk to the music therapy area one time each week. Continue movement to music.

Encouragement of Vocalization

Since so many children with cerebral palsy have brain damage which limits their ability to process or produce speech, the music therapist should include music activities to encourage and develop speech. The child with dysarthria has great difficulty even producing or maintaining lip closure so he will need to become more aware of his lips and then learn to close his lips. Some very helpful activities are to try to learn to blow like the wind, in response to songs about the wind; or to blow away cotton balls, strips of paper, etc. Gradually, this can be developed into the child blowing a kazoo, single reed horn, and then the harmonica.

For the child struggling to produce any vocal sounds, the music therapist needs to hum or vocalize with the child to encourage him to try to make sounds. Usually a child is very responsive to hearing sounds and he will eventually try to match the sounds he hears. This may take place slowly, but the music therapist must be willing to move at the child's pace, allowing the matching to happen when he is ready. He should be exposed to much humming and vocalizing as he is being placed in comfortable positions such as lying over a large ball or in the therapist's arms.

Within a small group of peers, the child needs to be given time to produce his sounds. This may mean that the therapist must sing lyrics slowly to allow the child a chance to imitate vowel or animal sounds when it is his turn to respond. As Graham and Beer (1980) and Nordoff and Robbins (1977) have stressed, songs should be presented within the range of the child's musical ability. If the child can only discriminate pitches within a two- or three-step range, that is where he should be expected to vocalize. For the nonverbal child, to be able to sing softly within his range or match the pitches of tone bells, xylophone, or the piano can be a most satisfying, exciting experience.

As in other imitative behavior, the child usually likes to have his sounds imitated. The therapist can try to vary these sounds and introduce different sounds for the child to try to imitate.

The use of open-ended phrases is very helpful for the child who is having difficulty remembering words or who has unintelligible speech. The therapist must listen closely to recognize approximations of the words to acknowledge his attempts and then to help the child to sing them more clearly. From the music therapy assessment, the therapist can determine what sounds the child needs to improve. Then after consultation with the speech therapist, a program can be planned to include songs of activities to develop the needed sounds such as "buh," "puh," or "mm." Often the child with the most involved speech is the one most anxious or determined to sing. For the child with delayed language or with acquired cerebral palsy who is regaining his language, he should be encouraged to join his peers in singing the lyrics of age-appropriate songs. The very young child may join in on only a few words of a song and then gradually, with much positive encouragement, will spontaneously add more words. The older child with acquired cerebral palsy may attempt more lyrics by strumming the Autoharp or guitar as he sings with another peer or the music therapist.

Movement Therapy for the Child

Movement activities found most effective in working with children with cerebral palsy include unstructured creative movement (improvisation), highly structured movement, and relaxation which emphasize isolation of body parts. Creative movement often begins with mirroring in which the children face partners and take turns leading and following very simple movements involving just the head, hands, arms, or legs. The complexity of the movements will be determined by the mobility and confidence of each child. At times, the music therapist may need to help the more mobile child keep his movements simple enough so that the more involved child can approximate the movements. Children greatly enjoy the moving as different animals, balloons, or machines. As they become more confident in moving freely, they will enjoy music that stops suddenly, requiring them to "freeze," or music that changes tempo.

Many of the exercises from the F. and J. Robins' book, *Educational Rhythmics for Mentally and Physically Handicapped Children* (1968) are highly structured but can be adapted for physically handicapped children and still be very effective and appealing to perform. Initially, it is very helpful to use many of the visual aids those authors recommend in presenting the various exercises. After children have learned several of the Educational Rhythmics exercises, they do not need as many visual aids to stimulate their imaginations. The combination of the structured dance steps, the poetry or lyrics of the songs, and the appropriate music (usually classical or folk dances) seems to have a universal appeal to handicapped children and they attempt to participate on whatever level they are able.

Relaxation to soothing, sedative music or repetitive environmental sound is very important with some children with cerebral palsy. Not only do they learn to relax on the mat, but they are helped to relax isolated body parts while seated in their wheelchairs or seated on regular chairs. Children are usually more receptive to passive movement to help them relax when it is done gently with music. Children can be shown how to help each other to relax while lying on the mat, by slowly stroking each other's hands, necks, arms, etc., as the music therapist verbally instructs them to think about that particular part of their body. This technique has been most helpful in developing sharing between hyperactive, demanding children, and at the same time in providing much needed calming when the children are over-stimulated by their environment. Often, such children will request "to relax on the mat first." These children then can attend to other music activities following a few minutes of relaxation.

Generally speaking, the child with athetoid cerebral palsy will have more control in his movements with sedative, melodic music while the child with spastic cerebral palsy will have more control in his movements with stimulative, strongly rhythmic music. However, responses vary with each child (Schneider, 1968).

Case Study: Lisa[15]

When the child is restricted by casting following orthopedic surgery, it may be necessary to modify the program in music therapy. The following case study describes the creative adapting by one music therapist.

Lisa was a 14-year-old Latin American girl with cerebral palsy, tension athetosis, in a residential school. She was functionally nonambulatory but was able to propel a wheelchair with her feet. Lisa had very limited movement in her arms. Prior to a surgical operation, her arms usually assumed a flexed position with the palms of each hand resting slightly in front of her shoulder regions. Lisa had a flexor release of her left elbow to increase her range of motion (ROM). It was anticipated that her left arm could be rotated to an adductive or abductive position and used for various activities such as holding onto the handle of a walker and performing fine motor tasks. After the surgery, a cast which placed her arms in a supine position was placed on Lisa's left arm for approximately four weeks.

During Lisa's placement at this school, she had been receiving individual music therapy sessions. Initially, she had learned how to play an electric chord organ using a headpointer to reinforce her typing skills. However, at the team's recommendation, the music therapist developed a new program to reinforce Lisa's use of her left arm rather than the headpointer. Since she could not play the chord organ using her casted left arm, the music therapist introduced a smaller electronic instrument to Lisa. She worked on music therapy goals of strengthening and increasing the range of motion in her left arm by playing an electronic instrument called the Magical Musical Thing designed by Mattel. This instrument is 21 inches long and displays a color-coded keyboard on one side. When one of the 25 keys is pressed, an electronic sound is heard. To play the Magical Musical Thing, Lisa sat in front of a mirror and held the instrument in the palm of her left hand. The mirror allowed Lisa to see the color-coded keyboard, since the cast restricted her arm from moving to a more flexed position.

Lisa also read her music by looking into the mirror. She learned how to play songs like "London Bridge" and "Down in the Valley." The musical compositions consisted of a series of colored squares, each representing a different musical pitch. The squares were arranged in reverse order, so that when Lisa viewed the image of the music in the mirror, the "notes" (colored squares) were correctly arranged. The therapist also adapted the Magical Musical Thing by covering up some of the keys with dark tape. The therapist placed her own color stickers on the instrument, since the instrument revealed a color scheme utilizing colors which were difficult to discriminate.

When the cast was removed, Lisa's forearm assumed an extended position parallel to the floor. She used her arm in this position to play the electric chord organ again. As Lisa gained strength in her arm, she was able to adduct the arm so that the index, middle, and ring fingers of her left hand rested on the surface of the white keys of the organ. The therapist frequently had to assist Lisa when she played black notes by physically guiding her hand to a position over the keys. Lisa also exercised her left forearm by strumming the strings of a portaharp in a circular motion when the instrument rested against the trunk of her body. Continual progress and improvement was made by Lisa on the chord organ and on the portaharp until her discharge one month later.

Case Study: Jim[16]

Although a child with cerebral palsy may make great strides in his physical and occupational therapy goals, he may fail to adjust to a public school placement if his family provides inadequate emotional support. This case study exemplifies how music therapy can help such a child increase his security and self-esteem to bridge that gap of inadequate family support.

Jim was a 12-year-old male with cerebral palsy, spastic diparesis with an IQ of 65, ambulatory with two forearm crutches, and with good use of his arms and upper body. He was admitted to a small residential school for the second time due to regression in physical and social behavior at home.

Jim's home environment fostered feelings of insecurity and poor self-esteem. He was rejected by his family and frequently told he was "dumb" and "retarded." His family referred him for readmission after he began crawling and acting out at home. Initial evaluations found him to be very withdrawn, exhibiting little eye contact, and having a tendency to mumble in his interactions. In his music therapy group, Jim laughed and talked inappropriately and exhibited poor on-task behavior. His leisure time was spent fighting, bullying, and sexually acting out.

It was decided that Jim's needs could best be met individually in music therapy. Since he had expressed interest in playing guitar, he was given guitar lessons four hours per week. The two major music therapy goals were (1) to increase security and self-esteem and (2) to provide a medium for productive use of leisure time.

Initially, Jim's frustration tolerance was very poor; if he could not play a chord correctly the first time it was presented, he would begin acting out by rolling on the floor, verbally "putting himself down," and refusing to try again. The music therapist spent the first month on one- and two-chord songs (therapist and Jim alternating chord changes). After two months, Jim began asking for new chords and songs. His frustration tolerance also increased in that he would keep trying to play a chord until correct. He began "bragging on himself" to other staff. Auditory discrimination exercises were introduced to help Jim learn to tune the guitar independently.

Two 30-minute practice periods were provided for Jim in the evenings. The music therapist was in the room with him, but they were separated by a room divider. Jim was supplied with song sheets and could ask for assistance if needed. At first, he would call to the therapist every two minutes and complain about not being able to play by himself; soon be began to play longer and complain less frequently.

In his third month of music therapy, Jim initiated teaching guitar to the other boys in his dorm. He organized informal sing-a-longs during the evening. There was a notable decrease in acting-out behavior after school hours. After three months, Jim was added to a group with one other student to encourage appropriate group social skills. In addition to guitar, this group worked on creative activities that revealed a different side of Jim. He was found to be very creative in songwriting activities. His compositions were distributed around the school so that he could receive additional reinforcement from staff. After five months in music therapy, Jim gave a concert with the other student for the entire school. This concert was evidence of Jim's increased security and self-esteem. He participated in planning and organizing the details (i.e., program, choosing ushers, extra rehearsals, costumes, etc.). During the concert, he consistently sang and played. He kept eye contact with his audience and thanked them appropriately. When Jim's parents were informed of his progress, they bought him a guitar. His increased security and self-esteem helped him overcome his physical regression and encouraged more positive social interactions and leisure-time skills.

Case Study: Dick[17]

At times, the handicapped child learns to accept his limitations more readily than his family does. This may be seen with the orthopedically handicapped child who is mainstreamed (placed in a regular school classroom). Discharge planning from a residential school may well need to include recommendations for positive peer interaction and suggestions for the music educator in the child's home school.

Dick was a 10-year-old boy with moderate spastic diparesis cerebral palsy and intermittent exophoria in a residential school for children with cerebral palsy. He was very verbal and personable with normal intelligence. He was manipulative and often instigated arguments with the staff and his peers. Although he could walk functionally in long-leg braces on short-arm crutches, his father was very demanding that Dick learn to walk as well as his normal brother. Dick had good bilateral hand usage and he wrote legibly but slowly.

Dick was seen two hours a week for individual music therapy. His long-term goals were to decrease his arguments and to teach him to play the Autoharp. Dick had requested to learn to play the Autoharp to accompany his own singing of folk songs. Initially, he was very shy about singing as he made the correct chord changes. However, with much encouragement from his music therapist, he learned to use his involved left hand to strum while holding a pick with a natural grasp. He was able to isolate the fingers of his right hand to accurately make the chord changes on the Autoharp by pressing the appropriate chord button on the instrument.

Prior to his return to his home school and regular classroom, the music therapist found a suitable Autoharp for Dick and requested that his father purchase it. In spite of Dick's apprehension, his father was convinced that this would be beneficial to his son, and he purchased it. Dick was now playing the Autoharp in the evenings at the residential school to avoid frequent arguments when bored, and he had volunteered to play the chord organ with a severely handicapped peer. He would help to position this peer properly at the organ, fasten his headpointer, and secure his upper limbs in the chair.

While Dick had a much improved self-image upon his discharge, it was not possible to help him maintain this when he returned home. His father and brother did not adequately accept the importance of music in Dick's life, and they did not encourage him to play. The father could only see his own expectations for his son, and constantly pressured him to keep up in his homework for his regular classes. In spite of a verbal report to the father in the team discharge meeting and a written discharge summary and home program in music therapy, the father failed to recognize the emotional value of music therapy for Dick.

It might have helped if the music therapist had communicated directly with the music teacher in Dick's public school. Since Dick was placed in a regular music class, his reports from the residential school were not channeled to that music teacher. Only occasionally do orthopedically handicapped children find music teachers within the community who are willing to teach them.

Therapeutic Music Program

This author visited a unique program at the Settlement Music School in Philadelphia, Pennsylvania in March, 1981. The Moss Rehabilitation Hospital in Philadelphia was seeking alternative modes of therapy for their increasing pediatric population. Instrumental music study was seen as an inexpensive alternative to traditional therapies which would also be attractive to the chilren and their parents. The Settlement Music School collaborated with Moss Rehabilitation Hospital to initiate a program, funded by the U.S. Office of Education, to provide instrumental music education for the children which would, at the same time, provide therapy for their physical handicaps. *A Guide to the Selection of Musical Instruments with Respect to Physical Disability* was written under this grant and is soon to be published.[18]

The *Guide* enables a pediatrician to write a prescription for a specific musical instrument as therapy for a particular handicapped child, and specifies the measurements of torso or arm flexibility required and the positions needed to play each musical instrument, and identifies the muscles or nerves it can strengthen and what it demands of the player's fingers, arms, body, and legs. The data in the *Guide* are the result of observation and measurement of professional musicians actually playing each instrument. The research was done by experienced occupational therapists and staff at Moss Rehabilitation Hospital.

The children participating in the Therapeutic Music Program attend public schools and, in most cases, are being mainstreamed in their respective schools. The intention of the Settlement Music School is to provide an opportunity for physically handicapped children to have a normal experience of instrumental music lessons from professional musicians. The musicians who are involved in the program receive an orientation to disability from the Moss Hospital staff prior to teaching the children. The musicians then have frequent consultations, as needed, from the occupational therapist or other specialists such as psychologists, speech therapists, or pediatricians during the school year.

This is one approach for meeting the needs of physically handicapped children who are less involved and who are motivated to study instrumental music in a traditional manner of private lessons within a conservatory setting. For these children, lessons provide normalization through music study.

In addition to the information contained in the guide available from the Therapeutic Music Program, a music therapist can find further information about the use of playing musical instruments to achieve specific goals such as range of motion in specific joints of the body, coordination and endurance, in a book by Karen J. Miller (1979) and in an article by Barbara Denenholz (1959).

CHILDREN WITH SPINA BIFIDA

Spina bifida, a serious handicapping condition in children, refers to open defects in the child's vertebral column resulting from abnormal fetal development. *Myelomeningocele* is the "outpouching of the spinal cord through the back of the bony vertebral column that has failed to form," while the *meningocele* is "the outpouching of the coverings of the spinal cord and not the cord itself" (Bleck, 1975e, p. 181). In contrast, *spina bifida occulta* has no outpouching of spinal cord or meninges, but is "the failure of formation of the back arches of the vertebra" (p. 181). This deformity is seen in "between 0.1 and 4.13 of 1,000 live births . . . . Myelomeningoceles are five to four times as common as meningoceles" (p. 181). It is thought that viruses or other noxious agents cause the neural tube to stop developing completely and to close in the first 30 days of pregnancy.

Disabilities and Treatment of the Problem

Disabilities commonly seen in a child with spina bifida (myelomeningoceles) are:

- Flaccid paralysis of the lower limbs and trunk. Weak or no muscle function dependent upon the level of the spinal cord damage.
- Bony deformities resulting from muscle imbalance from partial paralysis in lower limbs. Club foot, dislocation of hip, severe rocker bottom, scoliosis (spinal curvature), lordosis (swayback), and/or kyphosis (humpback).
- Complete loss of skin sensation to temperature, pain, and touch. Extent of the problem determined by level of spinal cord damage. Frequent decubitus (pressure ulcers) and burns.
- Bladder paralysis due to injury above the level of major nerve supply to bladder. Usually paralysis of bladder and muscles controlling urination. Results in incontinence (absence of emptying of bladder), frequent bladder and kidney infections, and eventual loss of kidney function.
- Bowel paralysis. Frequent paralysis of rectum and spincter (anal muscles) causing frequent soiling.
- Hydrocephalus. An associated deformity seen in 90-95% of these children. A blockage of spinal fluid circulation in the brain with resultant mental retardation, seizures, and sometimes spastic paralysis of the lower limb (Bleck, 1973e).

A child with spinal bifida receives treatment from birth from many medical specialists prior to any contacts with other therapists. These medical specialists work as a team to manage the child through his life:

1. *Neurosurgeons.* The surgeon usually closed the defect of myelomeningoceles in infancy as a life-saving matter. Then hydrocephalus is treated promptly through the insertion of shunts (permanent drainage systems): plastic tubes and an interposing valve between the ventricle and the heart (ventriculoatrial shunt) or the ventricle and the abdomen (ventriculoperitoneal shunt) (Bleck, 1975e, p. 186).

2. *Urologists.* It is mandatory to regularly monitor the child's urine content through urinalysis and culture of the urine for bacteria. Continuous attempts are made to help the child learn to empty his bladder through special techniques or through the use of a catheter and collector.

3. *Orthopedic Surgeons.* Early use of self-standing braces for support of trunk and lower limbs is prescribed. Several orthopedic surgical procedures are used to keep the child straight and to keep the disability from becoming worse. Surgeries are done to prevent dislocation of hip and to correct foot deformities and the spinal deformities of lordosis, scoliosis, or kyphosis. The treatment for flaccid paralysis found in the child with spina bifida is similar to that for poliomyelitis, and the treatment for spastic paralysis is comparable to that for cerebral palsy.

4. *Pediatricians.* These specialists care for the general health of the child and specialize in the child's bowel management through the use of medications, suppositories, and diet.

5. *Occupational and Physical Therapists.* These specialists begin therapy early with the child to teach activities of daily living, strengthening of weak muscles, gait training with crutches, using wheelchairs and transfers.

With early treatment and consistent medical care through childhood, many children with spina bifida exhibit borderline or average intelligence. However, the mental functioning of other children may be limited by the extent of brain damage caused by hydrocephalus. This may be manifested in developmental delays, or learning and language disabilities. Verbosity in some children with hydrocephalus is misleading as to expectations of academic achievement. Furthermore, the child with spina bifida is limited in his ability to physically explore his environment due to the paralysis or deformity of his lower limbs. He will need extra opportunity to "scoot about" as best as he can to discover his environment. He, or his family, may also develop emotional problems as a result of an enlarged head, shunts, or the wearing of helmets (for protection).

Due to frequent hospitalizations for surgery or medical tests, the child will miss a considerable amount of schooling, which will interfere with his academic, social, and emotional development. Often the child with spina bifida will experience several shunt revisions which will require his head to be shaved each time. The acceptance of his shaved head or the wearing of a wig while new hair grows may be very traumatic for the child, his family, and his friends.

As with the other orthopedic handicapping conditions, the greater the severity of the handicap, the more complex the acceptance by the child. The child with spina bifida will be readjusting to his many handicaps as he passes through different developmental stages of childhood. During many stages of his life, he will have a difficult adjustment period concerning his urinary incontinence or frequent soiling. He may react to these frustrations with regression, aggression, and/or frequent manipulative behavior.

Case Study: Susie[19]

One effective method of dealing with some of the manipulative behaviors seen in several children with spina bifida has been the use of contractual agreements. One such case is that of Susie.

When first seen in music therapy, Susie was a 5-year-old child with spina bifida and arrested hydrocephalus. During her year as a student in a residential school for orthopedically handicapped children, she underwent orthopedic surgery and a shunt revision. She was of normal intelligence and spoke very clearly in age-appropriate language. She had moderate visual-perceptual disabilities, and she was very demanding with her peers, staff, and family.

She learned to play the chord organ compatibly with a peer and then in individual music therapy, she learned to play with both hands simultaneously. By matching colors, she could press the chord buttons to make appropriate chord changes with her left hand while matching numerals to play simple tunes with her right hand on the chord organ. She learned to use three fingers in isolation in her left hand and five in her right hand before her discharge. She was mainstreamed into a regular first grade in a public school. About three years later, she was attending a regular class in a public elementary school, singing in a children's choir in a large church, and continuing to play her chord organ at home.

Susie was able to walk unassisted in short-leg braces on forearm crutches, but she was still manipulating others by wanting to avoid taking part in the opening procession with the church choir. The choir director consulted with her former music therapist (a member of the adult choir) and it was arranged, with Susie's agreement, that she would process on crutches next to a peer who would carry her books, if she wanted to sing with the choir. She cooperated by following through on this arrangement.

She then asked to learn piano, like her sister, and individual music therapy was arranged in her home (with the same former music therapist). Her parents indicated that Susie needed an emotional outlet since she was experiencing some adjustment problems in the public school. After a few assessment sessions, a contract was made with Susie that she would (1) be taught to read and play piano music, (2) be assisted in writing her own songs, (3) be agreeable to practicing between lessons, and (4) be ready for her lessons at the appointed time. She began to appear promptly for her music sessions and she would eagerly improvise her moods on the keyboard. Her improvisations were free form, both in rhythm and melody. On a few occasions, her father questioned this "misuse" of the piano (as he perceived her improvisations as "loud banging"). When the music therapist explained the therapeutic value and its necessity in helping Susie prepare for formal piano study, he accepted this, albeit reluctantly. Each music therapy session was closed with the therapist assisting Susie in writing new lyrics and tunes. She often verbalized her pleasure about the beginning and ending periods of her sessions, and she expressed her frustration about her handicaps less frequently as she gained confidence in her improvisations.

Typical Music Therapy Goals

While priorities will change with each individual and with each developmental stage, typical goals in music therapy for the child with spina bifida include the following (Fischer, 1977):

1. Increasing upper extremity strength and coordination to compensate for limited use of lower extremities; for maximum development of ADL skills; to play musical instruments and participate in movement activities to music to increase range of motion and muscular strength, and develop bilateral coordination.

2. Improving body awareness/image to improve functional use of his body; to develop awareness of body parts; to accept the parts of his body which do not function as a "normal" child's do; and to learn to move isolated parts of his body and then the total body through space to music.

3. Improve self-concept to recognize his strengths; to de-emphasize his handicaps; through individual or group participation in creating vocal or instrumental music, gain confidence, learn to lead, follow, and share; and through music therapy or music education, to learn to develop as a "normal" child develops through these positive music experiences.

4. Maintaining or increasing vital capacity to improve breathing by singing, making loud or strong sounds in a music activity, or playing wind instruments which are nonthreatening and pleasurable.

5. Improving interpersonal skills to decrease manipulation; to increase positive inter-actions; and through the security of a pleasant music therapy group, to develop skills of social interaction which will help him to cope in relating to family members, other nonhandicapped classmates, teachers and therapists, and strangers in his home environment.

6. Increasing attending behavior to decrease distractibility; to increase attention span; and through structured musical experiences, to develop on-task behavior.

PARAPLEGIC OR QUADRIPLEGIC CHILDREN

The paraplegic child has paralysis of both legs, or lower limbs, due to injuries below the first thoracic vertebra. The quadriplegic child has paralysis of both legs and both arms due to injuries above the thoracic vertebra. Although it is uncommon to see spinal cord injuries at birth, the child may experience such injuries during a breech birth. Most spinal cord injuries are the result of automobile accidents, and are usually seen in children over the age of 13 (Meyers, 1974).

Causes and Symptoms of the Problem

The causes of paraplegia or quadriplegia are varied or multiple. If there is a traumatic cause, the onset of the paralysis is acute and immediate. This may be due to a direct injury, such as a gunshot wound or knife stab, or to an indirect injury "associated with fractures or dislocations of spine and central herniations of the intervertebral disc" (Salter, 1970, p. 254). In contrast, the paralysis develops gradually if the cause is due to infections (tuberculosis), diseases of the spinal cord (multiple sclerosis), or neoplasms (tumors) of the spinal cord.

In complete traumatic paraplegia, there will be a complete lesion with two stages of paralytic development. In the initial state of shock lasting several weeks, the child will experience flaccid paralysis. This will affect all muscles innervated at that level of the spinal cord and below, with complete sensation loss, absence of deep tendon reflexes in the affected muscles, and flaccid paralysis of urinary bladder and rectal sphincter. After several weeks, this initial shock will be replaced by a residual spastic paralysis state which will then be permanent. The former symptoms are replaced by hypertonicity in the affected muscles, increased clonus and deep tendon reflexes, and extensor plantar cutaneous reflexes. The complete loss of sensation remains. There will be no voluntary control below the lesion, and massive reflexive spasms in response to painful stimuli may result in emptying the bladder.

In incomplete traumatic paraplegia where there are incomplete lesions, some recovery may be possible due to some tracts not having permanent, severe damage. In the gradually progressing paraplegia of diseases, infection, or neoplasms, spasticity will be seen throughout.

Treatment for the Child

As with the cases of spina bifida, poliomyelitis, and acute burn cases, the total treatment and management of paraplegic and quadriplegic children require a very skilled, dedicated team of specialists which includes physiatrists, or rehabilitation physicians, neurosurgeons, urologists, orthopedists, plastic surgeons, nurses, trained nursing assistants, occupational and physical therapists, special educators, social workers, vocational counselors, and a devoted supportive family. Complications, which can be fatal, are those of urinary tract and decubitus ulcers of the skin. Without daily gentle range of motion exercises, joint contractures can develop which greatly interfere with a child's rehabilitation.

Today there are an increasing number of young paraplegics and quadriplegics in rehabilitation settings or special schools due to the increased incidence of automobile accidents, diving accidents, and contact sports injuries. However, with the improved vigorous treatment and management of these cases, the mortality rates have decreased considerably. There is a great need for avocational outlets as well as vocational training for these individuals.

The overall goal for the quadriplegic and paraplegic child is to become as independent as possible. Music therapy can play an important role in helping the child achieve this goal. This overall goal may be subdivided into six parts. Appendix I includes music therapy activities supplementing the following comparison of music therapy and other therapies as related to these six sub-goals:[20]

Music Therapy	**Concurrent Therapies**
Goal 1: Strengthening Muscles	
Music therapy offers a graded program of playing a variety of musical instruments, moving toward faster and stronger movements incorporating spontaneous, purposeful movement.	P.T. and or O.T. and nursing personnel supervise children through a program of active exercises to help children reach their maximum of independence in daily living activities.
Goal 2: Increasing Vital Capacity	
Music therapy offers pleasure and satisfaction through playing wind instruments, singing, or stretching to music while deep breathing.	Respiratory therapy offers function through practice of glossopharyngeal breathing. Triflo Respiratory Exerciser is used to assess vital capacity.
Goal 3: Expressing Emotions	
Through listening to music or singing songs of their choice, children find an appropriate outlet for their emotions. Music can serve as the vehicle for children talking about their injuries and their anger about the imposed altered lifestyle.	Psychotherapist, psychologist, or counselor provides verbal and play therapy.
Goal 4: Increasing and Maintaining Mobility of Joints	
Music therapy uses music activities which stress the flexion and extension of the wrists, elbows, and shoulders.	P.T. and O.T. usually move children through passive range of motion exercises to increase joint mobility. O.T. makes splints for fingers or hands.
Goal 5: Improving Coordinated Movements	
Music therapy encourages participation in music activities requiring proper timing and steady rhythm.	O.T. supervises children in practicing independent feeding and typing.
Goal 6: Developing Recreational and Avocational Interests	
Music therapy provides a variety of musical experiences for beneficial use of free time.	O.T., nursing, or recreation therapy staff offer reading, watching T.V., listening to the radio, or handicrafts.

At times it is appropriate for the music therapist to send a home program to a child's home school to encourage follow-up of music therapy goals begun during a hospitalization. Appendix J contains such a home program for a quadriplegic boy.

CHILDREN WITH BURNS

Types of Burns

While there are three types of burns—first, second, and third degree—the types that produce orthopedic handicaps are deep second and third degree burns. The deep second degree burn is quite painful and produces severe scarring but can heal spontaneously in several weeks. A third degree burn involves the three skin layers (epidermis, dermis, and subcutaneous layers), and it may involve muscles, tendons, and even bones. This burn is not initially painful, due to nerve damage, and it does not heal spontaneously like the deep second degree burn. The third degree burn requires skin grafting and also produces severe scarring.

Of the four categories of agents causing burns—electrical, chemical, radiation, and thermal (scalds, direct contact with hot objects, and flame)—most burns fall into the thermal category (Parks, Carvajal & Larson, 1977).

Treatment of Burns

Infections immediately after a severe burn and resultant loss of body fluids are life-threatening for the child. As a result, he must receive highly specialized treatment as quickly as possible. This treatment may last for many weeks or months, and it is very painful and emotionally and physically stressful. The treatment of the acute burn injury consists of "daily tubbings in a bleach solution, debridement of dead tissue, dressing changes, blood tests, and numerous surgical procedures" (Knudson-Cooper, 1981b, p. 103). Because the child feels extreme pain during the tubbings and the debridement (removal of the dead tissue or skin), he is anxious and fearful. He often has misconceptions about the meaning of this treatment.

While the child in an acute period of hospitalization suffers much pain, little medication can be given. Since the child must have an extended hospitalization, the use of narcotics could be addictive, plus depressing the respiratory and digestive system (Knudson, 1979).

To maintain "respiratory function, muscle tone, and joint flexibility," the acutely burned child must be kept moving in spite of the pain of movement (Knudson-Cooper, 1981b). In addition, the child also undergoes skin grafts to induce healing and to reduce infection: When skin grafting begins, the child must be immobilized in uncomfortable positions, perhaps for weeks at a time. Skin grafts are made from donor sites taken from the child's healthy skin. (It is important for the music therapist to be aware of the tenderness of donor sites.) Sometimes the grafted limbs or digits are immobilized in skeletal traction to help prevent contractures at joints.

Contractures present a major complication as the burns and grafts begin to heal. The burn scar itself has contractile properties which may cause contractures of the crippling joint resulting in disabilities or deformities. The most common ways to help prevent contractures in burns are splints or braces, range of motion exercises, and then skin grafts for repairing and releasing scars that are contracted. To prevent scarring as much as possible, the child is placed in splints and pressure bandages. Without this aftercare, the burn scars can continue to grow, become raised and disfigured due to hypertrophy (buildup of scar tissue).

The child then faces a very long period of reconstructive surgery. Only a little reconstructive treatment can be done at a time. The child returns home for months or years before returning to the burn center for further treatment. The child may experience functional and/or cosmetic plastic reconstructive surgery, probably many times during his life. Functional surgery refers to plastic surgery to maintain function, e.g., joints and growth. Cosmetic surgery refers to reducing the appearance of scars on the face, arms, hands, etc.

Reaction to Burn Injury

Just as the child who has suffered the trauma of an amputation, a severe head injury, or spinal cord injury faces a major emotional adjustment to his altered body, the child experiencing a severe burn injury after the age of infancy faces a major emotional adjustment to the permanent visible stigma of his burn scars. With proper treatment and follow-up care, severely burned children may not experience functional handicaps nor lasting orthopedic handicaps.

Knudson-Cooper (1981a) has reported on a retrospective study of adjustment to the visible stigma of the severely burned. Only 13% of 89 young adults who had suffered severe burns in childhood mentioned the presence of physical disability some 4-23 years after burn injury. While most of these individuals indicated they had emotional problems when starting to school or returning to school after the burn accident, they also felt positive emotional adjustment to their burn injuries. They expressed the importance of time, internal acceptance and strength, and external support of caring people. While members of the family, especially the mother, were the most important persons in helping them cope with being burned, the burned subjects also specified members of the hospital staff who had helped.

Music Therapy for the Child

The child in the acute care burn unit of a hospital will experience sensory deprivation, due to the sterile atmosphere necessary as precautions against infection, the painful ongoing treatment of many weeks or months, and the limitations of movements due to tight bandaging, splinting, or tractions. According to Christenberry (1979), some patients react to such sudden sensory deprivation with hallucinations or delusions. Christenberry shows that music therapy can play an important role in providing needed auditory and visual sensory stimulation, through encouraging the child to watch the therapist strumming a guitar or Autoharp. It is important for the therapist to position himself within "comfortable range of vision of the patient so that the auditory stimulation can be enhanced by the visual" (p. 140).

Correspondingly, Smith (1979) noted seven problems of hospitalized burned children: pain, poor self-image, misconceptions about condition and treatment, guilt, loss of control, separation from family, and interruption of normal developmental processes which leads to immature personality development. In response to these problems, the child may display depression, regression, aggression, anxiety, or fear. While in the hospital, the music therapist can help the burned child deal with these problems by developing trust, helping the child to relax, creating body awareness to improve body concept, offering a means of self-expression, providing a means of control, decreasing anxiety and fears, providing developmental activities during hospitalization, and developing renewed self-confidence.

Music is nonthreatening and provides security to the patient suffering from delirium during the initial stage of physiological emergency. Familiar tunes, repeated rhythms, and predictable cadences in the harmony of music can help to reorient the delirious patient to reality (Christenberry, 1979).

Sepsis, a systemic bacterial infection, may occur during the acute phase of treatment of the severe burn and may cause marked changes in the sensorium of the child. Listening to audio tapes can be most helpful at this time. For example, Knudson (1979) has used commercial relaxation tapes which verbally describe restful mountain or ocean scenes to calm and sooth children in an acute burn ward.

To help individual adolescents in an acute ward of a burn hospital to relax, a music therapist recorded music chosen by individual patients. Based on the iso-moodic principle of matching the mood of the patient to the "mood" of the music, each of the patients was

- test

moved toward the desired mood or level of activity. Since many of these acutely burned adolescents felt very tense, the music therapist usually presented rock or disco music. The effectiveness of the music was noted by observed relaxation of facial muscles and limbs, decreased rate of breathing, and the patients requesting the staff to play the music for them. For patients suffering from considerable pain and unwelcome treatment procedures, listening to nonthreatening music of their choice was a welcome means of controlling their environment.

For children who have recently had reconstructive plastic and orthopedic surgery, participating in a few minutes of guided imagery (Bonny & Savary, 1973) while lying with a group of peers on the floor can be very satisfying. They are encouraged to relax and to allow themselves to imagine a scene or a trip somewhere while listening to music. Often in the verbal sharing following the guided imagery, the children begin to tell some of their feelings about their homes or families as they describe the journeys they took while listening to the music.

Movement Therapy for the Child

Participating in movement therapy sessions helps ambulatory burned patients to improve their range of motion of their limbs while making them more aware of their bodies. Most of these patients, from preschoolers to teenagers, enjoy dancing and with little prompting, will begin to lead the others in new dance steps or movements.

Usually burned children are very accepting and supportive of one another. When they are emotionally comfortable within a group, they enjoy moving by isolating different parts of their bodies. At times, it may be helpful for the children to gently pat or massage each other's shoulders, neck, arms, etc., prior to moving isolated body parts. Some children may prefer having someone move their parts for them initially, then they will move them independently within the group activity. Burned children readily urge their peers to move freely, even those with prostheses or splints.

Adaptation of Musical Instruments

Adapting instruments for the burned child is a very individualized project. By involving the child in the decision-making and planning of the adaptation, he is given a means of control. Robert, a 14-year-old boy, had lost his fingers in a burn accident when 2 years of age. He had expressed interest in learning to play a steel guitar some day. As a preparation for this, the music therapist demonstrated playing a small standard guitar using a metal guitar slide to bar the chords after retuning the guitar to the key of C major (Slyoff method[21]). Robert rather quickly demonstrated that he could move the guitar slide with one hand, but he needed a strap around his hand and through the slide to allow him to lift the slide off to strum the open strings. He then explained to the occupational therapist and music therapist what type of adaptation he needed to strum with his other hand. Sketches of the two adaptations for Robert are seen in Figure 2.

FIGURE 2
Adaptations for Robert

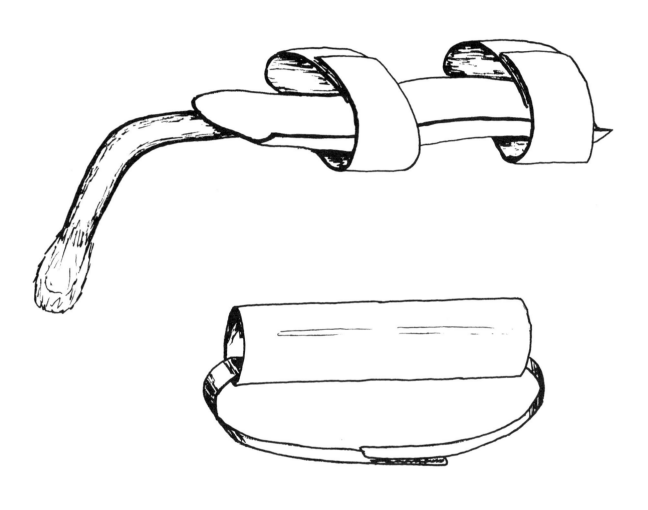

Lupe, a small 7-year-old Latin American girl, had learned to play melodies on the piano using the two remaining fingers of her "best hand." She welcomed the opportunity to play the pianica when she was confined to her bed later with both arms immobilized with wrappings and splints. Lupe told her music therapist she thought she could play tunes on the pianica with her big toe of her right foot (her left leg had been amputated). A double length of the flexible mouthpiece extension was used to place the pianica at the proper distance for Lupe to see the keyboard while lying on her back. Once the mouthpiece was placed in her mouth by the music therapist, Lupe could then play familiar tunes with her big toe by matching letters on the keyboard to letters in a book. She expressed her pleasure with this adaptation through frequent laughing between tunes and through verbally thanking the therapist at the end of each session.

Case Study: Ronny[22]

Ronny was an 11-year-old white male who was severely burned in a gas leak explosion. Eighty-five percent of his body was burned; approximately 45% was third degree, the remainder was second degree. Following two months of initial acute treatment in an adult setting, Ronny was transferred to a children's burn treatment center. There his medical treatment was continued, along with educational tutoring and physical, occupational, music, and child-life therapies.

Ronny's movements were limited due to extensive wrapping, pain, muscular stiffness, and swelling. He was referred to music therapy by the team as a part of a structured treatment plan developed for him. Music therapy for Ronny included relaxation with music, movement to music, and improvisation on various music instruments.

It was difficult for Ronny to get adequate rest, and as a result, he often had a frustrated temperament. Relaxation exercises, consisting of tightening and releasing parts of the body beginning with the toes to the top of the head to sedative music, were initiated. Ronny would respond by falling asleep by the time he was instructed to tighten and release the top of his head. He would sleep or rest quietly until the music had stopped.

Ronny's anxiety about tubbing and the debridement treatment caused the process to take an extensive amount of time, thereby lengthening his periods of anxiety. Following a two-week exposure to the music/relaxation, the exercises were employed during Ronny's tubbing time. Ronny could choose the type of music he wanted to listen to during redressing and wrapping following the tubbing. The first treatment, with music, was shortened by 20 minutes. The remaining tubbing and debridement treatment with music continued at the shortened period of time.

Much of Ronny's movement was stiff and labored; therefore, a variety of movements was encouraged in music activities. A maraca, jingle bell, or stick castenet was fastened by an ace wrap to either arm conformer or the ankle and Ronny would improvise rhythms to various styles of music. Since Ronny's feet were not burned, he utilized them in most fine motor activities. An Autoharp or omnichord was placed on the floor for Ronny to play by strumming with his toes or a pick attached to his foot with tape, while he was seated. Ronny pressed the chord bars with his big toe while strumming with his other foot. Strumming with alternate feet was encouraged to allow equal movement for both legs. Ronny also was encouraged to play/improvise on keyboard instruments, i.e., piano, pianica, and chord organ, to encourage finger dexterity and arm movement. Guided (directed by the music therapist) or free (improvised by Ronny) movement to music encouraged movement of Ronny's total body. As a result of these activities, Ronny established a close relationship with the music therapist and often sought emotional support from her.

Ronny adapted lyrics about his family and home to "Country Roads." He sang it and accompanied himself on the omnichord, while the therapist played the guitar and sang to a group of Ronny's friends at the hospital.

Prior to his discharge, Ronny could walk up and down the stairs with ease, he had noticeably increased movement in his arms, and could move more quickly overall. He appeared to have more self-confidence and his temperament had improved.

CHILDREN WITH HEAD TRAUMA

Head trauma (brain trauma) is the result of sudden mechanical force. Head trauma in children may result from accidents within the home or at school, sports accidents (especially diving accidents), birth injuries, child abuse, or most often, from motor vehicle accidents.

Of the head traumas resulting from vehicular accidents in the USA, "75% die from the primary and secondary effects of trauma on the vital centers of the central nervous system" (Woodford & Reeves, 1981, p. 193). For the 25% who survive major head trauma accidents, the prognosis is surprisingly good, but there may be residual central nervous system functional defects.

Types and Symptoms of the Problem

According to Woodford and Reeves (1981), there are two categories of major effects of head trauma: primary and secondary effects.

1. Primary effects resulting directly from the head trauma:
   a. *Concussion.* Often "a reversible state of diffuse cerebral dysfunction associated with a transient alteration in consciousness" (p. 183). Two types of amnesia are associated with concussions: (a) retrograde amnesia which is the loss of memory of recent events from several seconds or minutes to (rarely) days or weeks prior to the injury, and (b) anterograde amnesia which is the variable period following recovery of consciousness in which the patient is unable to learn new material. The patient may be unable to remember any early post-injury events.
   b. *Contusions.* Bruises of the brain under the site of the severe blow to the cranium or opposite the site of the blow.
   c. *Lacerations.* Either the result of skull fracture with penetrating trauma to the brain by fragments of skull or foreign objects, or the result of severe shearing forces. Usually an epidural, subdural, or intracerebral hemorrhage is associated with a laceration of the brain.
2. Secondary effects complicating the severe head trauma: Include "edema, hypoxia, hemorrhage, infection, and epilepsy" (Woodford & Reeves, 1981, p. 184). Since all of these secondary effects can be life-threatening or may result in severe residual dysfunctions, prompt examination and treatment by neurosurgeons is critical.

The music therapist who works with the child with head trauma will see some common symptoms. The severity of the symptoms will depend upon the severity, extensiveness, and/or location of the head trauma. Also, the symptoms will be more severe the closer to the comatose period. The child with head trauma may well have:

- hemiplegia (paralysis and/or sensory loss of one side of his body).
- limited range-of-motion (mostly cerebral), ataxia (mostly cerebellar), and rhythmic incoordination (either cerebral or cerebellar).
- lability (sudden mood changes).
- residual pain or fears of pain.
- limited attention span.
- hyperactivity.
- distractibility or loss of short-term memory.
- seizure activity (petit mal or grand mal seizures) or sleepiness due to seizure medication.
- speech disturbance (slow monotonous speech with little inflection, aphasia, or no verbal speech).
- resistance to attempting new tasks or experiences.

Case Study: Pedro[23]

It is very helpful to have early intervention by a music therapist in the hospital setting or rehabilitation center. The following case study describes such early intervention.

Pedro was admitted to the long-term care and rehabilitation center one month before his fifth birthday. He had fallen off a gate at the ranch where his father worked and sustained a right skull fracture and closed head trauma. At the time of his admission, he moved all extremities, although movement was more purposeful on the right side. His alertness increased daily.

There were several problem areas upon which Pedro's treatment focused. He was admitted with a tracheostomy tube and a nasal feeding tube. He needed to regain muscle strength and acquire more purposeful movement in his extremities. An additional factor in planning and treatment was that Pedro seemed to understand very little English. He was scheduled for physical, occupational, music, and recreational therapies, as well as education services.

Pedro was scheduled for both group and individual music therapy sessions for five months. Initially, his participation during group sessions was limited to occasionally playing a rhythm instrument. He always responded more during individual sessions, but the amount of participation seemed affected by his moods. He gradually became more verbal and increased his participation during both group and individual sessions.

Music therapy goals for Pedro are listed below, with a brief summary of Pedro's progress.
1. Sing two- and three-word phrases in songs. Pedro learned short phrases ("hello, hello," "1,2,3") in 10 preschool songs which he sang about 75% of the time.
2. Identify rhythm instruments. Pedro identified drum, bell, maraca, tambourine, triangle, and wood block with 80% accuracy.
3. Improve rhythmic coordination. Pedro stamped his feet or clapped his hands with the beat about 50% of the time. He played rhythm instruments with the beat most of the time when using both hands.
4. Imitate actions to body-part songs. Pedro learned the actions to five body-part songs which he performed inconsistently during group sessions and more consistently during individual sessions.

Pedro was discharged when he learned to walk and to eat without assistance. He continued to be stronger on his right side. He was developmentally delayed about one year in social and self-help skills; his language skills were delayed more than two years in both Spanish and English. At the time he left the rehabilitation center, Pedro showed more peer-group interaction and less hesitancy to try new experiences. He usually seemed to enjoy music sessions, even when he did not actively participate. Recommendations were sent to his school to continue his involvement in music for both therapeutic and educational goals.

Case Study: Barry[24]

As with other children who have orthopedic handicaps, the primary goal for a child with a brain trauma is to help prepare the child to return to his home and the least restrictive environment for his schooling. This may not always be successful with the child with severe brain trauma. The residual maladaptive behavior may be such that he will need to be placed in a residential institution with a program to cope with his behavior with little emphasis on his orthopedic handicaps. However, music therapy can be very important in working with such a child, in his assessment, direct therapy, and discharge planning.

At the time of admission to a residential school, Barry was a 7-year-old boy who was three months post-comatose following a severely closed head trauma resulting from an automobile accident. He also had suffered fractures of his legs and hips. Barry was an attractive but very hyperactive boy who utilized a walker and wore a protective helmet. He constantly complained of pain at the end of his spine, and he exhibited limitations in his range of motion in his left upper extremity. He had good speech, but he frequently cursed and used other inappropriate language. He was very volatile and related poorly to his parents, peers, and staff.

Initially, he was assigned to a small group in music therapy with a long-term goal of improved interpersonal skills and short-term goals of improved peer interaction and appropriate expression of feelings. However, this quickly became a fearful experience for the two young boys in his group due to Barry's physical and verbal outbursts during therapy sessions. He was then seen individually two hours a week with a revised short-term goal of appropriate expression of feelings. He often walked some distance to the music therapy cottage, complaining loudly the entire way. The therapist tried to channel his excess energy and verbal behavior into song by first singing familiar songs and then gradually improvising songs with him while walking to the cottage. His sessions were highly structured to curb his distractibility and tendency to throw instruments and materials about the room. He began to initiate loud rhythmic patterns on the drum, which the music therapist then repeated. For many sessions, Barry beat the drum for 30-45 minutes of his hour session. Gradually, he was able to verbalize his anger while playing the drum: He was required to beat out whatever he verbalized. His former behavior of striking at and cursing the therapist gradually decreased.

There was still some problem in walking directly to the cottage or the main building. He eventually was rewarded with collecting rocks on the trip out, to toss in an adjacent pond on the trip back, if he was cooperative during his session. As a result, Barry showed much more creativity in his rhythm and lyrics. He preferred singing his own words to songs, and he now needed only a few minutes on the drum before exploring other instruments appropriately (without throwing or hitting them against something). He learned to play dozens of long-short patterns from DLM (Developmental Learning Materials) cards with a buzzer board, using a finger of each hand. He tried, but rejected, learning to play a baritone ukulele. While his behavior improved within the individual music therapy sessions, he still demonstrated his maladaptive behavior most of the day between therapies and especially at home on weekends. He was discharged to another residential institution which could provide a more consistent 24-hour program for coping with his maladaptive behavior.

CHILDREN WITH
JUVENILE RHEUMATOID ARTHRITIS

According to Miller (1975), juvenile rheumatoid arthritis may occur in infants as early as 6 weeks of age; between 100,000 and 300,000 children have this problem in the USA. However, after 10 years of active disease, 60-70% of the children will experience remission. Only about 10% of these children are left with functional limitations.

Types and Characteristics of the Problem

While the cause of juvenile rheumatoid arthritis is unknown, it is believed to be an autoimmune disease of abnormal antibodies attacking normal body materials. Due to its variable presentation, this disease is often difficult to diagnose. Three types of juvenile rheumatoid arthritis have been identified:

1. Systemic. This type affects 20% or less of children with juvenile rheumatoid arthritis. Its signs and symptoms include a characteristic rapidly changing flat, pink rash, a fever curve of "spiking" high fevers once or twice a day, enlarged spleen, generalized fatigue and malaise, visibly enlarged lymph nodes, anemia, and eventual appearance of arthritis. While the outlook for these children is good, some will develop polyarticular arthritis.

2. Polyarticular. This most common type affects 50-60% of children with rheumatoid arthritis. In addition to rash, fever, anemia, malaise signs and symptoms are five or more severely involved joints, usually the ankles, knees, and wrists, then the neck, shoulders, elbows, and fingers. As it progresses, hip involvement will occur in about one-fourth of the children. In about 10%, there will be painful involvement in the jaw, interfering in growth of the jaw bone and producing a receding chin. Children afflicted with this type of arthritis are very uncomfortable, small for their age, and have limited range of motion, contractures, and subluxations.

2. Pauciarticular. In this type, four or fewer painful, swollen joints develop within the first three months of the disease. While little permanent damage occurs in this instance, it may develop into polyarticular disease. A serious secondary problem, which develops independently of the arthritis, is "iridocyclitis" or "anterior uveitis," (inflammation of the iris and the muscle controlling the lens of the eye) which lead to blindness.

Music Therapy for the Child

The music therapist may deal with certain factors with children with juvenile rheumatoid arthritis. Since they are often angry, depressed, introverted, or inhibited, these children substitute outbursts of acting out with expression of feelings through music. They also experience very changeable moods due to pain and stiffness fluctuating during the night and day. The music therapist should accept these mood swings and grade these changes of mood through appropriate choice of music.

"Jelling" causes inability to move joints freely for minutes or hours after waking or after prolonged sitting or maintenance in any given position. The children should be given more time to change positions or to move about rooms to counteract the "jelling" effect. Nevertheless, these children need regular rest periods each day, and suitably chosen music can enhance this rest.

The need for protection of joints from stress contraindicates gross motor activity that causes jolting or twisting of the joints; smooth sustained movements can be facilitated by appropriate music. Fine motor activity requiring use of the fingers and hands should be done only for short periods of time, and not at all when the joints are stiff. Playing of musical instruments should be alternated or preceded with play in soft clay or warm water.

Most children receiving large doses of aspirin have a high tone hearing loss; therefore, the music therapist should be sensitive to the types of music presented. Eye inflammation or blindness necessitates learning through sensory channels other than visual, such as auditory, tactile, and olfactory stimuli. Splinting or bracing to immobilize joints will limit the ability to move particular body parts; caution must be taken in movements during music activities. (**CAUTION:** Consult *directly* with the occupational or physical therapist before removing splints or braces temporarily or encouraging the child to move a limb that is immobilized.)

Case Study: Laura[25]

The following case study describes the beneficial role of music therapy with a teenager hospitalized on three different occasions for the treatment of juvenile rheumatoid arthritis (JRA).

When she was first seen in music therapy, Laura was a 16-year-old black female with a diagnosis of juvenile rheumatoid arthritis. She had received some music therapy and was able to read music. Laura began playing piano to attempt to improve finger dexterity and coordination, and to increase muscle tone. During this admission, she spent two-and-a-half months in the rehabilitation unit of the hospital and then underwent surgery.

Five months after surgery, Laura was readmitted to the rehabilitation unit. She was confined to a stretcher and required to stay supine. A portable organ and an Autoharp were used to help her work on increasing fine motor manipulative skills and coordination. (The piano was not accessible to her due to the stretcher and her positioning.) In addition to these physical goals, music was used to work on increasing memory skills and to provide a much needed acceptable outlet for expression of emotions as well as constructive use of leisure time.

Laura was transferred to the acute care section of the hospital after one month of rehabilitation. She was seen again in music therapy two months later. At this time, Laura was able to be in a wheelchair, but was very depressed. The main goal for her music therapy session was to encourage her to express her feelings. Work on strengthening her fingers and improving coordination continued through playing the organ. During her two-month stay she had good and bad times emotionally. During the bad times, she stated that she did not think her therapy was going to make her get better, and she consequently was less motivated to work. In music therapy, she was cooperative only for such activities as listening to music and making comments about what she had heard.

One year and three months later, Laura was readmitted to the rehabilitation unit prior to undergoing surgery. She asked to work on playing the piano and seemed quite motivated. After surgery, Laura was not able to play piano but expressed an interest in learning to play the Autoharp. She enjoyed this activity but tired easily and was not able to complete a song without stopping. Laura told the music therapist that she could not depress the Autoharp buttons; however, the therapist determined that she was strong enough to do this and insisted that she do it. She sang along while playing and was responsive to the insistence that she play the Autoharp independently.

Laura exhibited some manipulative behaviors which the music therapist felt were indicative of a feeling that she was losing control over her life. Laura was allowed to be in charge of certain aspects of her sessions but was required to continue working. She began to verbally express some of her concerns and even wrote a letter to the city to complain about the neighborhood sidewalks. Over a two-month period, Laura's endurance increased.

CHILDREN WITH AMPUTATIONS

Types and Treatment of the Problem

Amputation in children may be either congenital or acquired. The former means that a child was born without a part or a total limb, due to the failure of limb bud development in the fetus during the first trimester of pregnancy (Bleck, 1975a). Types of congenital amputations are:

1. Phocomelia. Refers to a small appendage in place of what should have been a limb.
2. Hemimelia. Refers to half of a limb.
3. Amelia. Refers to absence of the total limb.

Acquired amputation means a child was born with normal extremities, but a limb or part of a limb was removed due to an accident or surgery. Surgery to remove a limb is usually done for a malignant bone tumor but may also be done after trauma of a car accident or a serious burn. In cases of severe deformities from burns or other accidents, amputations are done to provide for more freedom or to maintain function of the remainder of the limb. Generally, amputations can be classified as follows:

1. Upper-limb absence. Above-the-elbow (A.E.) amputations will not be as functional as below-the-elbow (B.E.). The child will rely on the intact upper limb to its maximum and use the prosthetic (artificial) limb only as a helper. The child may become frustrated and discard the prosthesis. While this may not be harmful for activities if the child has a unilateral absence of his upper limb, it would be harmful for the child with a bilateral partial or loss of both upper limbs. He then must learn to use the artificial limbs. Often children develop compensatory methods of using their feet and toes adeptly to replace the absence of their upper limbs.

2. Lower-limb absence. Children with unilateral above-the-knee (A.K.) amputations can learn to walk well with prostheses. If not encouraged to remain active, they often become fat. Obesity itself promotes problems of movement and thereby further reduces activity. Children with bilateral above-the-knee amputations are severely handicapped, needing wheelchairs for part-time use to conserve energy. Often, it is difficult to recognize children walking with prostheses with unilateral below-the-knee (B.K.) amputations since they may walk very well. Children with bilateral below-the-knee amputations may also walk well with prostheses, but their participation in physical activities may be more limited. However, in spite of the motivation of the amputees to be active, there will be intermittent stump problems and adjustments for changing of the prostheses as the children grow. The treatment for amputations is to fit children with prostheses and to train them in their use. Special electrical prosthetics and devices are necessary with the absence of both upper limbs or lower limbs.

Early fitting of a prosthesis for an infant or toddler with an amputation, congenital or acquired, is recommended to match the motor readiness of the child. The prosthesis becomes an extension of the child's limb and thus a part of his body image. Through the assistance of the prosthesis, the child develops sensory awareness and motor control by being able to explore and manipulate toys, musical instruments, and objects with bilateral, or hand-prosthesis, usage. Currently, 20% of infants with limb deficiencies under 6 months of age are fitted with prostheses and 65% before 1 year (Challenor & Katz, 1974). In addition, early fitting of prostheses encourages acceptance by the child and family, decreases one-handed function, encourages efficient hand-prosthesis usage at midline, decreases tendency toward scoliosis through improving balance and symmetry of trunk, facilitates eye-prosthesis (as well as eye-hand) coordination and control, and decreases muscle and bone hypotrophy resulting from disuse.

In addition to the expected difficulties of dealing with the medical problems associated with the care of the child with amputations, the parents of the child face psychological problems. Following the initial shock, they often experience guilt, anger, anxiety, ambivalence and/or rejection toward the child. The parents and family will need counseling and support from the habilitation or rehabilitation team. They will need to be an active part of the team to face the years of emotional adjustment. The child with an acquired amputation often feels he is being punished by losing a limb, and his parents feel guilty that they had not protected the child sufficiently. Both the child and parents will need to work through this grief of the loss of limb while the child is relearning developmental and functional tasks. During this habilitation or rehabilitation process, the child needs to relate to his peers, amputees *and* nonamputees, to maximize his future placement in the "mainstream" of the public schools. The child's team will need to help prepare his teacher and the children in the school for acceptance of the child's limitations and needs.

Music therapy can play an important role in aiding the child with an amputation in overall body awareness (conceptual, proprioceptive, and kinesthetic), balance and symmetry of trunk, eye-hand coordination, fine and gross motor control, bilateral usage, improvement of self-esteem, appropriate expression of emotions, and acceptance of his handicap.

Movement Therapy for the Child

Movement therapy can prove to be a powerful rehabilitation tool for the music therapist to use. According to Bartenieff and Lewis (1980), there are three functional, expressive stages to the rehabilitation of movement:

1. The realization of sudden loss of function and analysis of its extent.

2. An intense effort to restore function or to create an adequate substitute for it.

3. Adjustment to permanent limitation of function, and discovery of new resources.

Children experiencing numerous hospitalizations for orthopedic surgery, plastic surgery, neurosurgery or extensive laboratory tests, may experience many periods in life when they are restricted from movement. Effective use of music therapy may help to restore the normal movement experiences of childhood.

Case Study: Karen[26]

The following case study tells of music therapy with a girl with both congenital anomalies and an acquired amputation.

Karen was a 7-year-old female of Mexican descent. She had scoliosis, low functioning kidneys, hypermobility of joints, a right radial club hand (right radial hemimelia), and an above-the-knee (A.K.) amputation of her left lower extremity. Karen had a developmental age of 10-12 months and exhibited low muscle tone. She could make all of her wheelchair transfers independently and could accomplish some movement skills by using normal movement patterns. However, because of her decreased muscle strength, Karen would compensate by substituting use of certain muscle groups with other muscle groups. Prior to coming to this institution, she had a prosthesis for her left leg; but because of obesity, she no longer could use it. Since admission, she was fitted with a new prosthesis which she was able to use to walk independently for short distances with a walker.

Karen was seen individually in music therapy, since her schedule did not permit placing her with a group of children. Until she became more adept with her new prosthesis, Karen was confined to mat activities or activities she could do while sitting in an ill-fitting wheelchair (prior to receiving a new, more suitable wheelchair). Karen was unable to reach the piano or chord organ or to play musical instruments at a table when seated on the piano bench or in a regular chair; her low muscle tone made her trunk too short for her to reach. However, she was able to play an electronic keyboard while seated in the wheelchair. The music therapist conferred with the occupational therapist who made Karen a hand splint to correct her right wrist from bowing to the ulnar side. Wearing the splint, Karen was able to learn to play the C scale and simple melodies on the electronic keyboard using her four remaining digits of her right hand and the fingers of her left hand. When cooperative, she was able to play with traditional piano fingering with only minor adaptation of the right hand.

In agreement with the therapeutic team's goals, the music therapist also worked on Karen's body awareness through action songs, mirroring activities, touching, moving, and naming parts of her body and playing rhythm instruments. Initially, Karen was resistive to being touched, and she needed much encouragement in bilateral hand usage. Although she made gradual improvement in these areas, she soon began to be very manipulative, complaining of physical discomfort, fearing that the girls in her dormitory disliked her or that her mother would forget to take her home. When placed in a special small group situation for a Girl Scout or Christmas program, Karen did not demonstrate the "attention-getting" behavior, but instead became rather passive. Again, when seen individually, Karen would sing along with recorded songs about feelings, but she resisted creating lyrics to songs about feelings when the music therapist played the guitar and encouraged Karen to create her own songs.

In a later reevaluation of Karen's program, it was decided by the team to place her in a music therapy group with emphasis upon group interaction. The music activities were to include vocal and instrumental participation, stressing expression of positive and negative feelings, body awareness, and bilateral usage. The music therapist was to work in cooperation with O.T. and P.T., incorporating music with gross motor activities such as rolling, jumping, and falling, using wedges, beanbags, and other appropriate equipment.

CHILDREN WITH MUSCULAR DYSTROPHY

Duchenne's type of muscular dystrophy (pseudohypertrophic muscular dystrophy) "is a progressive diffuse weakness of all muscle groups characterized by a degeneration of muscle cells and their replacement by fat and fibrous tissues" (Bleck, 1975d, p. 173). This disorder is found in 4 per 100,000 persons in the USA as well as having worldwide distribution (Chutorian & Myers, 1974).

Symptoms of the Problem.

The presenting complaints occur during the third year of life. The child may have a waddling gait and have difficulty in running or climbing stairs. The disease will move in distal progression, upward from the lower limbs. A classical symptom is Gower's sign, where the child "walks" up his legs with his hands to get up from a sitting position on the floor. The calves of the legs become enlarged. Obesity is often seen due to restricted activity of these children, but a few appear atrophic. Skeletal deformities develop due to unopposed weakness of muscle groups causing contractures at joints and scoliosis (Bleck, 1975d). Mental subnormality is present in about 70% of these children, whose average I.Q. ranges in the 80's. Children with Duchenne's muscular dystrophy become wheelchair bound in their second decade of life with death occurring between 15 and 35 years as the result of respiratory or cardiac muscular involvement.

Treatment and Maintenance.

Currently, there is no effective dietary or drug-oriented treatment. Important team members for maintenance of child with muscular dystrophy include the respiratory therapist, physical therapist, occupational therapist, speech therapist, physician, and nurse. These professionals will be especially helpful in advising the family and the staff of the child's needs to increase his vital capacity through correct positions or increasing duration of inhalations or exhalations. The occupational therapists and physical therapists also will be very important in advising on the child's needs regarding increasing his motor skills, or preventing disuse atrophy through gross motor coordination and strengthening, upper extremity fine motor manipulation, or lower extremity strengthening and coordination. Physical therapists are especially helpful in positioning joints, and they work in cooperation with occupational therapists, the child, and his family in maintaining maximum activities of daily living (ADL).

One must realize Duchenne's muscular dystrophy is a progressive and terminal disease. This makes the child with this problem different from children with other orthopedic handicaps discussed in this monograph. The music therapist must constantly be aware of the status of the child's condition. While the dystrophic child should not be overprotected, he also should not be overly fatigued. The expectations made of him must be realistic for his individual condition.

Music can be a very meaningful medium for working with this child. If the child cannot be an active participant, he can satisfy many emotional and intellectual needs through active listening. The child can maintain or develop his imagination and his creativity through listening to music, discussing it, writing about it, and writing songs to melodies played for him. For the child who is still able to participate physically, the music therapist should encourage him to participate to his maximum. It is very important that the music therapist consult with the other members of the child's team to know what to expect the child to do.

Case Study: Sam[27]

The following case history of Sam, a boy with muscular dystrophy and possible learning disabilities, describes his individual music therapy program plan and sample individualized educational program (IEP).

Sam had a medical diagnosis of Duchenne's muscular dystrophy. He entered school at age six; since that time, academic progress had been slow. A previous psychological evaluation suggested average intelligence with the possibility of a learning disability noted. Sam was wheelchair dependent, and as he could not wheel himself, had obtained an electric wheelchair. He fed himself independently, but required maximal assistance for the remainder of his self-care activities.

Currently, Sam appeared to be functioning within the low average range of measured intelligence. There was a significant difference between verbal functioning and performance functioning. Relative strengths were suggested in visual interpretations of social situations, analytical ability, and visual reasoning. Sam seemed to have the most difficulty with immediate auditory memory. Language testing indicated close to age level in receptive processes involving single words and short phrases. Severe deficits in memory for sentences were noted, which would interfere with his ability to remember extensive receptive material. Substantial delays in expressive language abilities were noted in word order and word confusion. Auditory discrimination of speech sounds was tested as deficient. However, Sam responded well to verbal directions which required a visual response. His primary learning style appeared to be visual/kinesthetic.

It was noted that Sam should be encouraged to participate with one or two children in class activities to diminish his feelings of isolation. Accordingly, he was evaluated for possible inclusion in a music therapy program, and the following results were noted: Sam would continue in an academic setting that took into account his physical limitations and the prognosis of his condition. Therefore, it was imperative that normal life experiences be offered to him, and at the same time, that his individual learning style be considered. Due to the progressive nature of muscular dystrophy, many physical activities had been discontinued, including swimming and physical education activities that could not be performed in an electric wheelchair. Sam's social/emotional development and well-being were also considered in establishing the following music therapy program for him:

1. Sam will maintain maximum physical functioning in a leisure time activity by participating in music lessons on the electric organ.
   a. Use electric organ because of simple touch sensitivity, chord and rhythm possibilities.
   b. Adapt instruments as necessary.
   c. Allow opportunities for performance for peers, staff, etc.
   d. Use large print music (Nash Recorder Method).

2. Sam will develop socially accepted individual skills which will provide him with peer acceptance and a means for involvement in group activities.
   a. Develop skills that will carry over to group experiences, such as rhythmic integration, vocalization of melody, assertiveness, self-esteem, alternatives for responses in creative or practical situations.
   b. Monitor progress and allow for memorization of tunes.

3. Sam will improve in the area of auditory discrimination and memory.
   a. Use individual time for intensive work in this area, and a group setting for reinforcement.
   b. Use rhythms coupled with words; do imitation exercises; have Sam repeat directions or observations of other members of the group.
   c. Introduce timbre differences of instruments, voices, etc.
   d. Use individual preferences in popular music to reinforce skill growth in this area.

After one year in this program, it was noted that Sam made significant progress in the areas of social/emotional development, of developing leisure time skills in music, and in coping skills for participating in normal activities. He completed the first method book and had begun another book with standard size music notation (Snyder Guitar Method). He learned to read a full octave and one half. Sam tended to practice songs until he memorized them and could accompany himself with chords. His rhythmic integration had improved by 40% overall, and especially in the area of kinesthetic repetition (75% improvement). The development of specific social skills, coupled with factors of maturation, had provided Sam with coping skills which he used to become as involved in individual and group activities as he desired, and as time allowed.

Sample IEP for Sam. Long-range goal: Sam will develop skills in using music activities for occupation of leisure time.

One-year objectives:
a. Sam will learn three new songs at the upper beginner level of adapted keyboard skills and he will accompany his right hand with his left hand playing chords. *Procedure:* Play from Snyder book and aim for periodic performances. *Measurement:* Observation by a music therapist.
b. Sam will develop skills in auditory discrimination and memory. He will learn to play, "by ear," melodic patterns of at least three notes in length. *Procedure:* Use list for first 15 patterns. Have Sam sing pattern back first, then attempt to play pattern. Assist him to find note. Develop a continuum for playing a familiar tune after practice. *Measurement:* Observation by a music therapist, and reevaluation at three-month intervals.

CHILDREN WITH OTHER ORTHOPEDICALLY HANDICAPPING CONDITIONS

Arthrogryposis.

Arthrogryposis is a congenital disease readily diagnosed at birth. This disease causes deformities due to stiff joints and weak muscles. While the cause is unknown, the disease process begins in early fetal life. The lack of muscle contraction and development limits early movement of joints in the developing fetus which may explain the deformities and stiffness of the newborn infant's joints.

While the muscle abnormality is nonprogressive, changes around and in the joints may become more severe with the child's growth. The child may have a shoulder adduction deformity (turned inward) and elbow extension deformities. His forearms may be pronated (palm turned downward) with wrist and finger flexion. The hips usually will be dislocated and the knees will be flexed or entended (sometimes with resulting knee dislocation). There may be severe clubfeet (turned inward and downward). If the trunk is involved, there will be scoliosis (curvature of the spine). There will be limb atrophy (wasting of muscle) and joint enlargement and stiffness, especially during the growing years. The child only rarely has deformities of his hands and feet. Fortunately, speech and intelligence are usually normal (Salter, 1970).

Associated conditions may include "congenital heart disease, urinary tract abnormalities, respiratory problems, abdominal hernias, and various facial abnormalities" (Bleck, 1975b, p. 23). A child with arthrogryposis may require several types of orthopedic surgeries, such as bone operations, osteotomy (for the hips), and arthrodesis (for the feet), as well as early spinal fusion for the scoliosis.

As mentioned in the section on amputations, the parents of the child with arthrogryposis will need much emotional support and counseling to accept their child and his many handicaps. Again, the family must feel they are not alone in dealing with their child, but that they are part of a specialized team.

Case Study: Lolita[28]

The following case study describes a girl with arthrogryposis who has good social interactions with her peers and used music therapy as a means of self-expression.

Lolita was an 8-year-old girl with atrophy of her four distal extremities and had flexed knees with contractures. When admitted to a residential intensive care center, she was able to write cursive legibly even though her wrists were habitually flexed, and she could push a wheelchair by sitting on the foot rest to use her feet. While at this residential school, she received orthopedic surgery: bilateral hamstring releases and bilateral Achilles tendon lengthening. However, her wrist remained in the flexed position with her hands in front of her.

Lolita had normal to above average intelligence and she was performing at grade level academically. She was very verbal and cooperative, and was quite sociable with adults and peers. She used a mouth stick for typing on an electric typewriter. Since she was unique among a population of children primarily handicapped with cerebral palsy and often mental retardation, Lolita was an inspiration to the other children. In music therapy, she played the chord buttons on the chord organ by pressing them with her mouth stick, as a younger peer played simple tunes by matching numbers on the large note music to the numbers above the keys. Lolita could also strum the strings on the Autoharp with her mouth stick as a peer pressed the chord buttons, or she would efficiently change chords by pressing the buttons with the mouth stick as a peer strummed the strings. Lolita further demonstrated her independence by initiating the blowing of a pianica through an extension and fingering the notes with her right hand. This was made possible by the music therapist holding the instrument close to Lolita's shoulders since both wrists were held in a flexed position with hands in front of the chest.

Upon discharge from this residential school, Lolita was walking independently in long-leg braces. She returned to a regular fourth grade class in her home public school, and participated in a regular music class. Her family purchased a chord organ for her to play in her leisure time.

Poliomyelitis.

Poliomyelitis ("infantile paralysis" or "polio") is a viral infection which affects the anterior horn cells of the spinal cord, the motor cells. It can be life threatening and can cause permanent paralysis. While it is rare in countries where vaccination programs are widely used, poliomyelitis still exists today. Boys are affected more often than girls, and lower limbs more than the upper limbs or trunk.

The poliomyelitis virus enters the body through the gastrointestinal tract, spreads through the bloodstream to the anterior horn cells of the spinal cord and the brain stem. Two vaccines, a killed virus vaccine by Salk and a live virus vaccine by Sabin, are effective and safe as prevention against poliomyelitis (Salter, 1970). Types of poliomyelitis are:

1. *Abortive.* No symptoms.
2. *Nonparalytic.* Temporary inflammatory edema or reversible damage to anterior horn cells causing a transient paralysis.
3. *Paralytic.* Irreversible damage to anterior horn cells, possible destruction of cells producing "permanent lower motor neurone type of paralysis of muscle fibers which they innervate" (Salter, 1970, p. 249).

Four phases of paralytic poliomyelitis have been determined:

1. *Prodromal phase.* Lasts two days. Common viral symptoms of malaise, headache, general muscular aches.
2. *Acute phase.* Lasts about two months. Severe headache, fever, tenderness and painful spasm of affected muscles, rigidity of neck; gradual development of flaccid paralysis of affected muscles; may weaken only one muscle or all muscles of four limbs and trunk, even to muscles of respiration (if brain stem is affected).
3. *Convalescent or recovery phase.* From six months to two years; slow recovery of any transient paralysis. About one-third of patients recover completely during this phase.
4. *Residual paralysis phase.* Lasts remainder of patient's life with no further recovery. Half of patients with residual paralysis have moderate involvement, half have extensive paralysis.

There are a variety of post-poliomyelitis paralytic deformities which vary according to the severity and distribution of the paralysis. These deformities are caused by muscle atrophy, muscle imbalance or muscle contracture, and retarded longitudinal bone growth in the affected limb.

No treatment can affect the extent of paralysis or the degree of recovery. During the acute phase, passive range of motion exercises are done after muscle spasm subsides, followed by hot packs and removable splints used to prevent joint contractures. During the recovery phase, active strengthening range of motion exercises are done, and appropriate bracing is used for stabilization (especially of knees and ankles) to prevent contractures and to improve function of limbs (Bleck, 1975f).

Treatment of residual paralytics includes:

1. Preventing musculoskeletal deformities through daily passive range of motion exercises, splinting or bracing, or orthopedic surgery.

2. Correcting existing musculoskeletal deformities through passive stretching or orthopedic surgery.
3. Improving muscle balance through appropriate orthopedic surgery.
4. Improving function through bracing.
5. Improving appearance through cosmetic prosthesis or orthopedic surgery on shorter or longer leg.
6. Rehabilitating through combined efforts of a team of professionals, the patient, and family support.

Since spinal curvature caused by poliomyelitis often cannot be controlled by bracing, the child may have a plaster cast or orthopedic surgery for spinal fusion.

A music therapist may see the child with poliomyelitis in a hospital setting during the recovery phase, but he would more often be seen during post-convalescence. The child might be restricted to a bed or stretcher following orthopedic surgery such as spinal fusion. Depending upon the severity of his paralysis, he might be walking independently, with or without crutches and braces, or confined to a wheelchair or a motorized wheelchair. The music therapist should consult with the occupational and/or physical therapist to learn what muscle strength limitations the child has prior to designing his therapy program. The music therapy goals for paraplegics on page 67 and in Appendix I would be equally appropriate for the child with poliomyelitis.

Case Study: Peter[29]

Peter was a 14-year-old boy who had poliomyelitis at age 11 months. Prior to admission to a residential school he had had spinal fusion with poor post-surgery care at home and was unable to tolerate sitting upright. Initially, he came to music therapy on a gurney (a wheeled stretcher), either lying on his stomach or back. Although fearful of being touched or moved, Peter was very cooperative and attempted whatever he was asked to do. He was quite weak for many weeks and his breath support was poor. For several months, Peter concentrated on increasing his breath control through daily practice with a Triflo II (Incentive Deep-Breathing Exercise) to improve his inhalations and through playing tunes on the pianica. He gradually met his goal of getting the three balls to rise on the first inhalation on the Triflo II, and he learned to play complete phrases within simple tunes using one breath while blowing the pianica. As reinforcement, he improvised briefly on the harmonica, finding desired notes by inhaling or exhaling into the instrument. Initially, Peter could only use his left hand efficiently and independently to finger melodies on the pianica. He needed to support his right hand or arm with his left to be able to position his fingers in such a manner to reach the keys. Sixteen months later, Peter was sitting upright in an electric wheelchair, able to use all ten fingers to play many tunes on the pianica or on the electronic keyboard; he was more proficient on the pianica since he could better position it within his reach. Throughout his stay at the residential school, Peter had little contact with his family and rarely was taken home for visits. He frequently seemed lonely and depressed and verbalized concern about his father. He expressed a desire to practice the pianica in his leisure time in his dormitory; after practicing regularly for several days, Peter could play two-finger chords in his left hand on the pianica while playing a tune with his right hand. Although he had learned to read from regular printed music, he played most tunes from memory, after being exposed to the tune by reading the music.

Peter memorized many tunes, but he forgot them if not played recently. Because he did not remember to practice independently, Peter did not progress as much as he and the music therapist had desired. Since he seemed too preoccupied for independent practice, Peter was seen in a group of four to seven younger children in music therapy who were on a token system of reinforcement. Peter accepted this system well, and quickly became the leader within the group. Often, he acted as the big brother to the others. Within this group, they received music education by learning to identify instruments of the orchestra, different styles of music, and simple rhythmic patterns. Peter especially enjoyed competitive music games in the class.

Peter's singing and speaking voice changed considerably during his stay at this residential school. His sweet, soprano voice became a strong deep voice of an adolescent, and his soft, shy speaking voice changed to a confident, mature voice. He did very well in speaking roles in two music programs of the school and also helped his peers learn their speaking and singing lines.

Peter had had many periods of depression during his residency, but these periods decreased as he became more involved in individual and group music therapy sessions. He learned to share his feelings and to express them more openly. Overall, he was a very personable, sensitive adolescent who greatly enjoyed music of all kinds. Upon discharge to another residential school, it was recommended that he receive group music education. A pianica was donated for him to take with him since his family could not purchase one for him.

GLOSSARY

In parentheses after each term in the Glossary is a code [in letter(s)] identifying the reference source for the definition which follows the term. Code letters and their corresponding sources then are identified toward the conclusion of this Glossary in a section, "Code to References in Glossary."

Abduction (HS): Movement of a limb outward (away) from the body.

Acquired (S): Denoting a disease, predisposition, habit, etc., that is not congenital but has developed after birth.

Activities of daily living (R): Those tasks that people do routinely in their everyday encounters, i.e., writing, dressing, eating.

Adduction (HS): Movement of a limb inward (toward) the body.

Anoxia (S): Absence of oxygen in inspired gases, arterial blood, or tissues.

Anterior (C): Situated in the front or belly surface of the body; opposite of posterior.

Anterior uveitis (M): Inflammation of the iris and the muscle controlling the lens of the eye; may led to blindness (also, iridocyclitis).

Aphasia (A): The inability to speak and, sometimes, difficulty in understanding the written or spoken word.

Astereognosis (S): Loss of the power of judging the form of an object by touch.

Ataxia (UC2): Incoordination of voluntary muscular movements.

Athetoid (UC1): Characterized by continuous involuntary writhing motion, particularly involving changes of positions of the fingers, toes, hands, and other parts of the body.

Atonia (C): Lack of sufficient muscle tone; a characteristic of cerebral palsy.

Auditory memory (L): The ability to store and recall what one has heard.

Auditory sequencing (L): The ability to remember the order of items given orally in a sequential list.

Autoimmune (M): Diseases of abnormal antibodies attacking normal body materials.

Central programming (A): The neural functions that are innate within our central nervous system; they do not have to be learned. Creeping on hands and knees and walking are good examples of centrally programmed actions.

Clonus (US2): Spasm in which rigidity and relaxation alternate in rapid succession.

Cocontracture (A): The simultaneous contraction of all the muscles around a joint to stabilize it.

Congenital (S): Existing at birth; referring to certain mental or physical traits or peculiarities, malformations, diseases, etc.

Contracture (HS): Permanently tight muscles and joints.

Corralling reach (C): To grab with a sweeping motion of the fingers.

Cylindrical grasp (C): The entire palmer surface of the hand grasps around a cylindrical object; the thumb closes in over the object.

Debridement (SBI): Removal of whitish-colored dead skin or eschar, to prepare the burn for grafting. This is usually done surgically (escharectomy).

Decubitus (S): A pressure ulcer or sore.

Deep tendon reflex (S): An involuntary muscular contraction following percussion of a tendon or bone.

Digit (UC1): Finger or toe.

Diplegia (UC1): Major involvement (paralysis) in the lower limbs, and minor involvement in the upper limbs.

Directionality (C): The property of directional selectivity or precision; maintenance of direction.

Distal (S): Situated away from the center of the body, or from the joint of origin; specifically applied to the extremity or distant part of a limb or organ.

Donor site (SBI): Site of normal or nearly normal skin from which a piece of skin (graft) is taken for use on another area of the body.

Dorsiflexion (C): The lifting of the foot up toward the body.

Dysarthria (UC2): Imperfect articulation in speech.

Dyskinetic (S): Related to dyskinesia. Difficulty in performing voluntary movements.

Dyspraxia (A): Poor praxis or motor planning. A less severe, but more common dysfunction than apraxia.

Dystrophy (HS): Weakness or degeneration of muscle.

Embolism (S): Obstruction or occlusion of a vessel by a transported clot or vegetation, a mass of bacteria, or other foreign material.

Encephalopathy (UC2): Any degenerative disease of the brain.

Esotropia (S): Cross-eye or internal or convergent squint.

Eversion (C): Turning outward.

Exophoria (S): A tendency of one eye to deviate outward.

Extension (UC1): Straightening of the arm, leg, head, or trunk.

Extensor (S): A muscle, the contraction of which tends to straighten a limb.

External rotation (R): The rotation of an extremity away from the midline of the body.

Extremity (S): Limb, member, one of the arms or legs.

Eye-hand coordination (R): The coordination of visual perception with fine and gross motor movement.

Fine-motor coordination (R): Coordination requiring precise control of the hands and fingers.

Fist grasp (C): A prehension in which the fist closes over a comparatively narrow object and the grip is secured by the thumb over the other digits.

Flaccid paralysis (G): Paralysis in which the affected muscles are limp, with little resistance to passive movement.

Flexion (US2): Bending of the joints of the arm, leg, head, or trunk.

Flexor (S): A muscle, the action of which is to flex (bend) a joint.

Gag reflex (S): Contact of a foreign body with the mucous membrane of the fauces (space between the cavity of the mouth and the pharynx) which causes retching or gagging.

Gait (S): Manner of walking.

Glossopharyngeal breathing (H): A substitute method of breathing which uses muscles of the mouth, tongue, soft palate, and throat to force air into the lungs.

Gradation (W): A series forming successive stages.

Gross motor (L): Activities involving the total musculature of the body and the ability to move various parts of the body on command.

Hemiplegia (S): Paralysis of one side of the body.

Herniation (S): The process of formation of a protrusion, a rupture.

Hook grasp (C): Digits two to five are used as a hook; the thumb is not necessarily active.

Hydrocephalus (HS): Congenital condition in which the accumulation of the fluid in the brain causes enlargement of the skull.

Hyperextension (UC1): Extreme or excessive straightening of an arm or leg, or of the neck or trunk; straightening beyond neutral.

Hyperopia (S): Farsightedness.

Hypertonic (C): Having greater than normal muscle tone; tight.

Hypertrophy (S): Overgrowth; general increase in bulk of a part or organ, not due to tumor formation. In the case of severe burns (SBI), buildup of scar tissue.

Hypotonic (C): Having less than normal muscle tone; floppy and loose. Prevents maintenance of posture against gravity and difficulty in starting a movement due to lack of fixation.

Hypoxia (S): Decrease below normal levels of oxygen in air, blood, or tissue short of anoxia.

Internal rotation (R): The rotation of an extremity toward the midline of the body.

Inversion (C): Turning in.
Iridocyclitis (S): Inflammation of both iris and ciliary body of the eye.
Kinesphere (B): The reach space around a person's body.
Kinesthetic (S): Relating to sense perception of movement, the muscular sense.
Kyphosis (S): Humpback; an abnormal curvature of the spine, with convexity backward.
Labile temperament (S): Denoting free and uncontrolled expression of the emotions; emotionally unstable.
Laterality (C): Sidedness; preferential use of one hand, one eye, or one foot more than the other; assumed dominance of one side of the brain over the other with respect to motor functions of the individual.
Lordosis (S): A bending backward; hollow back, saddle back; anteroposterior curvature of the spine, generally lumbar with the convexity looking anteriorly.
Meningitis (UC2): Inflammation of the membranes that envelop the brain and spinal cord.
Midline (R): That line which divides the body longitudinally into left and right sides.
Monoplegia (S): Paralysis of one limb.
Motor planning (S): The ability of the brain to conceive of, organize, and carry out a sequence of unfamiliar actions. Also known as praxis.
Muscle tone (C): The state of tension in muscles at rest and in movement.
Myopia (S): Shortsightedness, or nearsightedness.
Neoplasm (S): Tumor; new growth; an abnormal tissue that grows by cellular proliferation more rapidly than normal and continues to grow after the stimuli that initiated the new growth cease.
Nystagmus (A): A series of automatic, back-and-forth eye movements. Different conditions produce this reflex. A common way of producing them is by an abrupt stop following a series of rotations of the body. The duration and regularity of postrotary nystagmus are some of the indicators of vestibular system efficiency.
Opposition movement of limbs (C): Moving each limb in the opposite direction from the other (as in moving each arm away from midline simultaneously); or holding one limb steady while the other acts upon it (as in hammering a nail).
Orthopedic (C): Pertaining to the correction of deformities of the muscular skeletal system.
Orthotics (C): The field of knowledge related to orthopedic appliances and their use.
Palmer prehension (C): A grip used to pick up and hold small objects; the thumb opposes one or more of the other digits; contact is made by the palm side of the distal parts of the fingers.
Paraplegia (S): Paralysis of both lower extremities and, generally, the lower trunk.
Paresis (C): Slight or incomplete paralysis.
Percept, or **perception** (A): The meaning the brain gives the sensory input. Sensations are objective; perception is subjective.
Perceptual-motor (L): A term describing the interaction of the various channels of perception with motor activity. The channels of perception include visual, auditory, tactual, and kinesthetic.
Perseveration (R): Once under way, a behavior which remains persistent, i.e., repetitive even when inappropriate.
Pincer prehension (C): A grasp in which the tip of the thumb is used against the tip of one of the other digits to pick up a small object.
Plantar cutaneous reflexes (S): Responses to tactile plantar (sole of foot) stimulation; normally plantar flexion of the toes.
Plantar flexion (C): The pointing of the foot downwards.
Posterior (FW): In man, pertaining to the dorsal side of the body; the buttocks.
Prehension (C): The act of seizing or grasping objects by the hand.

Primitive reflexes (UC 1): The stereotyped first movements that normally appear and disappear and control the distribution of postural tone throughout an infant's body.

Pronation (HS): Turning of the palm downward or backward; opposite of supination.

Prone (A): The body position with the face and stomach downward.

Proprioception (G): The ability to sense the position of the limbs and their movements, with the eyes closed.

Prosthesis (S): A fabricated substitute for a missing part of the body, as a limb, tooth, eye, or heart valve.

Protective extension (A): The reflex that extends the arms to provide protection when the body is falling.

Protraction (C): Movement of the shoulder girdle toward the front of the body; the opposite movement from retraction.

Proximal (S): Nearest the trunk or the point of origin.

Quadriplegia (UC1): Paralysis of all four limbs (both arms and both legs).

Radial (C): Toward midline.

Rake grasp (C): Fingers held in garden-rake position.

Range of motion (R): The distance through which a joint can move.

Receptive language (L): Language that is spoken or written by others and received by an individual. The receptive language skills are listening and reading.

Receptive vocabulary (R): The words understood by the receiver.

Reflex (A): An innate and automatic response to sensory input. We have reflexes to withdraw from pain, startle at sensations that surprise us, and extend our head and body upward in response to vestibular input.

Residual (W): A disability remaining from a disease or operation.

Rigidity (S): Increased tone of the extensor muscles (cerebellar rigidity).

Righting (HS): Ability to put or restore the head and body to a proper position when in an abnormal or uncomfortable posture.

Rotation (S): Turning or movement of a body round its axis.

Scissor gait (S): One leg crosses in front of the other, so that the imprint of the left foot is on the right and vice versa.

Scoliosis (UC1): A lateral or side-to-side curvature of the spine in the shape of an elongated letter S.

Sensorimotor (C): Pertaining to motor activity caused by sensorial stimuli, feeling one's own movement.

Sensory integration (A): The organization of sensory input for use. The "use" may be a perception of the body or the world, or an adaptive response, or a learning process, or the development of some neural function. Through sensory integration, the many parts of the nervous system work together so that a person can interact with the environment effectively and experience appropriate satisfaction.

Sepsis (SBI): Presence of bacteria or their toxins in the blood or tissues which causes poisoning.

Shunt (BL): Permanent drainage system of plastic tubes and an interposing valve for treatment of hydrocephalus.
   a. Ventriculoatrial shunt—connects between the ventricle and the heart.
   b. Ventriculoperitoneal shunt—connects between the ventricle and the abdomen.

Spastic (UC1): Having increased tension in a muscle, so that the muscles are stiff and movements are awkward.

Spastic paralysis (G): Paralysis with a coinciding stead and prolonged involuntary contraction of the muscles affected.

Spherical grasp (C): The grasp is adjusted to a round object.

Supination (C): Turning of the arm with the palm side up; opposite of pronation.

Supine (UC1): Lying with the face upward.

Symmetrical tonic neck reflex (UC1): A proprioceptive reflex normally present during infancy. When head is raised, there is maximal extension of arms and flexion of legs and when head is lowered, there is maximal extension of the legs and flexion of the arms.

Tactile defensiveness (A): A sensory integrative dysfunction in which tactile sensations cause excessive emotional reactions, hyperactivity, or other behavior problems.

Tactile discrimination (R): The discrimination of shapes, textures, sizes, etc., through touch.

Tip prehension (C): A grasp in which the tip of the thumb is used against the tip of one or the other digits to pick up a small object.

Thrombosis (W): The formation or presence of a blood clot within a blood vessel.

Tremor (W): A quivering or vibratory motion.

Trunk (HS): The human body excluding the head and limbs; torso.

Ulnar (C): On the side of the forearm opposite the thumb; away from midline.

Verbalization (W): An act or process of expressing something in words.

Ventral (C): Pertaining to or situated at the anterior or belly surface; opposite of dorsal.

Ventricle (S): A normal cavity, as of the brain or heart.

Vestibulary system (A): The sensory system that responds to the position of the head in relation to gravity and accelerated or decelerated movement.

Visual memory (R): The ability to recall visual images.

Visual-motor coordination (L): The ability to coordinate vision with the movements of the body or parts of the body.

Visual perception (L): The identification, organization, and interpretation of sensory data received by the individual through the eye.

Vocalization (W): An act or process of expressing something through sounds produced in the larynx.

Code to References in Glossary

A: Ayers, A. *Sensory integration and learning disorders* (5th ed.). Los Angeles: Psychological Services, 1977.

B: Bartenieff, I. & Lewis, D. *Body movement: Coping with the environment.* New York: Gordon & Breach Science, 1980.

BL: Bleck, E. & Nagel, D. *Physically handicapped children: A medical atlas for teachers.* New York: Grune & Stratton, 1975.

C: Clark, C. & Chadwick, D. *Clinically adapted instruments for the multiply handicapped.* Westford, MA: Modulations Co., 1979.

FW: *Funk & Wagnalls standard encyclopedic dictionary.* Chicago: J. G. Ferguson Co., 1968.

G: Goldberg, S. *Clinical neuroanatomy made ridiculously simple.* Miami: Medmaster, 1979.

H: Hopkins, H. Occupational therapy management of spinal cord injuries—paraplegia and quadriplegia. In H. Willard & C. Spackman (Eds.), *Occupational therapy* (4th ed.). Philadelphia: J. B. Lippincott, 1971.

HS: Kieran, S., Conner, F., von Hippel, C. & Jones, S. *Mainstreaming preschoolers: Children with orthopedic handicaps* (DHEW Publication No. 78-31114). Washington, DC: U.S. Government Printing Office, 1978.

L: Lerner, J. *Children with learning disabilities* (2nd ed.). Boston: Houghton Mifflin, 1976.

M: Miller, J. Juvenile rheumatoid arthritis. In E. Bleck & D. Nagel (Eds.), *Physically handicapped children: A medical atlas for teachers.* New York: Grune & Stratton, 1975.

R: Russell, S. *Simulation techniques with teaching music therapists and music teachers of physically handicapped.* Unpublished master's thesis, University of Kansas, 1976.

S: *Stedman's medical dictionary.* Baltimore: Williams & Wilkins, 1976.

SBI: Shriners' burns institute inservice information. Galveston, TX, 1979.

UC1 Umbreit, J. & Cardullias, P. (Eds.). *Educating the severely physically handicapped: Basic principles and techniques* (Vol. 1). Columbus: Special Press, 1980.

UC2 Umbreit, J. & Cardullias, P. (Eds.). *Educating the severely physically handicapped: Basic principles and techniques* (Vol. 2). Columbus: Special Press, 1980.

W: *Webster's new collegiate dictionary.* Springfield, MA: G. & C. Merriam Co., 1977.

REFERENCE NOTES

1. While it is impossible to locate accurate statistics regarding the number of children served in public school programs according to their specific handicapping conditions, we do know the number of children *reportedly* served through Special Education. In the 1980-81 school year, over 4,000,000 children with handicapping conditions were served. This represents approximately 8% of the total population between the ages of 5 and 17 years in the public schools of the USA. Of this national statistic, over 60,000 children, or 0.12%, were classified as orthopedically impaired. The majority of these children were those with cerebral palsy; those with spina bifida, second. (See Appendix A for a categorical and statistical breakdown.)

2. Demonstration lessons from Dellinda Henry, RMT; formerly Music Therapy Consultant, Region 18, Educational Service Center, Midland/Odessa, Texas. (Note: Names in this and all case studies related in the present monograph have been changed to protect confidentiality.) (See Appendix B)

3. IEP's from Joanne Pasquinelli, RMT; D. T. Watson Rehabilitation Hospital for Children, Sewickley, Pennsylvania. (See Appendix C)

4. Home program from Lee Anna Rasar, RMT; Children's Hospital, New Orleans, Louisiana. (See Appendix D)

5. Case study from the author; Moody State School, University of Texas Medical Branch, Galveston.

6. Music therapy interns (MTI's) are students participating in six months of full-time clinical training supervised by a Registered Music Therapist (RMT) in a clinical facility approved by the National Association for Music Therapy (NAMT). The internship follows completion of academic coursework.

7. A Registered Music Therapist (RMT) is a person who is registered by the National Association for Music Therapy (NAMT). Registration comes after successful completion of a minimum of four years of academic work from a NAMT-approved college or university, followed by successful completion of a NAMT-approved six-month internship.

8. Case study from Jeannie D. Weiss, RMT; Moody State School, University of Texas Medical Branch, Galveston. The study is presented in the form used at the institution.

9. Case study and IEP (Individualized Educational Program) from Faith L. Johnson, RMT; F. J. Gaenslen School, 1301 East Auer, Milwaukee, Wisconsin.

10. The *Bayley Scales of Infant Development* (1969) was developed by Nancy Bayley, and measures performance on a mental scale of 0-30 months, with a scale of motor development and characteristic behavior patterns. The *Scale* is used at the F. J. Gaenslen School in Milwaukee for testing children, ages 3-6. (From written communication with Faith L. Johnson, RMT.)

11. Description provided by Faith L. Johnson, RMT.

12. See the Glossary for an explanation of various terms used throughout this monograph. For terms not included in the monograph Glossary, refer to the source references used in compiling the Glossary.

13. The materials in Appendices F, G, H, and I were provided by Laurie A. Farnan, RMT; Central Wisconsin Center for the Developmentally Disabled, Madison.

14. Case study from Jeannie D. Weiss, RMT.

15. Case study from Melinda L. Boyd, RMT; Colonial Manor Nursing Home, PO Box 1554, Cleburn, Texas.

16. Case study from Linda F. Smith, RMT; Region 10, Educational Service Center, Richardson, Texas.

17. Case study from the author.

18. For further information, contact Robert Capanna, Assistant Executive Director, Settlement Music School, 3745 Clarendon Avenue, Philadelphia, Pennsylvania 19114. Phone: (214) 637-1500.

19. Case study from the author.

20. Based on a comparison by Ellen C. Miller, MTI; Children's Hospital, New Orleans, Louisiana. Also, reference is made to *Treatment with Music: A Manual for Allied Health Professionals* by Karen J. Miller, RMT, OTR, which can be ordered from the Department of Occupational Therapy, College of Health and Human Services, Western Michigan University, Kalamazoo 49008.

21. Refers to a method of Martha Slyoff whose method books are available from Rhythm Band, Inc., in Ft. Worth, Texas.

22. Case study from Sheryl Matthews, MTI; Moody State School, University of Texas Medical Branch, Galveston.

23. Case study from Anne Buvinger, RMT; Edmond, Oklahoma.

24. Case study from the author.

25. Case study from Lee Anna Rasar, RMT.

26. Case study from the author.

27. Case study from Faith L. Johnson, RMT.

28. Case study from the author.

29. Case study from the author.

REFERENCES

Baken, J. Positioning and handling. In J. Umbreit & P. Cardullias (Eds.), *Educating the severely physically handicapped: Basic principles and techniques* (Vol. 1). Columbus: Special Press, 1980.

Bartenieff, I. & Lewis, D. *Body movement: Coping with the environment.* New York: Gordon & Breach Science, 1980.

Bayley, N. *Bayley scales of infant development.* New York: Psychological Corporation, 1969.

Bleck, E. Amputations in children. In E. Bleck & D. Nagel (Eds.), *Physically handicapped children: A medical atlas for teachers.* New York: Grune & Stratton, 1975a.

Bleck, E. Arthrogryposis. In E. Bleck & D. Nagel (Eds.), *Physically handicapped children: A medical atlas for teachers.* New York: Grune & Stratton, 1975b.

Bleck, E. Cerebral palsy. In E. Bleck & D. Nagel (Eds.), *Physically handicapped children: A medical atlas for teachers.* New York: Grune & Stratton, 1975c.

Bleck, E. Muscular dystrophy—Duchenne type. In E. Bleck & D. Nagel, *Physically handicapped children: A medical atlas for teachers.* New York: Grune & Stratton, 1975d.

Bleck, E. Myelomeningocele, meningocele, spina bifida. In E. Bleck & D. Nagel (Eds.), *Physically handicapped children: A medical atlas for teachers.* New York: Grune & Stratton, 1975e.

Bleck, E. Poliomyelitis. In E. Bleck & D. Nagel (Eds.), *Physically handicapped children: A medical atlas for teachers.* New York: Grune & Stratton, 1975f.

Bobath, B. & Bobath, K. *Motor development in the different types of cerebral palsy.* London: William Heinemann, 1975.

Bonny, H. & Savary, L. *Music and your mind: Listening with a new consciousness.* New York: Harper & Row, 1973.

Challenor, Y. & Katz, J. Limb deficiency in infancy and childhood. In J. Downey & N. Low (Eds.), *The child with disabling illness—Principles of rehabilitation.* Philadelphia: W. B. Saunders, 1974.

Christenberry, E. The use of music therapy with burn patients. *Journal of Music Therapy,* 1979, *16,* 138-148.

Chutorian, A. & Myers, S. Diseases of muscle. In J. Downey & N. Low (Eds.), *The child with disabling illness—Principles of rehabilitation.* Philadelphia: W. B. Saunders, 1974.

Clark, C. & Chadwick, D. *Clinically adapted instruments for the multiply handicapped.* Westford, MA: Modulations Company, 1979.

De Obaldia, M. & Best, G. Music therapy in the treatment of brain damaged children. *Academic Quarterly,* 1971, *6*(3), 263-269.

Denenholz, B. Music as a tool of physical medicine. In E. Schneider (Ed.), *Music therapy 1958: Proceedings of the National Association for Music Therapy.* Lawrence, KS: The Allen Press, 1959.

Federal Register, August 23, 1977.

Fischer, T. *The spina bifida child and the role of music therapy in rehabilitation.* Unpublished manuscript, Children's Hospital, New Orleans, 1977.

Graham, R. & Beer, A. *Teaching music to the exceptional child.* Englewood Cliffs, NJ: Prentice-Hall, 1980.

Johnson, J. Programming for early motor responses within the classroom. In J. Umbreit & P. Cardullias (Eds.), *Educating the severely physically handicapped: Basic principles and techniques* (Vol. 4). Columbus: Special Press, 1980.

Kieran, S., Conner, F., von Hippel, C. & Jones, S. *Mainstreaming preschoolers: Children with orthopedic handicaps* (DHEW Publication No. 78-31114). Washington, DC: U.S. Government Printing Office, 1978.

Knudson, M. Where burn care also eases inner hurt. *Patient Care,* 1979, 86-109.

Knudson-Cooper, M. Adjustment to visible stigma: The case of the severely burned. *Social Science and Medicine,* 1981a, *15B,* 31-44.

Knudson-Cooper, M. Relaxation and biofeedback training in the treatment of severely burned children. *Journal of Burn Care and Rehabilitation,* March/April, 1981b, 102-110.

Meyers, S. The spinal injury patient. In J. Downey & N. Low (Eds.), *The child with disabling illness—Principles of rehabilitation.* Philadelphia: W. B. Saunders, 1974.

Miller, J. Juvenile Rheumatoid arthritis. In E. Bleck & D. Nagel (Eds.), *Physically handicapped children: A medical atlas for teachers.* New York: Grune & Stratton, 1975.

Miller, K. *Treatment with music: A manual for allied health professionals.* Kalamazoo: Western Michigan University Printing, 1979.

Nordoff, P. & Robbins, C. *Creative music therapy.* New York: John Day, 1977.

Parks, D., Carvajal, H. & Larson, D. Management of burns. *Surgical Clinics of North America, 57*(5), 1977, 875-894.

Putnam, J. & Chrismore, W. (Eds.) *Standard terminology for curriculum and instruction in local and state school systems.* Washington, DC: National Center for Educational Statistics, Government Printing Office, 1970.

Robins, F. & Robins, J. *Educational rhythmics for mentally and physically handicapped children.* New York: Association Press, 1968.

Salter, R. *Textbook of disorders and injuries of the musculoskeletal system.* Baltimore: Williams & Wilkins, 1970.

Schneider, E. Music therapy for the cerebral palsied. In E. Gaston (Ed.), *Music in therapy.* New York: Macmillan, 1968.

Smith, L. *The role of music therapy with burned children.* Unpublished manuscript, Moody State School, University of Texas Medical Branch, Galveston, Texas, 1979.

Stevens, G. *Taxonomy in special education for children with body disorders.* Pittsburgh: Department of Special Education and Rehabilitation, University of Pittsburgh, 1962.

Woodford, J. & Reeves, A. Cranial and spinal trauma. In A. Reeves (Ed.), *Disorders of the nervous system.* Chicago: Year Book Medical Publishers, 1981.

BIBLIOGRAPHY

Ayers, A. *Sensory integration and learning disorders* (5th Ed.). Los Angeles: Psychological Services, 1957.

Ayers, A. *Sensory integration and the child.* Los Angeles: Psychological Services, 1979.

Banus, B., Kent, C., Norton, Y., Sukiennicki, D. & Becker, M. *The developmental therapist* (2nd ed.). Thorofare, NJ: Charles B. Slack, 1979.

Bitcon, C. *Alike and different: The clinical and educational use of Orff-Schulwerk.* Santa Ana, CA: Rosha Press, 1976.

Bleck, E. *Orthopaedic management of cerebral palsy.* Philadelphia: W. B. Saunders, 1979.

Bobath, B. The treatment of neuromuscular disorders by improving patterns of coordination. *Physiotherapy,* 1969, *55,* 18-22.

Bobath, B. & Bobath, K. The facilitation of normal postural reactions and movements in the treatment of cerebral palsy. *Physiotherapy,* 1964, *50,* 240-252.

Brewer, D. & Cleveland, S. *Juvenile rheumatoid arthritis: Major problems in clinical pediatrics* (Vol. 6). Philadelphia: W. B. Saunders, 1970.

Chase, J. *Closed head injuries.* Unpublished manuscript, Children's Hospital, New Orleans, 1979.

Craver, P. Tying splints for the quadriplegic patient. *American Journal of Occupational Therapy,* 1975, *29,* 551.

Finnie, N. *Handling the young cerebral palsied child at home* (2nd ed.). New York: E. P. Dutton, 1975.

Fujita, M. The impact of illness or surgery on the body image of the child. *Nursing Clinics of North America,* December 1972, 7(4), 641-649.

Gaston, E. (Ed.) *Music in therapy.* New York: Macmillan, 1968.

Goodglass, M. Musical capacity after brain damage. In E. Schneider (Ed.), *Music therapy 1962: Proceedings of the National Association for Music Therapy.* Lawrence, KS: Allen Press, 1963.

Gregg, S. Rheumatoid arthritis in childhood. *Arizona Medicine,* 1971, *28,* 577-585.

Hartfield, D. *The uses of music therapy with the juvenile rheumatoid arthritic.* Unpublished manuscript, Children's Hospital, New Orleans, 1977.

Jacobson, S. *The post-traumatic syndrome following head injuries.* Springfield, IL: Charles C Thomas, 1963.

Kooker, C. *The use of music therapy in the team treatment of muscular dystrophy.* Unpublished manuscript, Children's Hospital, New Orleans, December 1979.

Larsen, B. *Experiences of physically handicapped children, ages three to six years.* Unpublished doctoral dissertation, State University of Iowa, 1954.

Licht, S. *Arthritis and physical medicine.* Baltimore: Waverly Press, 1969.

Manning, A. Music for physically handicapped children. In E. Schneider (Ed.), *Music therapy 1958: Proceedings of the National Association for Music Therapy.* Lawrence, KS: Allen Press, 1959.

McNaughton, S. *Visual symbols: A system of communication for the nonverbal physically handicapped child.* A regional course presented by the American Academy for Cerebral Palsy, Palo Alto, 1975.

Miller, E. *The use of music therapy in the treatment of quadriplegia.* Unpublished manuscript, Children's Hospital, New Orleans, November 1977.

Nagel, D. Traumatic paraplegia and quadriplegia. In E. Bleck & D. Nagel (Eds.), *Physically handicapped children: A medical atlas for teachers.* New York: Grune & Stratton, 1975.

Nordoff, P. & Robbins, C. *Music therapy for handicapped children.* New York: Steiner, 1965.

Perlstein, M. *The exceptional child.* New York: Holt, 1960.

Pirtle, M. & Seaton, K. Use of music training to actuate conceptual growth in neurologically handicapped children. *Journal of Research in Music Education,* Winter, 1973, *21,* 292-301.

Rasar, L. *Uses of music therapy with physically handicapped children.* Unpublished manuscript, Children's Hospital, New Orleans, 1978.

Root, L. *The totally involved cerebral palsy patient.* Instructional Course Lectures, presented at the annual meeting of the American Academy of Orthopaedic Surgeons, Las Vegas, 1977.

Rouen, D. *The role of music therapy in the treatment of cerebral palsy.* Unpublished manuscript, Children's Hospital, New Orleans, date unknown.

Samilson, R. (Ed.) *Orthopaedic aspects of cerebral palsy.* London: Spastics International Medical Publications, 1975.

Snow, W. & Fields, B. Music as an adjunct in the training of children with cerebral palsy. *Occupational Therapy,* 1950, *29,* 147-156.

Stover, S. & Zeiger, H. Head injury in children and teenagers: Functional recovery correlated with the duration of coma. *Archives of Physical Medicine and Rehabilitation,* May, 1976, *57,* 201-205.

Taylor, D. Treatment goals for quadriplegic and paraplegic patients. *American Journal of Occupational Therapy,* 1974, *28,* 22-29.

Travis, G. *Chronic illness in children: Its impact on child and family.* Palo Alto: Stanford University Press, 1976.

Tucker, D., Seabury, B. & Canner, N. *Foundations for learning with creative art and creative movement.* Boston: Massachusetts Division of Mental Health, Department of Mental Health, 1976.

Vernazza, M. *Music plus.* Boulder, CO: Pruett Publishing, 1978.

SELECTED FILMS

1. "Changes"

   The Stanfield House
   12381 Wilshire Boulevard
   Suite 203
   Los Angeles, CA 90025

   29 min./16mm/color/sound
   Purchase—$335/Rental (2 days)—$35

2. "Emperor's Nightingale" by Fran Herman

   Ontario Children's Hospital
   Toronto, Ontario, Canada

   Rental—$30

3. "Mimi"

   Billy Budd Films, Inc.
   235 East 57th Street
   New York, NY 10022

   12-1/2 min./16mm/black & white/sound/1972
   Purchase—$150/Rental—$15

4. "Here's Looking at You, Kid"

   Biomed Arts Association
   350 Parnassus Avenue, Suite 905
   San Francisco, CA 94117

   Purchase—$400

5. "Motor Speech Disorders"

   Audiovisual Center
   Section of Photography
   Mayo Clinic
   Rochester, MN 55901

6. "Nicky: One of My Best Friends"

   CRM McGraw-Hill Films
   110 15th Street
   Del Mar, CA 92014

   15 min./16mm/color/sound
   Purchase—$230/Rental—$25

7. "Somebody Waiting"

   University of California
   Extension Media Center
   2223 Fulton Street
   Berkeley, CA 94720

   25 min./16mm/color/sound
   Purchase—$300/Rental—$20

8. "You Have Something to Offer (Individual Differences)"

   CRM McGraw-Hill Films
   110 15th Street
   Del Mar, CA 92014

   14 min./16mm/color/sound
   Purchase—$235/Rental—$28

APPENDIX A

Children Receiving Special Education in 1980-81

Handicapping Conditions	Total	Percentage of School Population Served
Speech Impaired	1,177,792	2.43
Mentally Retarded	849,890	1.75
Learning Disabled	1,455,135	3.01
Other Health-Impaired	995,246	.22
Deaf	41,372	.08
Hard of Hearing	41,212	.08
Orthopedically Impaired	60,695	.12
Deaf-Blind	2,955	.03
Visually Handicapped	33,631	.06
Multi-Handicapped	71,688	.14
Totals	4,729,616	7.92

Danielson, L. Personal communication, November 24, 1981.

APPENDIX B[2]

Samples of Demonstration Lessons

Demonstration Lesson #1 (September 24 & 29, 1981)
  1. Autoharp activities with Ida Hill.
  2. Rhythm instrument activities with Billy East.
  3. Instrument activities with Lupe Gonzales.

Ida Hill will (1) increase use of left hand/arm in strumming the Autoharp; (2) use right hand/fingers to press down two chord bars (G, D[7]); and (3) sing familiar, age-appropriate songs.

Billy East will (1) raise (against gravity) each arm/hand individually and (2) hit, touch, push, pull rhythm instruments suspended in the air or press down pianica keys.

Lupe Gonzales will (a) use one finger to play notes on the pianica; (2) blow air through the mouthpiece; (3) play only the black notes on the pianica; and (4) use both hands together in playing the toy accordion, cymbals, sticks, or other similar substitutes.

Demonstration Lesson #2 (October 1, 1980)
  1. Autoharp activities with Ida Hill.
  2. Rhythm instrument activities with Billy East.
  3. Instrument activities with Lupe Gonzales.

Autoharp activities for Ida Hill will follow those outlined in the demonstration in Lesson #1. Additional stretching and relaxing of her arms will be beneficial for strumming. Grasp the back of her upper arm with one hand and hold her hand with your other hand, then gently stretch forward. Also, rotate *slowly* and *gently* her upper arm/elbow/shoulder in a circle, both directions. This will help alleviate tension in the neck/shoulder area. Set behavior contingencies, such as: after you play one (short) song with your left hand, you may play two (or three) songs with your right. Emphasize singing to provide more pleasure. Send her out of the room when she refuses to try so the other children can enjoy their music activities, and so Ida cannot enjoy their activities without putting forth any effort.

Billy East should continue the activities outlined on September 24 and 29. Other objects can be substituted for the instruments to prevent boredom (i.e., various sizes of balls, Leggs containers, soft animals).

If Lupe Gonzales continues to be uninterested in playing the pianica, change the activities.

  1. Ask her to hum with the kazoo.
  2. Strum the Autoharp. Press down chord bars if possible.

Attempt to play the Autoharp in a slow, steady beat to encourage motor coordination (i.e., strum one time every other measure or one time every measure; teacher or aide can sing songs using one major chord, such as "Row, Row, Row Your Boat," "Are You Sleeping," etc.).

APPENDIX C[3]
Sample Individual Educational Plans (IEPs)

Instructional Area: __Music-Developmental A__ Student's Name _____ School Year_____

Annual Goal: __To develop a trusting relationship with the therapists through music activities._____

Educational Tasks	Evaluation Procedures/Conditions	Success Criteria	Progress
To respond by tracking or establishing eye contact when various sounds are presented (i.e., use of name, vocalizes instrumental sounds).	Periodic evaluation with therapist-made assessment list.		
To associate words with music materials by responding to directions involving these materials (rhythm instruments, pictures, etc.).	Performance on task.		

Instructional Area: __Music-Developmental A_____

Annual Goal: __To increase awareness through musical stimulation and respond in various ways to the stimulation._____

Educational Tasks	Evaluation Procedures/Conditions	Success Criteria	Progress
To vocalize when presented with a simple musical sound, source being an instrument or therapist's voice.	Periodic evaluation with therapist-made assessment list.		
To respond to music activities through voluntary movement of hand, arm, leg or head.	Periodic evaluation with therapist-made assessment list.		
To imitate therapist in gross body movements (arms, hands, head up and down; legs and feet where applicable).	Periodic evaluation with therapist-made assessment list.		

Instructional Area: __Music-Primary Level_____ Student's Name _____ School Year_____

Annual Goal: __To increase vocal production, motor coordination and peer interaction through music activities._____

Educational Tasks	Evaluation Procedures/Conditions	Success Criteria	Progress
To sing songs with a 3-note range.	Performance on task.		
To coordinate body movements with music and words of a song.	Given directions, student will imitate therapist and create own movements.		
The play simple rhythm instruments as accompaniment to songs and movement.	Student will play as directed or in a creative manner.		

Instructional Area: __Music-Primary Level_____

Annual Goal: __To increase body awareness, listening skills and language development through music activities._____

Educational Tasks	Evaluation Procedures/Conditions	Success Criteria	Progress
To associate parts of the body with words in a song.	Performance on task.		
To identify differences between loud/soft, fast/slow and high/low.	Performance on task.		
To increase knowledge of basic learning skills (i.e., songs with numbers, colors, alphabet, etc.).	Performance on task.		

Instructional Area: Music-Elementary Level Student's Name ______________ School Year ________

Annual Goal: To increase basic music skills, listening ability and vocal production through music activities.

	Educational Tasks	Evaluation Procedures/Conditions	Success Criteria	Progress
Short-Term Objective	To imitate simple rhythm patterns and follow tempo and dynamic changes.	Performance on task.		
	To listen with directed recall of sounds, words of songs, and directions.	Performance on task.		
	To sing songs by rote.	Performance on task.		

Instructional Area: Music-Elementary Level

Annual Goal: To increase group interaction, creativity and language development through music activities.

	Educational Tasks	Evaluation Procedures/Conditions	Success Criteria	Progress
Short-Term Objective	To participate in *movement activities which require peer interaction for successful outcome.	Performance on task.		
	To create individual ideas for songs and movement.	Performance on task.		
	To answer questions and discuss activities concerning musical experiences and materials.	Performance on task.		

*Movement activities such as circle games, simple folk dances, etc.

Instructional Area: Music-Intermediate/Secondary lev. Student's Name ______________ School Year ________

Annual Goal: To increase music appreciation, listening abilities and group interaction (socialization) through music activities.

Educational Tasks	Progress to Date	Comments
To participate in group projects of a musical nature.		
To listen to and discuss chosen musical compositions of different styles and eras.		
To express individual ideas on musical experiences and materials.		

Instructional Area: Music-Intermediate/Secondary lev.

Annual Goal: To increase creativity and music skills through music activities.

Educational Tasks	Progress to Date	Comments
To follow body movement sequences (i.e., disco, rock, modern or simple folk dances).		
To improve skills in learning to use musical signs and symbols.		

From Joanne Pasquinelli, RMT, D. T. Watson Rehabilitation Hospital for Children, Sewickley, Pennsylvania.

Home Program for a Parent of an Infant

(Note: some activities were omitted from the original program for brevity in this monograph.)

The following examples of activities are classified under goals which Michael may be expected to reach between 3 and 5 months of age.

Motor. Integration of reflex short-term goal: Child will keep both hands at the middle of his chest (midline) while he turns his head to either side (integration of asymmetrical tonic neck reflex).

Present a musical instrument to Michael at the midline and encourage him to take it with both hands or to transfer it from hand to hand.

Note: This activity is designed to break up the asymmetrical tonic reflex (ATNR), i.e., child assumes a "fencing" position when his head is turned to one side, the arm on the skull side bends, the arm on the face side straightens. This reflex should not dominate Michael's pattern of movements after the fifth month.

Fine Motor/Perceptual. Eye-hand coordination short-term goal: Child will reach for dangling musical instruments. Place a musical instrument or rattle in a place where Michael will make contact with it when he moves his arms. Dangle Michael's favorite musical instrument above his crib low enough so that he can touch it when he reaches up.

Hands in midline short-term goal: Child will bring his hands together in front of his body (at the midline). Play pat-a-cake with Michael. Move his arms through the actions, pausing to help him feel his other hand at the midline. Use his finger tips to feel his palm and other fingers.

Visual focusing short-term goal: Child will look at his hands. Bring Michael's hands into the field of vision and move them to make them clap and reach for musical instruments.

Grasp short-term goal: Child will hold an object in his palm using his thumb and index finger (radial-palm prehension). Gradually give Michael smaller instruments until he can hold surfaces as small as one inch in diameter using his thumb and index fingers. When Michael is holding the instrument with one hand, help him transfer it from one hand to the other. Gradually decrease your assistance until he can transfer the instrument on his own.

Language. Expression short-term goal: Child will vocalize on hearing the human voice. Give (or hold for) Michael a bell. Imitate the sound of the bell. Reward Michael when he makes any sound by patting him, smiling, talking, or using anything that serves as a reward to him.

Imitation short-term goal: Child will use objects to make noise. Place a bell or shaker in Michael's hand, and shake his arm to demonstrate how the music is made. Encourage him to shake his arm.

Reception short-term goal: Child will turn head to locate sounds to voices. Ring a bell or play an instrument in different parts of the room, being careful to stay out of Michael's range of vision. Reward him when he locates the sound.

Expression short-term goal: Child will vocalize sound patterns. Use words such as "oh-oh," and "bye-bye" with exaggerated pitch changes and encourage Michael to imitate.

Cognitive. When playing with Michael, sing nursery rhymes, children's songs, etc. Immediately imitate any sounds that Michael makes. Reward him with smiles, hugs or whatever is rewarding if he continues to vocalize.

Short-term goal: Child will combine two actions. Place a musical instrument in Michael's hands when he is not looking at his hands. Help him move the instrument into view or turn his head so that he can explore the instrument (grasping and seeing).

Object permanence short-term goal: Child will look at the place where a moving object has just disappeared. Set up a barrier or a tunnel. Slowly move a musical ball behind it. Call Michael's attention to the disappearance of the ball and then make it reappear. Encourage him to seek the ball.

APPENDIX E
Pictorial Examples of Instrument Adaptations

1. A fireplace bellow connects reed horn with rubber hose; used with children who cannot blow into a horn and used for improvement of bilateral upper extremity movement.

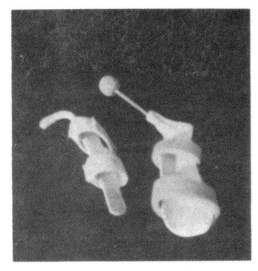

2a. A hand pointer made of polyform and velcro; used to play individual keys on a keyboard. 2b. Hand splint made of polyform with foam straps; used to hold a mallet in right hand.

3a. Hand splint made of polyform and foam; used to hold mallet in left hand. 3b. Universal cuff made of velcro; used to hold a mallet.

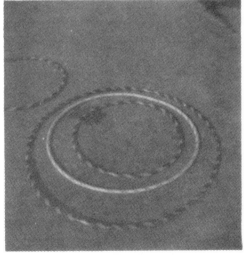

4. Hoops made of plastic tubing and colored tape, filled with popcorn; used for hand grasps and extension and flexion of upper extremities.

5. Headpointer made of polyfoam, velcro, dowel, silicon, and chalk holder; used to play individual keys on keyboard and reinforce head control.

6. Tilt-top table made of plywood and wingnuts; designed to adjust to heights of wheelchairs and provide proper positioning when playing resonator bells, drums, wood blocks or mini-harp.

7. Plexiglass cover designed for a child with a headpointer to operate a tape recorder.

Samples of Adapted Handles for Correct Hand Grasps

1

2

3

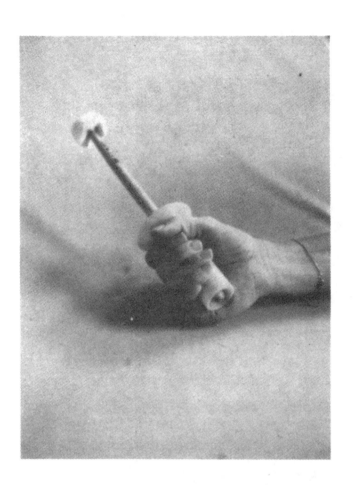

4

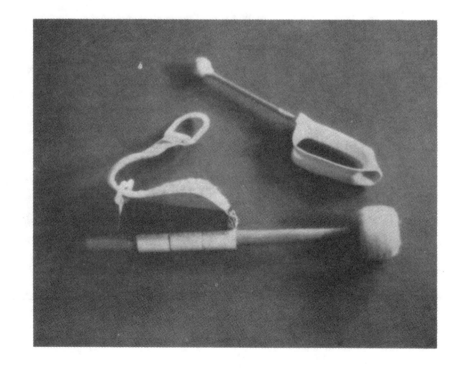

Fine Motor Skills in Music and Adapting Instruments

I. Characteristic grasp and hand patterns

    A. Developmental prerequisites

        1. Head stabilization
        2. Shoulder stabilization

    B. Cortical thumb

    C. Flexion patterns predominate

        1. More muscle tone on palmer surface
        2. Muscle on dorsal side stretched out
        3. Pulls wrist down
        4. Fingers curl
        5. Extensor tendons stretched out
        6. Hand deviates to ulnar side (ulnar deviation)

II. Points to consider when adapting instruments

    A. Consult O.T.

    B. Select correct materials
        1. Firm surfaces (plastic, wood, etc.) inhibit spasticity
        2. Soft surfaces (foam padding, "nerf" material, cotton, etc.) can increase spasticity

    C. Instruments should balance in hand to minimize slipping

    D. Instruments should elicit pleasant sounds and physical sensations when played

    E. The longer the mallet the greater degree of shoulder stability needed

    F. Grasp and release progression

        1. Spastic grasp should work with small diameter grips to gradually expand to larger grips to encourage finger extension
        2. Weak grasp should work with large diameter grips to progressively smaller grips to encourage finger flexion

APPENDIX G[13]
Materials and Adaptations of Musical Instruments

Instrument	Adaptation	Materials
Handle Bells	2 sets tied together	clothesline, electric tape
Cymbals	1. Enlarge handles 2. Suspend on tray	-spools, nuts & bolts, large pop beads -ping-pong net pole, with clamp
Large Mallets	Enlarge grip "Shorten" stick	cylindrical foam padding plastic spools
Small Mallets	Enlarge grip Prevent stick from falling from hand	-small pop beads -tape, bottle handles
Rhythm Sticks	Enlarge grip	cylindrical foam padding, quad-quip utensil holder
Handle Castenets	Balance Change plane	-tape -2 sets
Maracas	Prevent slipping through hand	tape, 2 maracas
Catalog	Fred Sammons, Inc. Professional Self-Help Aids Box 32 Brookfield, IL 60513	

APPENDIX H[13]
Ranking of Common Instruments in Terms of Difficulty in Producing Sounds

CENTRAL WISCONSIN CENTER FOR THE DEVELOPMENTALLY DISABLED
MUSIC THERAPY

RANKING OF COMMON INSTRUMENTS IN TERMS OF DIFFICULTY TO PRODUCE SOUND

INCREASE IN EFFORT NEEDED TO PRODUCE SOUND

BASIC
(MAXIMUM SOUND, MINIMUM EFFORT)
1. BELLS WITH HANDLES
2. WRIST BELLS
3. MARACA

INTERMEDIATE
1. DRUM
2. TONE BAR
3. TAMBOURINE
4. HANDLE CASTANETS

DIFFICULT
1. CYMBALS
2. CLAPPING HANDS
3. RHYTHM STICKS
(1, 2, 3 REQUIRE
2 HANDS TOGETHER
AT MIDLINE)
4. TONE BELLS
5. XYLOPHONE

Six Goals of Music Therapy and Concurrent Therapies For Para/Quadriplegic Children

Music Therapy	Concurrent Therapies

Goal 1: Strengthening of Muscles

Music therapy offers a graded program of playing a variety of musical instruments, moving toward faster and stronger movements incorporating spontaneous, purposeful movement. Types of activities include:

- Strumming stringed instruments of increasing size and difficulty, such as ukulele, guitar, Autoharp, etc.
- Beating drums and playing resonator bells for strengthening grasp and gross and fine motor control.
- Combining drums and other rhythm instruments, which require reaching and stretching to play (crossing midline, etc.)
- Using the bass drum, cymbals, and a trap set which require the use of a foot pedal.
- Using weighted rhythm instruments to strengthen wrist and arm.

P.T. and/or O.T. and Nursing personnel supervise children through program of active exercises to help children reach maximum of independence in daily living activities.

Goal 2: Increasing Vital Capacity

Music therapy offers pleasure and satisfaction through playing wind instruments, singing, or stretching to music while deep breathing. Types of activities include:
- Blowing kazoos.
- Blowing harmonicas by using a holder attachment around neck.
- Stretching exercises requiring deep breathing.
- Vocalizing and then singing complete musical phrases in one long breath.
- Blowing into a pianica while a therapist plays tune (fingers the keys).
- Blowing into a single-reed horn to increase decibel level of sound.

Respiratory therapy offers function through practice through glossopharyngeal breathing using muscles of mouth, tongue, soft palate, and throat to force air into lungs. Triflo Respiratory Exerciser is used to assess vital capacity: Child inhales to make three balls rise simultaneously.

Goal 3: Expressing Emotions

Through listening to music or singing songs of their choice, children find an appropriate outlet for their emotions. Music can serve as the vehicle for children talking about their anger about the imposed altered lifestyle. Types of activities (most effective in groups) include:
- Listening to recordings or to live music, and then discussing the music or lyrics.
- Composing songs, especially angry or sad songs, the blues, etc., to encourage sharing of feelings.

Psychotherapist, psychologist, or counselor provides verbal and play therapy.

Music Therapy	Concurrent Therapies

Goal 4: Increasing and Maintaining Mobility of Joints

Music therapy uses music activities which stress the flexion and extension of the wrists, elbows and shoulders. Types of activities include:
- Raising the work surface for more shoulder extension while playing resonator bell melodies on table top.
- Using finger splints to play piano, chord organ, or electric keyboard.
- Using finger splints to press buttons of Autoharp, using wrist action.
- Rotating plastic hoops of different sizes in circles, clockwise and counterclockwise.
- Creating rhythms on bongos, using wrist action for soft sounds and elbow action for louder sounds.
- Clapping in rhythm to recorded or live music.

P.T. and O.T. usually move children through passive range of motion exercises to increase joint mobility. O.T. makes splints for fingers and hands.

Goal 5: Improving Coordinated Movements

Music therapy encourages participation in music activities requiring proper timing and steady rhythm. Types of activities include:
- Beating a drum in steady rhythm to recorded music.
- Clapping splints or hands in rhythm to music.
- Strumming guitar, Autoharp, or ukulele with consistent beat.
- Using universal cuff or finger splint, pressing buttons of Autoharp to make chord changes at proper time in song.

O.T. supervises children in practicing independent feeding and typing.

Goal 6: Developing Recreational and Avocational Interests

Music therapy provides a variety of musical experiences for beneficial use of free time, such as:
- Singing.
- Listening to music and exploring new kinds of music.
- Playing harmonica, drums, Autoharp.
- Learning to read music.
- Creating music to express thoughts, feelings, and stimulate creativity.

O.T., nursing or recreation therapy staff offer reading, watching tv, listening to the radio, or doing handicrafts (weaving, painting, drawing, working with clay, etc.).

APPENDIX J

Home Program for a Quadriplegic Boy

Through playing harmonica, singing, and listening to music, Mark worked on the following goals over a period of seven months: improving his balance, increasing gross motor coordination and muscle strength, increasing vital capacity, increasing memory-sequencing skills, building his self-esteem, and learning a constructive use of his leisure time. Secondary goals included increasing independence in making assessments of his own progress and developing the ability to concentrate on more than one item at a time.

It is rare for a quadriplegic person to be able to hold a harmonica with his hands and play it independently. Mark worked extremely hard to learn to do this, and it was an accomplishment of which he was very proud. When he had trouble with any area of his musical work, Mark was reminded of his achievement in holding the harmonica by himself. Assistance was sometimes required when Mark dropped the harmonica because it had to be positioned at his mouth. When this occurred, he sometimes became frustrated and was afraid his dependence caused an inconvenience. Mark required constant reassurance that he was not a "bother." The music therapist tried to encourage him to become more critical of the physical aspects over which he had control.

Mark's progress was slow. While he could sightread music fairly well, he had only been able to memorize one song, "Oh, When the Saints Come Marching In." Mark needed associational cues to help him remember the sequences of numbers, i.e., to remember the sequence (5, 5, 4, 4, 4). We compared it to a full house in a poker hand. His ability to remember whether he should blow out or suck in on each note became better than his ability to remember numbers in the correct sequence.

Mark's difficulty with his memory work may have been related to his depression and feelings of frustration. When encouraged to verbalize his feelings, Mark vented some anger but was then able to relax and make progress more quickly. Approval by the music therapist was important to him, and at first he seemed to be working to please her. At this point, increasing independence in making assessments of his progress was added as a goal. Mark understood that he had to break tasks down into small units and master each one separately before chaining them together.

At the time of this writing, the next goal is to have Mark blow out on several different notes and time how long he is able to sustain a pitch. He should also do this by sucking in and timing how long he can hold each note. Presently, he is capable of sustaining the middle tones on the harmonica (4-6) for up to six seconds while blowing out and up to three seconds while sucking in. Hopefully, Mark can increase both of these and also learn to sustain notes on the high (above six) and low (below four) pitches.

MONOGRAPH 3

MUSIC THERAPY FOR OTHER HEALTH IMPAIRED CHILDREN

Lenore M. Schwankovsky
and
Perry T. Guthrie

ACKNOWLEDGMENTS

The music therapists listed below contributed to this monograph by offering comments and suggestions, reading and editing its context, submitting case studies, and in general, caring in its construction. The author is deeply grateful.

Cynthia Briggs, RMT
Philadelphis, PA

Michael Clark, RMT
Topeka, KS

Lloyd Davis, RMT
New Orleans, LA

Joan Fuery, RMT
Napa, CA

Mary Ann Froehlich, RMT
Benicia, CA

Ellen Griffith, M.A., RMT
Napa, CA

Judith Jellison, RMT
Minneapolis, MN

Faith Johnson, RMT
Milwaukee, WI

Wanda Lathom, Ph.D., RMT
Kansas City, MO

Linda Marley, RMT
Long Beach, CA

Terry McCarthy, RMT
New Orleans, LA

Alicia Nowicki, RMT
Porterville, CA

H. A. Padberg, RSCJ, RMT
St. Louis, MO

Susan Pasquale, M.A., RMT
Clinton, MA

Lee Anna Rasar, RMT
New Orleans, LA

Susan Tarver, RMT
Kansas City, MO

Caroline Zander, RMT

INTRODUCTION TO THE DISABILITY

The health impaired child historically has received much attention from the medical field. Research and treatment have focused on the prevention and cure of childhood illness to the extent that children who suffer from chronic or terminal illnesses are living longer and are less hampered by their conditions. As medical knowledge expands, more progress is being made toward further reduction of the deleterious effects of childhood illness. Along with medical advances, related fields have expanded their knowledge in the areas of emotional and developmental effects of illness upon children. Pediatric psychologists are continually searching for ways to facilitate optimum adjustment of the child and family to difficult, and sometimes devastating, issues that accompany chronic and terminal illnesses. Child life programs are becoming more frequent in children's hospitals, bridging the gap between the home and hospital. In additon, the *Education for All Handicapped Children Act (Federal Register,* 1977) recognizes that health impairments can cause a serious interruption in the education and subsequent success for a child.

Music therapists are becoming more involved in the treatment of health impaired children. Working with treatment teams which include physicians, anesthesiologists, registered nurses, psychologists, and social workers, music therapists are able to provide support and involvement, as well as a medium for self-expression to children and their families who are coping with temporary or chronic illnesses. The purpose of this monograph is to explore the primary needs of the health impaired child and the role of music therapy in the treatment and remediation of those needs. The format will include an examination of common characteristics of health impaired children, music therapy as one component of treatment intervention, the effects of hospitalization on children, issues of death and dying, and descriptions of 11 health disorders of children. The latter section will include a description of the illness, its etiology, psychological correlates, medical and psychological treatment, and description of music therapy intervention. The goals are to increase the reader's understanding of the major health impairments of childhood and the role of music therapy in treatment.

An initial definition of the health impaired child, as it will be addressed in this writing, is found in *Federal Register* (1977). *The Education for All Handicapped Children Act* became law in 1975 and was designed to assure a free appropriate public education in the least restrictive environment for all handicapped children, ages 3 to 21. As named in the law, this includes children who are mentally retarded, multihandicapped, deaf and hard-of-hearing, speech impaired, visually impaired, deaf-blind, orthopedically impaired, seriously emotionally disturbed, specific learning disabled, and other health impaired. The inclusion of health impaired children in this law is a recognition of the severe effects illness can have on the educational and developmental process. The law further defines health impaired as:

> Limited strength, vitality or alertness, due to chronic or acute health problems
> such as a heart condition, tuberculosis, rheumatic fever, nephritis, asthma,
> sickle cell anemia, hemophilia, epilepsy, lead poisoning, leukemia, or diabetes,
> which adversely affects a child's educational performance (p. 42478).

In addition to adverse effects on the child's educational performance, other factors that have a profound effect on the child include hospitalization; fear of pain, separation, and death; negative family responses; altered peer relationships; and negative self-image. Awareness of the difficulties the health impaired child encounters has led to the development of more effective treatment approaches. These approaches recognize the necessity of treating both the medical and nonmedical needs of the child.

The music therapist is trained to address the nonmedical needs of health impaired children. As a member of the treatment team, the music therapist is involved in assessing the need areas of the individual child and developing a treatment plan. This includes documentation of change and progress toward goals by writing progress reports and taking part in team meetings in which the overall progress of the child is discussed.

The treatment plan of the music therapist may focus on a variety of needs exhibited by the child. For example, the music therapist can provide a normalized environment which allows self-expression, release of tension, and relaxation. Group sessions can provide needed social involvement with peers and age appropriate activities. The music therapist can also address conditions related to the child's physical well-being, such as providing musical activities to strengthen the respiratory functioning of an asthmatic child. Emotional issues related to the illness and issues of death and dying might also be the subject of a music therapy session.

Music has a cultural base as well as personal quality which is specifically human. It is used by man as a medium of communication and expression of the full spectrum of emotions. Consequently, music becomes a valuable tool in treatment settings. The music therapist working with health impaired children uses the unique attributes of music to enhance recovery and facilitate healthy adjustment of the child and family to the illness.

Descriptions of music therapy intervention with health impaired children have been collected from Registered Music Therapists (RMTs) in various settings throughout the United States. Although a complete review of current treatment practices is not provided in this monograph, it is representative of present approaches to music therapy intervention with this specific population.

MUSIC THERAPY FOR DEVELOPMENT OF SKILLS

The National Association for Music Therapy (NAMT) was founded in 1950 and has developed curricular standards for the college and university training of music therapists. In addition to academic training, the music therapy student serves a six-month, 1040-hour clinical internship. NAMT grants registration to qualified music therapists who are then designated as Registered Music Therapists (RMTs). Additional information regarding music therapy curricula and certification is available from: The National Association for Music Therapy, Inc.

Music therapists are trained to use music as a tool to facilitate individuals in achieving and maintaining their maximum level of functioning. Music therapists work with a variety of child and adult populations including mentally retarded, geriatric, emotionally disturbed, physically handicapped, learning disabled, and acutely medically ill. Music therapists also work with the health impaired child. As a member of the treatment team, the music therapist works to facilitate optimum health and development of each child. To do so, an initial assessment of the child is compiled, which takes into account his medical condition, educational factors, family dynamics, communication and social skills, as well as related psychological variables. Additional information is obtained by referring to assessments by other team members.

Observation of the child by the music therapist in the treatment setting and possibly in the classroom, home, or other settings provides valuable perspectives. Also, information is gathered directly from the child by means of an interview. Interview assessment includes verbal questioning as well as engaging the child in musical activities. The child's responses indicate strengths as well as areas of need. Interaction between the music therapist and the child provides data regarding the child's developmental level, secondary effects of the health impairment, and indications of possible areas of trauma. This information provides direction for the establishment of an appropriate and effective treatment intervention plan.

Music therapy goals and objectives are then established for the child. Consequently, music activities are selected which address the child's specific needs. Through involvement in music, the child may be able to utilize his strengths, address areas of need, and alleviate secondary effects of the health impairment. Music therapy intervention can also contribute directly to medical treatment goals, such as respiratory control in cystic fibrosis. Goals of treatment correspond with major areas of development for the growing child including cognitive, motor, communication, and social skills, as well as emotional development.

Cognitive Skills

Cognitive skills include the following areas: concept formation, comprehension, and auditory/visual/motor association. Traditionally, cognitive skills are developed via school or other academic activities. Music therapy provides an additional resource in developing these skills. For example, some children have problems related to processing what they hear and incorporating auditory stimuli into existing concepts. Music therapy can assist the child by utilizing exercises which help develop listening skills, and provide a different modality of presenting information.

Motor Skills

Music therapy can be used to remediate developmental delays in motor skills, which may occur due to frequent hospitalization, reduction in activity, or organic factors. Range of motion, bilateral development, and fine motor skills can be exercised as a result of involvement in music activities. Practice of motor skills can be accomplished in a structured, motivating setting. The child can become involved in music activities which adapt to the physical abilities of the child, and which take into account the child's physical stamina and vitality. Music is also a vehicle for promoting development of sensorimotor integration in the child with neurological impairment secondary to the health impairment.

Communication Skills

Development of both receptive and expressive language skills can be facilitated through music therapy. For example, auditory perception can be increased by having the child learn to distinguish high and low tones as well as rhythmic sequences. Activities which require verbal responses are utilized along with such activities as song writing to exercise verbal expression and language development. Receptive skills can be reinforced by having the child follow verbal instructions in playing an instrument or musical game.

Social Skills

Interpersonal contact and interaction are among the most crucial needs of children, whether ill or healthy. Involvement in musical activities requires social skills, including listening, cooperating, and sharing. Participation in music assists the child in fitting into a group situation, and can help teach the child social skills. In addition, group activities also help relieve feelings of isolation and give the child a more normal social experience.

Emotional Development

The emotional development of the health impaired child plays a vital role in his response to a serious, chronic illness. Younger children have not yet developed strong egos and defense systems necessary in coping with stress. The music therapist is able to aid the child in self-expression, identification of emotions, and validation of his responses to a stressful life situation.

The music therapist takes into consideration specific goals and the dynamics and objectives of the individual child when planning therapy sessions. Participation in music is regarded as a normal childhood activity even when adaptations must be made to accommodate the health impaired child's limitations. Beyond the normal social experiences, the health impaired child who is involved in music activities can regard himself as being special in a positive sense. The child can gain attention through abilities rather than through medical needs.

CHARACTERISTICS OF HEALTH IMPAIRED CHILDREN

In *The Education for All Handicapped Children Act* the category of health impaired children has been included under the heading of severely-profoundly handicapped. This designation is determined when an illness significantly hinders the educational and developmental processes of the child. Hindrance is related to the child's inability to successfully participate and achieve in the normal classroom environment. "Health impaired children" is a most heterogeneous category, due to the wide range of illnesses it encompasses. Reynolds and Birch (1977) have discussed the artificiality of the category as related to the diversity of the illnesses and difficulty in establishing common characteristics among the children affected. For example, it is difficult initially to determine commonalities between a child with cystic fibrosis and a child who has sickle cell anemia. Both diseases affect different systems in the body and exhibit unrelated symptoms. In addition, health impaired children may have multiple illnesses or diseases which further compound their individual physical, emotional, and psychological difficulties. It becomes apparent that health impairment as a category covers a wide spectrum of symptoms and severity. Though the range and symptomatology of health impairment is diverse, there exist general characteristic needs of these children. The needs listed below are common to health impaired children (Petrillo & Sanger, 1980; Thompson & Stanford, 1981; Wright, Schaefer & Solomons, 1979). Careful attention to these needs by the health professional can facilitate healthy adjustment of the child and family to the illness.

1. *Adaptation to the illness and the limitations it imposes.* Health impaired children need assistance in understanding the nature of their illnesses. First, they need to be educated about the effects of the illness and the treatment regime required to keep symptoms under control. Secondly, the child will have emotional issues related to the illness. Anger and frustration may arise from limits the illness imposes. For example, fears of an uncertain future may cause acting-out behavior or depression. Learning to express and process these feelings related to being ill is a necessary factor in adaptation to the illness.

2. *Adjustment of the family to the illness.* When a child is diagnosed as having a serious illness or disease, family dynamics are usually affected. Problems include the stress due to new, medically related financial burdens. In addition, the child or other family members, such as parents or siblings, experience a variety of conflicting emotions which may include feelings of guilt, thoughts of being the cause of the problem, anger, or resentment. Professional support is an important element in helping the family maintain emotional equilibrium.

3. *Dealing with hospitalization.* When illness results in hospitalization for treatment, specific age-related issues emerge including separation anxiety, fear of pain, and fear of loss of control. Consequently, careful preparation of the child for hospitalization is most important. Preparation may include a visit to the hospital and the opportunity to become familiar with hospital personnel, hospital equipment, and related medical procedures. The child also benefits from exploration and possible resolution of various feelings and concerns prior to and during hospitalization. This can be facilitated by involving the child in a positive, normalized hospital environment.

4. *Learning and use of age-appropriate defense mechanisms.* With the onset of a major illness as well as with prolonged illness, health impaired children may regress to immature behaviors as a result of fears and anxieties. Often children use more primitive, less appropriate defense mechanisms when experiencing stress. For example, a child who has acquired speech prior to the illness may stop talking or may regress to using "baby talk." Consequently, the child may need support and understanding in order to maintain healthy emotional development.

5. *Resolving fear-provoking fantasies.* The younger the child who experiences a health impaired illness, the more likely that he will experience nightmares and fear-provoking fantasies pertaining to illness and to treatment equipment. Young children have not developed the cognitive skills necessary for conceptualizing the parameters of the illness. As a result, they require reality-based information on their illness and medical procedures.

6. *Need for a normalized environment.* A health impaired child, like any child, needs a normal, structured environment which includes interactions with significant others as well as involvement in age-appropriate activities. The effects of individual differences due to illness are confounded when the health impaired child is treated differently from other children. Whether the health impaired child is in school, at home, or in the hospital, it is important for the child to be treated as normally as possible, maintaining normal patterns of child management. The emphasis needs to be on the child not on the illness.

7. *Continuation of school and social development.* Health impairments may restrict a child's environment as well as his social interaction with others. At one extreme, the health impaired child may temporarily leave his usual environment and enter a hospital setting. Along the treatment continuum, the child may be able to live at home but not attend school. At the other extreme, the child may experience long periods of isolation from all but a few people. The least restrictive situation may allow the child to attend school for a partial or full day, but not participate in all activities. Quite often the illness limits the number of days that a child can attend school. Various educational or remedial services such as homebound instruction or the services of a remedial learning specialist can be utilized to counteract the limitation of restricted school attendance. Restriction of school attendance may also affect the development of social skills. Care should be taken to prevent developmental or maturational lags in social development due to inconsistent school attendance.

8. *Prevention and remediation of developmental delays.* Developmental delays can result in health impaired children as a result of (a) low to moderte absenteeism from school, (b) limited social interactions with peers, (c) limited participation in sports and physical activities, and (d) limited participation in other recreational activities. While health impaired children demonstrate areas of normal development and maturation, the interruption of school, recreational, and social activities may significantly constrain or retard growth in other areas. Consequently, a modified, normalized environment provides an opportunity for the child to be involved in the work of growing and developing at age level. It may require a conscious effort on the part of family and professionals to facilitate the continuation of growth and development in these areas.

9. *Normalization of physical activity.* Health impairments can restrict the range of physical activities from limited participation to complete isolation and immobilization. Naturally, health impaired children and adolescents react to these imposed restrictions and require assistance in processing their feelings regarding their physical limitations. These children should be as active as possible. When physical activity must be restricted, alternative activities can be provided to facilitate healthy release of energy.

10. *Facing issues of death and dying.* Illness in childhood includes the possibility that the disease may be terminal, which evokes powerful emotional issues in the child and significant others, such as the family members and involved health professionals. The child's response to death is dependent on his developmental level and the family's style of coping. The child and family both need support and the

opportunity to express grief, fear, and anger related to death. To be available to the child and family, the health professional needs to come to terms with his own relationship to death and dying.

General characteristics of health impaired children appear in varying degrees of severity. In addition, specific illnesses cause unique conditions and problems. The health professional working with health impaired children is clearly presented with a wide spectrum of developmental, social, medical, and psychological issues.

When the general needs of a health impaired child are identified, a treatment approach can be determined. Various professionals, who make up a treatment team, utilize their knowledge and skills to plan and implement a treatment program. The music therapist is qualified to be a member of the treatment team and to provide direct service to health impaired children.

HOSPITALIZATION OF CHILDREN

Hospitalization is experienced periodically by health impaired children, and many of them spend extended amounts of time in the hospital setting. Some of these children respond constructively and show growth as a result of hospitalization (Langford, 1961, 1966; Shore, Geiser & Wolman, 1965). Nonetheless, most show signs of psychological distress and maladjustment before, during, and after hospitalization (Becker, 1972; Belmont, 1970; Dombro & Haas, 1970; Erickson, 1972; Kenny, 1975; Langford, 1961, 1966; Mason, 1965; Robertson, 1962). The following factors contribute to the stress and difficulties of the hospitalized child.

1. Separation from home and family (Becker, 1972; Heinicke & Westheimer, 1965).

2. Unfamiliarity of the hospital environment (Billington, 1972; Kenny, 1975; Vernon, Foley, Sipowicz & Schulman, 1965).

3. Fear-provoking fantasies that are not reality based (Becker, 1972; Belmont, 1970).

4. Absence from school and noncompletion of academic work (Kenny, 1975).

5. Restriction of physical activity or immobilization which exacerbate feelings of vulnerability (Becker, 1972; Erickson, 1972; Langford, 1961).

6. Forced dependency and other psychological regressive states or behaviors (Becker, 1972).

7. Unanticipated medical procedure (Becker, 1972; Burling & Collipp, 1969).

8. The fate of other patients on the wards (Erickson, 1972).

9. The prolongation of hospitalization (Davenport & Werry, 1970; Vernon et al., 1965).

In addition to physical and medical conditions, the psychological stresses and related difficulties of the hospitalized child deserve careful attention. The importance and necessity of treatment of the whole child is recognized particularly in the settings of children's hospitals. Consequently, many children's hospitals incorporate specialized programs, such as Child-Life programs, activity programs, play therapy, recreation therapy, or child development programs (Wright et al., 1979). The primary goals of such programs are to help children cope with the stress and anxiety of the hospital experience, and to promote the child's normal growth and development while in the health care setting and after returning home (Thompson & Stanford, 1981). Four major areas of focus for the staff in treating the nonmedical needs of the hospitalized child are: (a) preparation and education of the child and family, (b) maintaining a normalized environment, (c) giving the child a means of establishing mastery over the illness and environment, and (d) consideration of the child's age and developmental level.

Preparing and Educating

With the onset of hospitalization, the child and his parents are normally apprehensive. Fear of separation, pain, and unfamiliar procedures can make the experience traumatic. Children's reactions to hospitalization can be active, such as crying, screaming, clinging to parents, as well as engaging in self-destructive behavior or resistance to medical treatment. Passive reactions include behaviors such as decreased communication, decreased activity, decreased eating, withdrawal, or depression (Thompson et al., 1981).

Because of the possible negative responses, careful preparation becomes an important factor in the child's adaptation to hospitalization, preparation for which often includes a "pre-op party." The Children's Hospital of Orange County, California schedules a pre-op party every Wednesday afternoon for the children who will be entering the hospital the following week. This party serves to familiarize the child with hospital personnel and with medical equipment and procedures. After punch and cookies are served, the children sit in a circle on the floor. Parents may join in or simply observe. Familiar musical activities are used to introduce the children to each other and hospital staff, and to establish a comfortable atmosphere. The children and parents watch a slide presentation and puppet show, which include identification of hospital staff, environment, and procedures. While parents have the opportunity to ask questions, the children are led in play by two recreation therapists. The children try on physicians' jackets and masks, take each other's blood pressure, and play with puppets of physicians and nurses. The children may play with the actual equipment which they will encounter during their hospitalization. In this way, they become better prepared for a positive adjustment upon entering the hospital the following week.

Once the child has entered the hospital, further preparation and education take place. The types of sessions range from explaining specific surgical procedures to telling the child where mother and father will be during surgery. In addition, the child is encouraged to ask questions and express feelings related to his individual needs (Petrillo & Sanger, 1980).

Music has been used successfully in the hospital setting to prepare patients for medical procedures as well as giving the children an opportunity to verbally and nonverbally express their feelings. In this regard, Taylor (1981) has provided an historical review of the use of music in the hospital setting from 1900 to 1950. Chetta (1981) supports the use of music in the preparation of children for anesthesia and surgery, whereas one component of preoperative sessions, music was successful in reducing the anxiety levels of the children.

Maintaining a Normalized Environment

In addition to the preparation and education of the child, maintaining a normalized environment is important in promoting a positive, or at least tolerable, experience. Although it is difficult to create a feeling of normalcy in a hospital, this goal is an important one for maintaining balance in the child's life.

In hospitals with Child-Life or recreation therapy programs, a well-equipped play room is available to the children for independent play and structured recreational activities. Planned daily programs are provided for both ambulatory and bedridden children. Holidays are celebrated with decorations and parties which include the participation of children, parents, and hospital staff. Preschool programs as well as academic programs are available to assist children in maintaining their academic levels. The value of these programs has been documented by Kenny (1975) who states that "play and recreational activities are not frills or idle diversions but are essential to psychological development" (p. 396).

Establishing Mastery Over the Illness and Environment

Hospitalized children experience major areas of concern, including the fear of pain and bodily harm, separation from family and peers, loss of control of the environment, and loss of normal routine (Wright et al, 1979). They continuously undergo various medical procedures. A strong feeling of helplessness and loss of ability to control their own lives and environment due to hospitalization can result in increased anxiety and unhappiness. The opportunity for children to deal with these situations and express concerns assist in the reduction of possible psychological harm (Becker, 1972).

Children need the opportunity to maintain or gain self-control through experiences that foster feelings of mastery (Dombro & Haas, 1970). Play is the child's natural way of exploring the environment and establishing mastery. Play facilitates self-expression and provides a mechanism for coping with stressful life situations (Thompson & Sanford, 1981). The following elements of play illustrate its value as a tool in treating hospitalized children:

1. Play is pleasurable.

2. Play has no extrinsic goals.

3. Play is spontaneous and voluntary.

4. Play involves some active engagement on the part of the player.

5. Play promotes nonplay development.

For the hospitalized child, interruption of normal play means interruption of the developmental process. This interruption also deprives the child of one of the major methods of coping with stress.

Another means of facilitating the child's sense of mastery is to provide an opportunity for the child to ask questions and express concerns (Becker, 1972; Belmont, 1970; Kenny, 1975; Shore et al., 1965). Individual and group music therapy sessions can provide the atmosphere for this process to take place. Music is particularly effective with young children whose verbal expression is less sophisticated and for children who find it difficult to verbalize emotional content. Music can create an atmosphere of play where tension is released, stress is reduced, and self-expression takes place.

Considering the Child's Age and Developmental Level

All children and adolescents, regardless of age, experience a certain amount of stress due to illness and hospitalization. Children's responses to illness, hospitalization, and their adaptation to illness are usually related to their developmental level. The following responses are common to the progressive stages of childhood to the stress of illness and hospitalization.

1. *Infants of less than 7 months* although affected, respond less severely to illness and hospitalization. They respond well to maximum parental participation and sensory stimulation (Scarr-Salopatek & Williams, 1973).

2. *Older infants* will exhibit an immediate and overt response to separation from parents and benefit from maximum parental participation in care and age-appropriate stimulation (Scarr-Salopatek & Williams, 1973).

3. *Toddlers* respond immediately to separation from parents. The child's new skills of ambulation, self-feeding, and toilet training may regress. Children of this age may feel they are the cause of the separation, and that they are being punished. They have a need for mastery and control which can be gained through play. Elements to be included in their play are familiar activities, exploration, and self-expression (Petrillo & Sanger, 1980).

4. *Preschoolers, ages 3-4,* are particularly vulnerable. Separation from parents is a major issue with these children who tend to view separation as punishment. At this age, children are susceptible to fantasies and fears and may have misconceptions of medical equipment and procedures. Parent-child interaction is very important for these children, and thorough preparation of the child and parents can facilitate a more successful recovery. These children benefit from expressive play, "medical play," and interaction with peers (Thompson & Stanford, 1981).

5. *School-age children* are past the most vulnerable age. Because they have usually developed socially and are able to develop relationships outside the family, separation is easier. Although they are subject to misconceptions, fantasies are fewer because their reasoning ability is more developed. However, maintaining control is very important for these children. Self-control has been a major variable for reaching important developmental milestones. Many school-age children have a fear of anesthesia because it is a threat to their hard-won control. Consequently, the parent-child relationship remains important. These children benefit from thorough preparation of a wide range of play activities including medical play and the maintenance of normal routines and activities (Thompson & Stanford, 1981).

6. *Adolescents* are busy with important tasks of becoming adults. Age-appropriate developmental tasks include: working to achieve independence from adults, exploring sexual relationships, struggling, for identity, as well as involvement in plans for the future (Hoffmann, Becker & Gabriel, 1967). For the adolescent, illness and hospitalization interrupt these tasks. They need a return to dependency, passiveness, and following orders. Future plans may have to be put aside. The adolescent is now different and cut off from his peer group. Recognition and alleviation of this dilemma can aid the ill or hospitalized adolescent. A separate unit in the hospital and an adolescent lounge where age-appropirate activities are available can minimize the stress of hospitalization for this age group (Hoffmann et al., 1967).

MUSIC IN THE HOSPITAL SETTING

Historically, music has been associated with healing in ancient cultures, classic antiquity, during the Renaissance, and in the 19th century as well (Licht, 1946; Schullian & Schoen, 1948). During the 20th century, music also has been actively included in the treatment of the medically ill. As medical techniques have advanced, technical progress in music therapy has also occurred. With the invention of the phonograph especially, music has been used in hospital settings including the operating room for diversion, to aid sleep, and to reduce the levels of stress and anxiety (Boxberger, 1963). Since the early 1900's, experimental research has been conducted to explore the physiological effects of music, the use of music in surgery, and music as an analgesia for pain (Taylor, 1981).

Physiological Response to Music

Studies of the physiological responses to music generally focus on heart and pulse rates, blood pressure, respiration, skin responses, muscular and motor responses, and brain waves (Hodges, 1980). The research typically compares the effects associated with the use of sedating and stimulating music. Three comprehensive sources of information in this area are: *The Handbook of Music Psychology* (Hodges, 1980); *Psychological Foundations of Musical Behavior* (Radocy & Boyle, 1979); and *A Psychology of Music: The Influence of Music on Behavior* (Diserens & Fine, 1969).

Music in Surgery

Music has been used in preparation of children for surgery to aid in the familiarization of medical equipment and procedures (Chetta, 1981). Music has also been found to have positive effects in the operating room, although there is no consistent use of music in hospitals for this purpose. A carefully planned use of music in the operating room may benefit the patient as follows:

1. Music creates a warmer, more pleasant environment for the patient and the staff.
2. Music provides a diversion, distracting the patient from strange sights and treatments.
3. The patient undergoing regional anesthetic becomes less restless because discomfort from positioning muscle strains is lessened and time passes more quickly.
4. The use of headsets muffles extraneous noises and may also keep the patient from overhearing staff conversation.
5. Members of the surgical team work in closer harmony because of decreased levels of tension and fatigue.
6. Appropriate rhythms may stimulate rapid, coordinated movements.
7. The monotony of preparation and cleanup procedures is reduced, contributing to staff morale and efficiency (MacClelland, 1979, p. 258).

Music as Analgesia for Pain

Music has been found to reduce post-operative pain and to motivate patients to activity during recovery (Gardner, Licklider & Weisz, 1960; Locsin, 1981). Chronic pain rehabilitation programs have incorporated music to reduce pain, reinforce positive verbalization, and to motivate patients for increased activity (Wolfe, 1978). Several studies of the effect of auditory analgesia on pain have been conducted (Lavine, Buchsbaum & Poncy, 1976; Melzack, Weisz & Sprague, 1963). Results indicate that both music and the suggestion of music reducing pain, when presented together, successfully affected a reduction of pain. Guided imagery and music, as developed by Bonny (1978), has also been used with patients in the reduction of pain.

In addition to experimental research, a review of the literature on music and healing provides many ideas for clinical application. Examples include descriptive research of music and healing as employed by Native Americans (Densmore, 1948) and other ethnic groups. Recent contributions in the area of wholistic health provide a framework for the clinical use of music to renew and maintain health. In a comprehensive study, Kenny (1982) has examined the healing qualities of ritual, rhythm, magic, asthetic experience, and creativity provided by music. In addition, a unique exploration of the role of rhythm is available in *The Silent Pulse* (Leonard, 1978).

PERCEPTIONS OF DEATH AND DYING

Treatment of health impaired children includes the reality that some of these children may not survive childhood. The chronic and terminal nature of a disease, such as leukemia, makes death an inevitability for the child. In addition, terminal illness affects the family and professionals involved with the child.

The overall goals of treatment of a terminally ill child are to maintain and enhance the quality of the child's life until the moment of death and so facilitate the adaptation of the child's family (Wright et al., 1979). Because treatment of dying patients is emotionally painful, it is necessary that the therapist come to terms with his or her own mortality and eventual death (Kubler-Ross, 1969). In this section, a general review of the process of dying will be presented, as well as children's perceptions of death, the developmental process of the health professional who works with dying patients, and music therapy as it relates to the dying patient.

General Review of the Process of Dying

American society reinforces the tendency to ignore or avoid death as a real part of our lives. People protect themselves from the threatening possibility that their lives or the lives of significant others will, at some time, end. The study of death by Kubler-Ross (1969) has provided the opportunity to understand one's personal responses to the mysterious process of death, and to come to terms with personal fears and related denial. The result of the awareness of death may be to make more of life available in the present.

In her book, *On Death and Dying,* Kubler-Ross (1969) outlines five response stages to death, which take place when a person is confronted with the fact that he is dying.

Stage I: Denial and Isolation. Denial at the first shock acts as a defense which allows the person to process the information and mobilize other less radical defenses. Denial is usually a temporary defense. The patient may fluctuate between a state of denial and acceptance according to the ability at the moment to face the inevitability of death.

Stage II: Anger. When denial can no longer be maintained, the patient moves on to feelings of anger, rage, envy, and resentment. Anger rises from an interrupted life, realization that long-term projects will not be finished or will be finished by someone else; there is loss of control and loss of physical vitality. The anger may be displaced in many directions, making it difficult for family and staff. The patient will need respect and understanding and the feeling of being a valuable, cared-for human being.

Stage III. Bargaining. In the third stage, the patient may bargain in an attempt to postpone death. This stage is based on the assumption that there will be a reward for good behavior.

Stage IV. Depression. Following the previous stages, the patient begins to feel a sense of loss. Financial burdens may become a problem. Two types of depression are distinguished: (1) reactive depression which results from past loss and (2) preparatory depression which deals with impending death. Resolution of both types are necessary for the patient to move on to the next stage.

Stage V. Acceptance. The stage of acceptance is achieved when the patient has had enough time and help in working through previous stages. The patient will be neither depressed nor angry; however, it is not necessarily a happy stage. The acceptance stage provides a time of resting and reduction of outside stimuli.

Children's Perceptions of Death

The understanding of death for children varies according to the child's age and experience. Very young children equate death with sleep and may understand the death of a grandparent or family pet in those terms (Segerberg, 1976). Around age 3, the child begins to develop a concept of death which is equated with separation; the child does not understand that death is final and has no concept of his own death (Zelig, 1974). From ages 3-5, the child perceives death as another form of existence; death is personified in the forms of skeletons and ghosts. From ages 6-7, the child is more aware of the finality of death and the fact he will die one day. From age 9 on, the child accepts death as a part of life which is inevitable and final (Nagy, 1959; Segerberg, 1976; Zelig, 1974).

When it is determined that a child has a terminal illness, the decision must be made whether or not to tell the child. The ultimate decision is that of the parents. Not verbally informing the child does not usually prevent the child from knowing. The child is able to figure out his fate in several ways; for example, observation of other ill children includes recognition of their death (Bluebond-Langner, 1974). Children also are able to detect the parents' change in attitude after prognosis (Schowalter, 1970); the result of this can be that the child may be silent to protect adults, causing the child isolation, pain, and anxiety (Buhrmann, 1973; Kubler-Ross, 1969; Solnit, 1973; Vernick & Karon, 1965; Waechter, 1971; Wolters, 1973). If the child is told, the developmental level of the child in understanding death should be considered. The child should have the opportunity to talk freely and ask his own questions (Kavanaugh, 1972). There also should be an opportunity for the child to express personal feelings, particularly anger (Gyulay, 1978).

General guidelines for management of the dying child and family include (Wright et al., 1979):

1. Determine the child's level of intellectual and emotional development.
2. Determine the child's concept of death and his previous experiences with death and other forms of loss (divorce, foster home placement, etc.).
3. Determine other relationships of importance (siblings or grandparents).
4. Determine parents' attitudes toward what their child should be told, by whom, and in what manner.
5. Help parents and staff anticipate the child's questions, and help them respond appropriately.
6. Coach parents and staff on ways to help the child ask questions and express his concerns.
7. Prepare parents to anticipate child-rearing difficulties and identify means by which they can be helped with these problems.
8. Encourage parents to spend as much time as is feasible with the dying child taking into account the needs of other children in the family, and include the siblings in the care of the child.
9. Identify sources of emotional support for the parents, and assist them in establishing appropriate contacts, i.e., with other parents of dying children.
10. Assess probable impact of the child's illness and death on significant others (siblings) and provide supportive intervention as needed.
11. Promote attitudes of emotional involvement and honesty in all who come in contact with the child.
12. Provide means of continued support and modes of assistance for the bereaved (p. 195).

Health Professionals Working With Dying Patients

The difficulty in working closely with dying patients, particularly dying children, is greatly underestimated. Working as a health professional with dying children is described as emotionally stressful and painful (Wright et al., 1979; Kubler-Ross, 1969; Lascari, 1969). In spite of our caring and good intentions, we may unwittingly avoid an important conversation with a dying child and begin to withdraw attention. To prevent this and other professional errors, it is essential that the therapist come to terms with personal fears of death (Kubler-Ross, 1969; Lascari, 1969; Rantz, 1979). She requires initial and on-going support in order to adjust to the daily confrontation with death. Harper (1977) has developed a "Schematic Growth and Development Scale in Coping with Professional Anxiety in Terminal Illness." The scale consists of five progressive stages of response a health professional may experience in working with dying patients.

Stage I: Intellectualization. During the initial stage, the professional is involved in tangible services and brisk activity. This may serve as a means of avoidance and gives the therapist a sense of control over the situation.

Stage II: Trauma Accompanied by Guilt and Frustration. At this point, the therapist confronts the reality of the patient's death and of his own death. This stage is characterized by emotional involvement with the dying patient.

Stage III: Depression. Harper (1977) refers to this period as the "go or grow stage" (p. 57). This is a pivotal point for the therapist. It requires the therapist to accept his own feelings of pain and grieving. An acceptance of death must emerge along with an orientation to the reality of death and dying.

Stage IV: Emotional Arrival. This stage is characterized by accommodation and a sense of freedom. The therapist is relatively free from identifying with the patient's symptoms, preoccupation with his own death and dying, guilt feelings of having good health, and incapacitating feelings of depression. The therapist will still experience pain in working with dying patients, but the emotional response will be more in perspective.

Stage V: Deep Compassion. The final stage is a state of self-awareness and self-actualization. It contains all elements of Stages I, II, III and IV, as well as the therapist's own personal values, self-reliance, and realistic acceptance of illness and death. With this comes the ability to serve others and the ability to give dignity and respect to dying patients and families.

The Royal Victoria Hospital Manual on Palliative/Hospice Care, (Ajemian & Mount, 1980), addresses professional stress in detail. Their approaches to prevention and management of stress include encouraging awareness of personal stress, encouraging limit-setting, establishing team support meetings, encouraging distancing, recognizing the value of socializing, exercising and meditating, and keeping one's sense of humor. In regard to the therapist, Kubler-Ross (1969) states: "To work with the dying patient requires a certain maturity which only comes from experience. We have to take a good hard look at our own attitudes toward death and dying before we can sit quietly and without anxiety next to a terminally ill patient" (p. 269). Thus, an ongoing awareness of the stress involved for health professionals working with dying patients can prevent problems as well as enhance the quality of service.

Music Therapy with the Terminally Ill

The music therapist who works with a terminally ill child has a unique contribution to make in the treatment of that child and his family. As a member of the interdisciplinary team, the music therapist is aware of the course of the illness as well as the dynamics of the child. All members of the treatment team work to maximize the *quality of the child's life* and to facilitate an acceptance of and adjustment to the child's death. The motivating and often powerful effects of music give the music therapist a means of facilitating this difficult process with the child and his family.

Music in the care of terminally ill children can create an atmosphere where a variety of needs are met. Participation in and choice of musical activities provides a feeling of control over the environment (Rantz, 1979). Group sessions provide support and shared experience which reduce fear and isolation. Music can also be a vehicle for verbalization of emotions and ideas that may otherwise be threatening to express (Gilbert, 1977). In addition to participation in music making and listening, patients and music therapists spend a large amount of time discussing results and associations stimulated by the musical interaction (Munro & Mount, 1980).

In providing music for the terminally ill, the music therapist is often met with a variety of responses on different levels. Some children and families are receptive and involve themselves spontaneously with the music therapist. Discrete responses may begin with a smile which hides underlying feelings of bewilderment, resentment, or anger. Another response of the dying patient to music is: "I guess it's the end. They're giving me music now. Nothing else works." (Munro & Mount, 1980). Thus, it is important for the music therapist to be sensitive to the individual's receptivity, perceptions, and defense system. Consideration and understanding of a family's cultural background, both in the realm of music and rituals surrounding death, assist the music therapist in providing appropriate support for the child and family. Any of these elements may result in a reluctance or refusal of the child or family to participate in musical activities. It is the responsibility of the music therapist to respect the wishes of the child and family; however, flat refusal may indicate a person is very aware on some level of the depth that music moves them. Such a person needs to move at his own pace, and although the therapist must respect the refusal, he may gradually create a relationship of trust.

In evaluating a patient for music therapy and related development of a treatment plan, Munro and Mount (1980) offer the following uses of music therapy in palliative care of the terminally ill:

- Physical

    Promoting muscular relaxation;

    Breaking the vicious circle of chronic pain by relieving anxiety and depression and thus altering the perception of pain;

    Facilitating physical participation in activities to the degree possible;

- Psychological

    Reinforcing identity and self-concept;

    Altering the patient's mood, including easing anxiety and lessening depression;

    Helping the patient recall past significant events;

    Providing a nonverbal means of expressing a broad range of recognized and unconscious feelings;

    Reinforcing reality;

    Expressing fantasy;

    As a direct appeal to the emotions;

- Social

    As a means of socially acceptable self-expression;

    As a bridge across cultural differences and isolation;

    As a bond and sense of community with family members and others, past and present, through the mental associations aroused;

    As a link to the patient's life before the illness;

    Providing an opportunity to participate in a group;

    As entertainment and diversion;

- Spiritual

    Providing means of expressing spiritual feelings and feeling comforted and reassured;

Providing an avenue for expressing doubts, anger, fear of punishment, and questions of the ultimate meaning of life (p. 259).

Literature on successful music therapy methods used with the terminally ill is limited. Gilbert (1977) discusses the implications of music therapy with the terminally ill and cites the work of Edwards (1977) who uses the approach of singing to patients, attempting to involve them in music performance and in discussions about death. A presentation by Rantz (1979) included a discussion of the role of the music therapist in the treatment of terminally ill children, as addressing fears of hospitalization, isolation, loss of control, physical involvement due to the illness, and dealing with dying.

Munro and Mount (1980) have presented the most comprehensive written source on the use of music therapy with the terminally ill to date. Methods described include drawing to music, making collages to music, use of live music, singing, instrument accompaniment, breathing, touch and massage, and guided imagery. They also discuss use of taped music available 24 hours a day to the patient; the patient determines how and when the music is used.

As the uses of music therapy in relation to death and dying are examined, it should be kept in mind that there are no fail-proof techniques or approaches which will assure the music therapist success. Each situation presents complex and inconsistent parameters. Munro and Mount (1980) bring into perspective theory and practice, providing a challenge to take another look at music as well as the concept of therapy. Music is a human behavior which is more than pitch, frequency, rhythm, intervals, and harmony. It is deeply entrenched in our history and human culture. This gives music a meaning which cannot always be anticipated. The music therapist evaluates each child and his family from a variety of perspectives which are based on a deep respect for the individuality and dignity of each person.

———

The planning of effective treatment with health impaired children requires that the music therapist have an understanding of individual health disorders. The health disorders examined in this monograph have been included based upon their description in the *Education for All Handicapped Children Act*. One exception has been made in the interest of providing useful information; instead of tuberculosis, cystic fibrosis (a respiratory disorder) is examined, due to its more common occurrence in childhood. Each disorder is examined according to the following outline: description, etiology, psychological correlates, medical and psychological components of treatment and music intervention.

CHILDREN WITH ASTHMA

Description

Asthma is a condition characterized by wheezing and shortness of breath resulting from spasms of the smooth muscle of the bronchi. Severe reactions of this type are referred to as status asthmaticus, a severe shortness of breath, leading to exhaustion (Nelson, Vaughan & McKay, 1969). Asthma has been found to be sex-linked, occurring 1.5 to 2 times more in males than females (Eriksson-Lihr, 1955; Schiffer & Hunt, 1963; Smith, 1961; Wilson, 1958). Of the children who are diagnosed having asthma, 50% outgrow the condition and are symptom-free 20 years after the onset of the condition; 30-40% have only mild difficulties with 10% continuing to have severe difficulties (Nelson et al., 1969). Furthermore, it has been found that 75% of all asthmatic children improve within five years of onset with or without treatment (Smith, 1971b).

Etiology

Review of the research literature indicates that the causes of asthma are difficult to pinpoint. Wright et al. (1979) state:

> The physical, intellectual and emotional correlates of asthma are more difficult to differentiate from its causes than is the case with most other diseases. This is because of confusion regarding whether asthma causes certain problems or the problems cause the asthma (p. 71).

Studies of the etiology of asthma have pinpointed four types of asthma:

1. Purely allergic.
2. Primarily allergic.
3. Primarily emotional.
4. Purely emotional (Wright et al., 1979, p. 65).

It has been determined in one type of asthma that allergies to household dust, molds, or food were directly related to the condition. In other situations, onset of asthma was precipitated by a traumatic emotional experience, such as loss or separation from a parent. Even a cause of asthma which is allergy related can be aggravated by chronic or recurrent emotional tensions (Nelson, et al., 1969).

Psychological Correlates

Anxiety and emotional tension play a significant role in asthma. Psychologists offer perspectives in an attempt to understand how emotions contribute to asthma. Included in those perspectives are psychoanalytic, classical and operant conditioning, and behavioral theories.

Children with asthma are faced with several physical and social problems. Anxiety can arise from the fear of an asthma attack occurring. In addition, fear of losing control and of suffocating contribute to the anxiety. Asthma attacks can interfere with a child's social development; for example, the child may anticipate a negative reaction from his peers following an asthma attack (Wright et al., 1979).

Psychological tests, such as the *Minnesota Multiphasic Personality Inventory (MMPI)*, the *Eysenck Personality Inventory,* and *Cattell Self Analysis Form,* indicate that asthmatics rate high on anxiety scales (Oswald, Waller & Drinkwater, 1970). Correlations were also found between respiratory distress and anxiety (Wright et al., 1979). Whether or not anxiety and emotional tension aggravate an asthma attack or are the result of one, the two appear to be linked in most cases.

Treatment

Medical treatment of asthma consists primarily of treating the allergies and the inflammation and spasms of the bronchi. Desensitization shots, diet, and monitoring of the home environment for allergens such as dust and mold are approaches which have been effective in relieving symptoms for many children. When the symptoms become severe, several classes of drugs, including epinephrine, antihistamine, ammophylline, and corticosteroid, may prove effective (Nelson et al., 1969).

Since traumatic emotional experiences or chronic recurrent emotional tension are closely related to asthma, attention and treatment of emotional symptoms is indicated. Awareness of precipitating factors is important in developing an approach to help alleviate these symptoms. It is important to understand the situations which cause asthma attacks for the individual child. In the development of a treatment plan, observation of patterns of behavior and emotional states of the child while in the school and home environments may provide significant information. The parent-child relationship is vital in facilitating the reduction of anxiety-producing situations. There may also be dynamics in the school and home environment which reinforce the symptoms. In certain situations, the child can learn to use the illness to meet his personal needs; for example, special attention to or being excused from an unpleasant task may actually reinforce the frequency of asthma attacks (Wright et al., 1979).

Due to the role of anxiety in the asthmatic condition, relaxation training can become one focus of treatment. Relaxation techniques, when practiced on a regular basis, appear to decrease the number of asthma attacks (Wright et al., 1979). Other modes of intervention include the development of a structured environment, consistency in child management techniques, and assisting the child in learning how to express his feelings and apprehension in an appropriate mode which does not affect his asthmatic condition.

Music Therapy Intervention

In the treatment of the child with asthma, there are three areas on which the music therapist may focus. These areas are the development and/or maintenance of respiratory capacity, minimization of developmental delays and releases of emotion (McCarthy, 1980). The following outline can aid the music therapist in developing the assessment of the child and a treatment plan. This tool was developed by McCarthy (1980) for the use with children at New Orleans Children's Hospital.

- Assessment

    Respiration:
    a. Breath control (record seconds for both inspiratory and expiratory).
    b. See respiratory therapy evaluation to record vital capacity, peak flow, result of pulmonary function test, and inspiratory and expiratory forces.

    Emotional status.
    Response to environment on social-emotional level.
    Fine motor skills.
    Gross motor skills.
    Cognitive skills.
    Expressive language skills.
    Receptive language skills.
    Musical history and interests.

- Long Term Goals

    Maintain maximum level of respiratory status.

    Obtain optimum level of upper extremity strength and functional gross motor skills.

    Develop appropriate expression of emotions.

    Obtain optimum level of functional gross motor skills.

    Develop independent pursuit to further own cognitive development.

    Develop maximal levels of functional communication.

    Develop healthy self-image.

    Develop interest and independent participation in musical activities.

- Treatment Plan

    Use of playing wind instruments and singing to develop optimum level of respiratory status.

    Use of playing musical instruments and participating in musical activities to increase upper extremity strength and obtain optimum levels of motor skills.

    Use of singing, playing musical instruments and participating in musical activities to provide appropriate outlet for expression of emotions.

    Participation in musical activities to provide opportunities in which the child can be successful.

In addition to these factors, the music therapist addresses the role anxiety plays in the asthmatic child's condition. Music listening, as a form of relaxation or in association with other relaxation methods, is a method to be used with these children.

The following is an example of music therapy sessions involving a 12-year-old girl hospitalized due to respiratory distress. Music therapy was incorporated in the treatment plan to address these goals: to increase the amount of time in a relaxed state, to reduce the level of anxiety related to the illness and hospitalization, to increase upper extremity strength, to increase level of respiratory status, and to increase self-esteem. During hospitalization, the girl was required to spend much time in bed, which limited her movement, choice of activities and social interaction. Bedside activities utilizing relaxing music and moderate participation were introduced by the music therapist. The girl was involved in listening to and singing of favorite songs as well as playing rhythm instruments in accompaniment. Her family was also involved in the sessions giving the girl and her family the opportunity to interact in a relaxed, enjoyable way (Marley, 1982).

CHILDREN WITH CYSTIC FIBROSIS

Description

Cystic fibrosis is a congenital, genetic disease that is present at birth but sometimes, because of disease variables, is not diagnosed until the child is an adolescent or young adult. The disease is characterized by pancreatic deficiency, chronic pulmonary disease, and abnormally high sweat electrolyte levels. Children with cystic fibrosis have difficulty with intestinal absorption; consequently, problems with nutrition and maintenance of body weight develop due to insufficient excretion of necessary pancreatic enzymes (Nelson et al., 1969).

Most children with cystic fibrosis have a history of coughing and wheezing. Secretions from the lungs are thick and the passageways become partially or completely obstructed with mucus, resulting in wheezing. Coughing is both an attempt to clear the passageways and a response to the accompanying repeated infections and bouts of pneumonia which are common to cystic fibrosis. Difficulty with intestinal absorption, repeated lung infection, and body tissues receiving inadequate oxygen often cause a delay in growth and short stature in children with cystic fibrosis. In addition, the sweat of these children contains an over-abundant amount of sodium chloride; consequently, children with cystic fibrosis are more prone to heat prostration, especially in hot weather (Nelson et al., 1969).

Etiology

Cystic fibrosis is a genetically transmitted disease. Experts in genetics estimate that 1 in every 20 adults is a carrier of the gene producing cystic fibrosis (National Cystic Fibrosis Research Foundation, n.d.). Presently, there is no way to detect a carrier of the gene. When both parents contribute the gene for the disease, the child is born with cystic fibrosis. This child is believed to lack a single specific chemical needed for important functions within the body. Presently, there is no known cure. Because of improvements in medical treatment, however, the life expectancy of children with cystic fibrosis has been extended.

Psychological Correlates

A variety of problems accompany this disease due to its chronic, terminal nature. These problems include vicarious detrimental effects on the family and related financial burdens, as well as various developmental difficulties of the child. Certainly, the determination that a child has cystic fibrosis has a strong impact on the family. The disease can be difficult initially to diagnose and the parents often are angry and frustrated with the inaccuracy of previous diagnoses. There are responses of relief at having an accurate diagnosis but also of shock that the disease is fatal (Wright et al., 1979). Most parents struggle with feelings of guilt, resentment, and devastation. In addition, treatment of the symptoms or the disease requires the parents' intense involvement which can leave them feeling deprived of privacy, energy, and leisure time (Turk, 1964).

Children with cystic fibrosis are generally of normal intelligence. They live with the knowledge that they are neither healthy nor normal and that they never will be. These children may have strange and unpredictable body sensations which can result in feelings of insecurity. They often simply do not feel well. In coping with the fact that they have a terminal disease, the children often suppress thoughts of death (Cytryn, Moore, Van & Robinson, 1973). There seem to be two dominant modes of psychic defenses for these children: healthy and unhealthy (Wright et al., 1979). The healthy children exhibit reaction formations by becoming involved in strenuous activity. They fantasize about such things as becoming a doctor to help children with cystic fibrosis or about being wild, free animals. The unhealthy defense is characterized by regression, withdrawal, and avoidance (Tropauer, Franz & Dilgard, 1970).

Treatment

Since a cure is not presently available, treatment for cystic fibrosis centers around four main objectives:

1. Maintenance of good nutrition;
2. Control of pulmonary infection;
3. Prevention of restoration of abnormal salt losses;
4. General care of the child (Nelson et al., 1969).

Dietary therapy is employed to insure that the child receives adequate nutrients to maintain health and weight. A wholesome, well-rounded diet is recommended to maintain the child's health. To aid digestion, necessary enzymes are taken at mealtime in the form of extracts of animal pancreas (National Cystic Fibrosis Research Foundation, n.d.). Because the child may experience abnormal salt loss from excessive sweating, an increase in salt intake may be required, particularly during hot weather.

Prevention of pulmonary infection is a major goal in treatment. Antibiotics are used as well as expectorants, antihistamines, and bronchodilators. Aerosols and mist tents are implemented to thin and loosen mucus in the lungs. Physical therapy is used to promote bronchial drainage by having the child positioned on his or her back with the head lowered and feet raised. Breathing exercises are also practiced to promote health of the respiratory tract (National Cystic Fibrosis Research Foundation, n.d.).

In general, the child with cystic fibrosis should be assisted in leading as normal a life as possible. Physical activity need be restricted only by the child's own tolerance. For adolescents, developmental difficulties related to self-image and physical appearance often occur. Nevertheless, adolescents and young adults with cystic fibrosis are able to pursue careers, marry, and have children (Wright et al., 1979).

A multidisciplinary treatment approach is needed to help the child and family cope with medical, social, and emotional difficulties. For example, the parents may need assistance in achieving a balance between treatment of the child and normal family activities. Separation, loss, and death also may be prominent themes for the child, parents, and siblings (Wright et al., 1979). Contact with other parents of children with cystic fibrosis can often provide important information and support.

Music Therapy Intervention

The following goals for music therapy intervention with children with cystic fibrosis were developed by Zander (1980) for children at New Orleans' Children's Hospital.

Increase respiratory status:
   a. Breath control.
   b. Inspiratory forces.
   c. Expiratory forces.

Increase gross and fine motor skills.

Increase or maintain physical tolerance.

Provide breathing exercises.

Promote relaxation.

Increase educational skills.

Provide an emotional outlet for expression of emotions.

Provide emotional and psychological support.

Increase self-esteem.

Increase social interaction.

Provide successful experiences in music.

Provide a learning experience in music.

To increase respiratory status, the music therapy session may include singing and use of wind instruments. The woodwinds and brass instruments, though particularly applicable, are difficult to master at times. Wind instruments which provide immediate success are the harmonica and kazoo. Singing and instrument playing can be used to develop breath control and expiratory force, important functions for the child with cystic fibrosis (Zander, 1980). For example, a melodica placed on a table stand with keys coded by colors, letters, or numbers can be used for children who can match these items but do not read music notation. More breath control is needed to play long phrases, with tones connected to form a phrase. Thus, resistance can be increased by choosing songs requiring an appropriate level of breath control (Lathom, 1982).

Participating in action songs, playing rhythm instruments, and moving in activities can aid the child with cystic fibrosis in maintaining and increasing gross and fine motor skills and physical tolerance. In a group setting, these activities also provide the opportunity for peer interaction and the development of social skills. Zander (1980) makes the following suggestions regarding music therapy sessions.

Cystic fibrosis patients should attend music therapy sessions at least once weekly. Groups should be limited to five or six patients. Each session should last approximately one hour. However, those children whose endurance may not last that long will stop sooner. The activities during the music therapy session should follow a certain order. First, there should be activities requiring little exertion, progressing to activities which require more physical exertion. Breathing and relaxation exercises should follow and coughing should be encouraged (pp. 25-26).

CHILDREN WITH DIABETES

Description

Diabetes is a metabolic disorder in which a failure of the pancreas to secrete insulin prevents proper metabolism of carbohydrates in the diet. The disorder is marked by abnormally high blood glucose levels as well as by the presence of sugar in the urine. Accompanying symptoms are abnormal thirst, increased urination, loss of weight and weakness (Wright et al., 1979). Complications normally occur only in long-term or untreated cases of diabetes. Untreated, diabetes can lead to increased chemical imbalances which may result in coma and death. Progression of the disease can be checked by adequate treatment. Before the discovery and use of insulin, children with diabetes died within two years of the onset of the disease (Nelson et al., 1969). With careful management of the disease, most children today suffering from diabetes lead normal, healthy lives.

Diabetes may have childhood or adult onset. At times, it may precipitate life-threatening emergency situations, two of which are diabetic acidosis and insulin shock. Acidosis is characterized by a lowering of the carbon dioxide content of the blood resulting in a more acidic pH level. Symptoms include abdominal pain, tenderness, muscular rigidity, and vomiting. Insulin shock can be caused by an overdose of insulin, decrease in diet, or increase in exercise. Symptoms are sudden hunger, weakness, restlessness, pallor, sweating, and dilated pupils. Both situations require immediate treatment (Nelson et al., 1969).

Etiology

Although difficult to pinpoint its cause, diabetes is usually considered a hereditary disease. It may result from a combination of two or more defects, including (a) impaired response of the pancreas to hyperglycemia, (b) an abnormal amount of insulin, (c) an increase of a normal insulin antagonist, and (d) an abnormal insulin antagonist (Nelson et al., 1969).

Psychological Correlates

Most diabetic children are of average intelligence (Wright et al., 1979). There is no apparent personality characteristic of children who are diabetic (Koch & Molnar, 1974), however, the willingness of the child to comply with treatment affects the course of the illness (Sterky, 1963).

Management of disease symptoms is a major factor leading to a normal healthy life. The child and his family must be knowledgable and consistent to be successful in controlling the symptoms. The condition can produce emotional responses in the child that makes maintenance of health difficult. "If the disease produces apathy or depression, then neglect may ensue and create a vicious cycle of disease-produced neglect and neglect-produced disease" (Wright et al., 1979, p. 249).

Adolescent rebellion resulting in noncompliance with the treatment regimen is one of the developmental problems which can lead to management difficulties with the adolescent diabetic.

Treatment

Because there is no known cure for diabetes, treatment consists primarily of management of the disease. The following list outlines objectives for successful management of diabetes.

1. Maintenance of balance of intake and use of sugar in the body through diet, hypoglycemic agents (insulin or oral medication), and exercise (Hunt, 1955).

2. Education of the child and family to an understanding of the disease and its management.

3. Assumption by the child (with assistance when appropriate) of the responsibility for day-to-day decisions regarding insulin dosages and urine testing.

4. Development of a positive attitude on the part of the child and family regarding future health and participation in a meaningful career.

5. Promotion of optimal physical health including normal growth and development.

6. Full participation in activities appropriate to age and interests. (Drash, 1971).

The crucial element in treatment is cooperation and consistency on the part of the child and parents. When compliance with the medical regimen is a problem, a carefully planned behavioral program can be implemented to encourage the child's responsible involvement in the management of the illness (Wright et al., 1979).

Exercise is an important part in the routine of the child with diabetes in that it helps stabilize the intake of sugar and insulin. Because a sudden increase in exercise may result in insulin shock, the child, parents, and therapist must be aware of the child's accustomed level of activity. It is also preferable for any strenuous activity to occur after meals rather than before meals (Hunt, 1955).

Because of the diabetic's high susceptibility to skin infection, precautions should be taken to prevent minor cuts, abrasions, or blisters. Cleanliness is essential. Any skin infection should be treated by a physician immediately (Hunt, 1955).

Music Therapy Intervention

Christina was a 15-year-old girl with diabetes (insulin dependent). She led a normal life until the fourth grade, when she began having recurring episodes of vomiting and weakness in 5-week cycles. Symptoms gradually worsened over the next 6 months, resulting in hospitalization with the diagnosis of diabetes. A 2½-month coma left her with cerebellar damage, right-sided hemoplegia, flexion of the right tendon, opticatrophy in the right eye, hyperphagia, slowed speech, and an uneven gait. These physical disabilities were compounded by emotional disturbance and depression resulting from her mother's suicide attempts and from abandonment by both parents following the coma. Christina was placed in a state residential treatment center for emotionally disturbed children.

The evaluation by the speech and language pathologist pinpointed a right brain lesion in the parietal lobe, which interfered with tone recognition and facial/vocal expression. There was damage to cranial nerves V, VII, VIII, IX, XI, and XII, resulting in inadequate functioning of lips, tongue, and velum. She showed vocal intensity weakness, lack of pitch variation, harsh and breathy vocal quality, and insufficient respiration for speech.

Music therapy assessment corroborated these findings from which it was further concluded that Christina's self-esteem was very low and that her peer relationships poor; consequently, she tended to isolate herself. When frustrated or taunted by peers, she would throw temper tantrums. As a result of this evaluation, Christina was enrolled in chorus consisting of a group of 12 children who met five days a week for one hour. Goals for Christina in this group were set in conjunction with speech therapy goals:

• To increase respiratory capacity.

• To improve breath control and prolonged exhalation.

• To develop tonal variety.

• To increase speech rate.

Due to the daily exercise of singing and speaking in rhythm with her peers, noticeable improvement was made in these areas. Christina was less resistive to practicing speech in this manner because she found it enjoyable. Participation in chorus also helped to improve her peer relationships and to increase her frustration tolerance. She also began to show a more positive attitude, indicating improved self-esteem (Griffith, 1981).

CHILDREN WITH EPILEPSY

Description

Epilepsy is a condition characterized by seizures or sudden, involuntary changes or loss of consciousness caused by disorganized electrical discharge in the cerebral cortex. There are seven basic types of seizures: grand mal (tonic clonic), petit mal (absence), myoclonic, akinetic, psychomotor, temporal (complex-partial) focal, and self-induced (Wright et al., 1979).

Grand mal (tonic clonic) seizures often are preceded by an aura or by warning sensations, such as irritability, digestive disturbance, headache, or mental dullness. During the seizure, which usually lasts 20-40 seconds, the eyeballs may roll up or to one side, the face distorts, glottis closes, abdominal and chest muscles become rigid, limbs contract and the tongue may be bitten from contraction of the jaw muscles (Nelson et al., 1969). During the second phase of the seizure, breathing appears difficult, the body jerks, saliva may accumulate in the mouth and the bladder may empty (Abbott Laboratories, n.d.). Following a seizure, the child may be confused and disoriented and may sleep heavily. Because the child does not remember the seizure, it is difficult for him to understand personal or social rejection that may follow (Wright et al., 1979).

Petit mal (absence) seizures are common in childhood and adolescence, and are generally outgrown. They are characterized by a brief loss of consciousness and can either occur infrequently or up to 100 times daily. Convulsions do not occur but there may be a drooping of the head or slight quiver in the trunk or limbs (Wright et al., 1979).

Myoclonic epilepsy is a brief loss of consciousness accompanied by minor jerks of the arms and legs. Akinetic seizures cause a sudden slump of the head or a nod. The child may fall to the ground but will get up again, and he may also have a blank stare and pale look. Focal seizures are limited to one part of the body and are not accompanied by loss of consciousness (Wright et al., 1979).

Psychomotor or temporal seizures (complex-partial) are difficult to recognize and control. These seizures cause purposeful repetitious motor acts, such as lip smacking, buttoning and unbuttoning, or fingerpulling. The child may be fearful, angry or hostile following this type of seizure (Abbott Laboratories, n.d.).

Self-induced (psychogenic) seizures can be brought on by the child, usually to draw attention. The child may hyperventilate, watch a stroboscopic light, or perform another learned behavior which will induce a seizure. Seizure activity can be detected by monitoring the electrical activities of the brain by means of electroencephalography (EEG). Abnormalities which indicate seizure activity appear as high-voltage spike discharges (Nelson et al., 1969). In most cases, epilepsy can be controlled by means of medication and usually does not cause injury or death.

Etiology

Epilepsy which has a known cause is referred to as symptomatic, or organic, epilepsy. Idiopathic epilepsy has no known cause. Seizures are not inherited; however, a child may inherit a predisposition for seizures. Seizures clearly are not contagious but are caused by organic lesions in the brain resulting from intracranial hemorrhages, birth trauma, arteriosclerosis, subdural hematomas, and contusions of the brain. Seizures may also result from metabolic-based chemical imbalances, toxic states, inflections, and neurosyphillis (Wright et al., 1979).

Psychological Correlates

Although epilepsy occurs in highly intelligent people, studies indicate that, in general, the IQs of school children with epilepsy fall 10-15 points below average (Keating, 1960). Emotional difficulties are related principally to reactions from others and to developmental obstacles resulting from limited activities. These factors, along with general apprehension about having seizures, may cause anxiety. Betts (1972) concluded that to help control seizures, anxiety must be controlled. Thus, it appears that emotional factors can precipitate seizure activity.

The main problems for the epileptic child center around school and peer relationships. Betts (1972) lists the following problems which occur frequently among epileptic children:

1. Frustration and embarrassment from having to be accompanied by an older sibling in case of seizure.
2. Exclusion from school athletics.
3. A desire to change schools.
4. Refusal to take medication.
5. Parents' feeling they have to sleep with the child in case of seizure.
6. Exclusion from school.
7. Depression and failing marks in school.
8. Expulsion from school because of problem behavior.

Treatment

The major approach to controlling seizures is the administration of specific medication. With medication, the seizures of 60% of epileptic children are completely controlled and 25% experience partial control. The remaining 15% of epileptic children obtain no control of their seizures in this manner (Livingston & Pauli, 1973). Common drugs used to control seizures are phenobarbitol, Mysoline (primidone), Dilantin (phenytoin sodium), Mebaral (mephobarbitol), and Tegretol (carbamazepine). Medication is usually continued until the EEG is consistently normal (Wright et al., 1979).

Ongoing treatment includes reducing the number of seizures, encouraging the child to function at his or her own level, promoting acceptance at home and school, and educating the child about the illness. Seizures during physical, or athletic activity are rare so the child should be encouraged to participate. If psychogenic seizures occur, parents may benefit from training in methods of giving attention for adaptive behavior incompatible with seizures and of ignoring the seizures themselves (Gardner, 1967). When seizure occurs, the following procedures are recommended:

1. If you or the person with epilepsy senses an impending seizure, help the person lie on the ground.
2. Do not try to restrain the person. The seizure must run its course and cannot be stopped once it has begun.
3. Clear the area. Particularly, remove hard or dangerous objects so the person experiencing the seizure will not be injured by them.
4. If the person is wearing glasses, remove them.
5. Loosen clothing in the neck and head area.
6. Turn the person on the side to allow saliva to drain from the mouth.
7. Do not place any hard object in the mouth or between the teeth. (Choking or damage to the mouth or teeth could occur.)
8. When the person regains consciousness and the seizure ceases, help him find a place to rest and become oriented (Abbot Laboratories, n.d.).

Most persons recover spontaneously. Thus, it is usually unnecessary to call a physician. However, if the seizures last more than 10 minutes, or if one seizure follows another, medical help should be sought.

Children with epilepsy should be encouraged to take part in physical activities. The type of activity depends upon the extent of seizure control for the individual child. Swimming is one activity which requires constant supervision. Activities which increase falling possibilities, such as horseback riding, bicycling, climbing, or swinging, should be evaluated and supervised carefully (Hunt, 1955).

Music Therapy Intervention

The music therapy treatment plan will vary according to the needs presented by the individual child. The following are goals which the music therapist may work toward when treating the child with epilepsy:

- Promote lowered anxiety through self-expression and relaxation.
- Promote developmental growth by providing age appropriate music and movement activities.
- Promote development of peer relations and social skills through involvement in musical activities.
- Promote awareness of events or feelings that precede seizures.
- Provide the opportunity to express feelings related to the condition of epilepsy.

The case study which follows, an example of music therapy treatment for a child with epilepsy, is provided. Cliff was a 9-year-old boy of normal intelligence who had epilepsy which cycled every month, culminating in several grand mal seizures. Although drug therapy was utilized, the cycling remained a problem which interfered with his concentration, performance, and attendance at school. Cliff was enrolled in the regular school program but was absent an average of five school days each month. His classroom teacher noted that, for several days prior to a seizure, Cliff became hyperactive and was difficult to handle in the classroom. Cliff was referred to the music therapist to deal with the acting-out behavior. A long-range goal was set for Cliff to accept and work with the cycles of his handicap. An annual objective was to reduce Cliff's absences from 5 to 3 days per month.

The following treatment plan was developed to achieve the goals. The first (1) objective was for Cliff to recognize signs of increase of his own frustration level which was a signal of an approaching seizure. As Cliff's frustration level increased, the music therapist used vocal improvisation to facilitate awareness of behavior and feelings. The second (2) objective was for Cliff to understand his cycles of hyperactivity and to be able to ask for assistance in channeling his hyperactivity in constructive ways. The music therapist helped Cliff become aware of external cues from adults that indicated his behavior was not under control. Cliff learned to ask for special materials from his classroom teacher and parents to channel his extra energy. Special materials included a jump rope, large ball, and a drum pad and drum sticks, as well as puzzles and crayons and drawing paper. Evaluative criteria for determination of progress toward these objectives were the number of days Cliff attended school, the number of difficulties which arose in the school day, and reports from teacher and parents about reduction of acting out behavior.

After eight weeks, Cliff was able to begin developing an awareness of the cycles of his seizures. His increased ability to take responsibility for his hyperactivity began to relieve behavior problems in the classroom and gave him a sense of mastery over his condition (Feury, 1981).

CHILDREN WITH CONGENITAL HEART DISEASE

Description

Congenital heart disease is characterized by structural defects of the heart and/or vessels carrying blood to and from the heart. The defects are present at birth, having occurred during fetal development. Different types of malformation include atrial and ventricular septal defects which consist of holes in the walls separating the atria or ventricles. Blood flow may be obstructed by narrowed or nonexistent openings, a disorder referred to as aortic stenosis or pulmonary atresia (Wright et al., 1979).

Congenital heart disease (CHD) cannot always be detected immediately at birth. Symptoms include difficulty in breathing, failure to thrive, vomiting, swallowing difficulties, and reduced physical endurance. Other more obvious symptoms are a bluish color of the lips and fingernails. Although CHD is the leading cause of illness and death in infancy, surgical techniques have resulted in a high success rate in preventing death and complications (Robinson & Gasul, 1959).

Etiology

Defects in the heart and vessels, which are categorized as CHD, develop during the first trimester of pregnancy (Robinson & Gasul, 1959); the actual cause is known in only 5% of all cases. Potential factors involved in the development of CHD are the mother contracting rubella or taking such drugs as thalidamide or LSD during pregnancy (Engle et al., 1970). Although there is some evidence linking hereditary factors to the disease, such a relationship has not been firmly established (Wright et al., 1979).

Psychological Correlates

Children with CHD are generally of normal intelligence but may perform below their developmental level because of environmental or social restrictions and excessive absence from school. Usually, CHD children appear normal in adjustment and degree of independence (Linde, Rasof, Dunn & Rabb, 1966). However, there are characteristic problems which accompany the condition of these children, one of which is the amount of anxiety resulting from the illness. Problems can arise in this area because the illness is a disease of the heart. Salk (1974) states that "cardiac conditions can result in severe anxiety, due to the great symbolic importance of the heart. Everyone knows that a functioning heart is synonymous with life" (p. 97). Sensitivity to this point can make it difficult for the parents to accept the disease and particularly the recommendation for surgery (Glaser, 1966; Glaser, Harrison & Lynn, 1964). Although surgery usually results in marked improvement of the child's condition, parents are understandably fearful. Prior to and following surgery, parents may be overprotective and may institute unnecessary restrictions. The child may respond by becoming withdrawn and depressed or may become angry and aggressive (Glaser, 1966). If children with CHD are treated too differently by parents, they may use their illness to manipulate for secondary gains (Linde et al., 1966). For example, the child may be able to avoid work or punishment by appealing to the parents' fear of the disease.

Treatment

Because the cause of CHD is usually unknown, prevention is difficult. Rubella vaccination and genetic counseling are two preventive measures which can be taken (Wright et al., 1979). Once the disease has been detected, however, corrective surgery may be recommended; this has been a successful remedy in the majority of cases. These practices have resulted in generalized positive effects which include increased school attendance and appetite and normalized sleeping habits (Boon, 1972; Landtman & Valanne, 1958).

Because of the emotional impact of treatment, parents need to be educated carefully about the pre- and post-operative conditions of the child. Individual counseling and/or parent groups are recommended so that parents may learn about the dangers of overprotection and overindulgence (Landtman & Valanne, 1958). In many cases, there is no physical restriction on the child who may be allowed to learn his or her own capacity for activity (Adams & Moss, 1969; American Heart Association, 1970; The American Public Health Association, 1960). Certainly, pre-operative preparation of the child can reduce significantly the effects of post-operative trauma. Pre-operative preparation includes acquainting the child with procedures and equipment and giving the child the opportunity to act out feelings verbally and through play with, for example, puppets (Cassell & Paul, 1967).

Music Therapy Intervention

The music therapist working with a child who has CHD must rely heavily on the physician's evaluation of the child's strength before and after corrective surgery. Choral singing, movement to a stimulating and strong musical beat, or prolonged dancing may be strenuous for the child (Hunt, 1955). Warning signals that cardiac reserve is being taxed include dyspnea (breathlessness), pallor of the lips, and signs of fatigue; the child may require a pattern of activity and rest. Goals the music therapist may address in treating the CHD child include:

- Preparation for surgery.
- Facilitation of relaxation and reduction of anxiety before and after surgery.
- Education of the child and family about the limitations of the condition.
- Increased physical stamina.
- Reduction of developmental lags.
- Expression of fears and feelings related to the illness.
- Development of social skills.

An example of music therapy treatment with a CHD child follows. Patty, age 4, had a medical diagnosis of congenital heart disease. She was cyanotic at birth; it was discovered that she had critical pulmonary valve stenosis. A valvotomy was performed. Due to continued problems, Patty remained in intensive care for eight weeks. Developmental progress was delayed, although she presently functioned within the 2-3 year range of intelligence. She was quite distractible and, at times, manipulative.

Patty was referred for music therapy assessment and the following strengths and needs were noted. Patty's strengths lay in the areas of verbal and visual imitation, although rhythmic imitation had not yet emerged. Patty demonstrated abilities in relating to people; however, new people would occasionally cause her to feel uncomfortable. Patty was able to participate successfully in structured group activities. She displayed developmental delays in gross and fine motor coordination skills. As a result, it was suggested that structured play situations be instituted, which would be oriented toward development of motor skills.

Because Patty worked well in group situations, she was placed in a group with four other children which met three times weekly. There, Patty participated in rhythm activities designed to help her develop in the areas of gross and fine motor skills. Movement and dance activities were also used. She made gains in accepting new people and in reducing manipulative behavior, since appropriate social development was also emphasized in the group. Patty developed the ability to imitate simple melodies and used auditory cues to determine her own involvement in music activities. A similar developmental program was recommended for Patty during the school year (Johnson, 1981).

CHILDREN WITH ACQUIRED RHEUMATIC HEART DISEASE

Description

Although there has been a decline in the incidence of rheumatic fever in recent years, it is still the leading cause of acquired heart disease in children. Rheumatic fever is usually contracted by children ages 5-15 years. During the acute phase, it is characterized by inflammation of the heart, joints, skin, and brain. Although such inflammation is a temporary condition, possible permanent cardiac damage, consisting of scarring of heart muscle or valves, may result. Rheumatic fever is unpredictable and can recur at any time (Wright et al., 1979). Symptoms include arthritis, fever, carditis, emotional instability, and in some cases, a skin rash (Nelson et al., 1969).

Rheumatic fever occurs in three phases: (1) the acute, active phase which can last for weeks or months, (2) the convalescent phase, and (3) the following phase of prophylactic therapy. The prognosis is dependent upon the presence and extent of heart disease. Most difficulties are related to recurrent attacks; hence, the importance of preventing additional infections. One-fourth of the children with heart disease due to rheumatic fever suffer relapse within 10 years of onset (Nelson et al., 1969).

Etiology

Rheumatic fever is usually preceded by a streptococcal infection of group A, beta-hemolytic type. Rheumatic fever may occur 2-3 weeks after an upper respiratory tract infection has occurred, or may happen due to an inherited genetic predisposition. Evidence also exists that socioeconomic factors, particularly crowded living conditions, result in higher incidence of rheumatic fever (Wright et al., 1979).

Psychological Correlates

Children who contract rheumatic fever have usually reached the age when they are beginning to spend more time outside of the home (Bauer, 1952; Hill, 1959; Shirley, 1952). The restriction of activity resulting from the illness leaves them, therefore, deprived of normal outlets of energy, assertiveness, and aggression. Frequent absences from school interrupt social development and can cause the child to fall behind in relation to his peers (Wright et al., 1979).

Thomas, Milman and Rodrigues-Torres (1970) suggest four characteristics which often cause the child and family emotional difficulties:

- The chronic nature of the disease.
- The threat of recurrence.
- The possibility of disability.
- The need for prolonged prophylaxis.

The two elements which seem to most affect the degree of success for the child and family are the resilience and adaptability of the child and the parent-child relationship (Wright et al., 1979).

Treatment

Initially, the child must have bed rest, either in the hospital or at home. Hospitalization can have the positive effect of putting the child in an atmosphere where he is not different from peers, as well as the negative effect of the separation and isolation from family (Wright et al., 1979).

Anti-inflammatory drugs are normally prescribed for rheumatic fever. Aspirin and corticosteroids usually are administered to reduce fever and inflammation of the joints. Antibiotics also are used to reduce the possibility of additional streptococcal infections. Although prevention is an essential part of the treatment, antimicrobial medication is often continued throughout childhood and adolescence to prevent recurrence of the disease and further damage to the heart (Nelson et al., (1969).

Intervention includes facilitating physical movement as soon as possible; 7-10 days of bed rest are typically required for children without heart damage, whereas children with carditis may need bed rest from 3 weeks to 3 months. In most cases, normal physical activity can be resumed after recovery is complete. Education about the disease is important for the child and family particularly, because of the frequent misunderstandings regarding the causes and nature of rheumatic fever. Since recurrence of the disease is potentially damaging, understanding of and adherence to a program of prevention is stressed (Nelson et al., 1969).

Treatment goals for rheumatic heart disease and congenital heart disease are similar; however, some differences do exist. The major differences involve the later onset of rheumatic heart disease as well as unpredictable nature of that disease.

Music Therapy Intervention

Music therapy sessions for the child with rheumatic heart disease require constant consideration of the physician's evaluation of the child's condition. The three phases of the disease (acute, convalescent, and prophylactic) present varying needs of the child. General goals which may be addressed by the music therapist in the treatment of this child are:

- Educating the child and family about the limitations of the condition.
- Providing an appropriate outlet for energy and aggression restricted by bed rest.
- Providing the opportunity to express feelings about the illness and restrictions.
- Providing the opportunity for peer interaction.
- Providing age-appropriate activities to prevent, as well as to remediate, social lags.
- Increasing physical stamina.

Children who require extended bed rest benefit from an active music therapy program. Music activities can be planned, which require minimal physical output while providing the child with a means of stimulation, interaction, and self-expression. In addition to bedside music therapy sessions, the child may benefit from having materials including a tape recorder, an instrument the child is learning to play, or paper for writing songs available for use at all times. As the child becomes more physically active, progressively increased physical involvement to music therapy activities can help strengthen the child and increase stamina. In addition to the emphasis on activity and stimulation, relaxation to music and guided imagery through music serves to relieve tension and anxiety which result from the illness and isolation that the child experiences.

CHILDREN WITH HEMOPHILIA

Description

Hemophilia is defined medically as "excessive bleeding into the soft tissues and joints whether spontaneously or induced traumatically" (Wright et al., 1979, p. 363). Hemophilia is a condition in which the blood does not coagulate properly because of a deficiency in one of the 13 clotting factors in the plasma. The problem can range from very mild to severe, depending upon the degree of deficiency. A severe degree of the disease, resulting in excessive bleeding into the joints, can cause crippling, referred to as "hemophilic arthropathy." Children with hemophilia often have extended periods when episodic bleeding does not occur. In one study, a group of children with hemophilia had a mean number of episodes in one year of 9.3, with 2.4 episodes requiring hospitalization (Olch, 1971a).

Hemophilia is a life-long disorder for which there is no cure. Life expectancy is dependent on the severity of the condition as well as on the quality of treatment.

Etiology

There are several types of the disease, but the two most common are "hemophilia A" and "hemophilia B." Both are caused by genetic transmission from a carrier mother with a recessive X chromosome and occur only in males (Wright et al., 1979). Hemophilia A is called "classic hemophilia," results from a deficiency in Factor VIII, and is responsible for 80% of the incidence of the disease. Hemophilia B, sometimes referred to as "Christmas disease," results from a deficiency in Factor IX and is responsible for 15% of the incidence (Nelson et al., 1969). There is often a history of hemophilia in the family, but it is also possible for the disorder to appear without previous history.

Psychological Correlates

Spontaneous bleeding appears to occur in cycles and, in some cases, the episodes have been related to emotional factors (Olch, 1971b). Anger and excitement can trigger an episode as well as anticipation of an upcoming event such as a holiday or a vacation (Mattsson & Gross, 1966). Bleeding episodes also are reported to be correlated with developmental milestones and stages, such as when a child begins to crawl or walk, or when he begins school. These stages stimulate increased physical activities, thereby increasing the possibility of physical injury due to falling or other trauma (Wright et al., 1979).

Intelligence levels of children with hemophilia are average to above average. These children tend to score high on information, vocabulary, and picture completion subtests but often score low on tests assessing social skills (Wright et al., 1979). Their education can be a problem because of frequent absences from school. As a group, hemophiliacs do not perform well in school or in vocational careers and they appear to have lower levels of motivation (Agle & Mattsson, 1968).

Socially, these children are often restricted and isolated. It is likely that hemophilic children are viewed as overly fragile by adults and peers. Therefore, a tendency exists for families to be overly protective, causing the child to be passive or rebellious (Connor, 1975). Families consequently experience much stress, due to the special needs of the child and the related financial burdens. The child must have access, for example, to immediate medical treatment (Boon & Roberts, 1970; Salk, Hilgartner & Granich, 1972); extra attention may be given to the ill child at the expense of siblings (Agle & Mattsson, 1968). The mother, in particular, may feel guilt, anxiety, anger, or resentment from taking responsibility for the child's dysfunction (Wright et al., 1979). Therefore, the parents' motivation in making the child's life as normal as possible is vital to the emotional, social, and physical well-being of the child.

The child with hemophilia is subject to specific psychological stresses. The child learns quickly about the bleeding and its consequences. From ages 6-7, these children often learn to monitor their activities in order to avoid bleeding episodes and the possible accompanying pain and immobilization. Also, they often are faced with repeated separation from the family during hospitalization and another negative result of the bleeding episode (Agle & Mattsson, 1968).

Negative responses related to the restriction of activity and possible over-protection include low achievement and motivation; feelings of inferiority, passivity and helplessness; dependence upon others; and guilt in relation to authority figures. These children also can respond with rebelliousness and risk-taking to counter their feelings of isolation and restriction (Agle, 1964; Poinsard, 1957; Spencer, 1971; Spencer & Behar, 1969).

Treatment

Hemophilia cannot be cured; it can be prevented only through genetic counseling and contraception (Favre-Gilly, 1957; Goldy & Katz, 1963; Merritt, 1975). Medical treatment consists of prevention of trauma and treatment of bleeding episodes. Minor episodes are treated in the home with application of ice and/or pressure, and by restriction of physical movement. During major bleeding episodes, however, an immediate transfusion of frozen fresh plasma containing the needed clotting factor as required (Salk et al., 1972; White, 1964). Frequent need for transfusion can disrupt the child's and family's personal lives as well as the child's attendance in school. Outpatient transfusion, though, can reduce the number of days in the hospital; one study showed a decrease in the mean number of school absences from 6.2 to 2.5 days as a result of outpatient treatment (Strawczynski, Stachewitsch, Morgenstern & Shaw, 1973).

Counseling is usually indicated to help the family understand the nature of the disorder and to relieve emotional stress (Agle & Mattsson, 1968; Spencer & Behar, 1969). One way in which counseling may be used to prevent negative effects of over-protection is by helping the parents to recognize a balance between protection and permissiveness. To assist in this, the child's home and school life should remain as normal as possible. Academic achievement and career training are important for the child's success as he progresses into adolescence and ultimately into adulthood.

Music Therapy Intervention

The hemophilic child needs to be included in appropriate activities as well as to experience an active role in them. Since motor activity discharges tension and contributes to a feeling of control, such activities can be implemented to relieve the child's feelings of passivity and helplessness and fear of immobilization (Wright et al., 1979). Music therapy provides a nonstrenuous means of meeting these needs. The following is an example of a child with hemophilia who was involved in music therapy as a treatment modality.

Christopher was a 1½-year-old male with frequent hospitalizations due to hemophilia. His parents were separated and he lived with his father and grandparents. The father was a frequent visitor and often spent the night in Christopher's room during hospitalization. When left alone, Christopher became restless and was in need of activities to keep him occupied and to reduce the anxiety of isolation. On one occasion, Christopher was admitted to the hospital due to a fall which resulted in a hemotoma on his forehead. Christopher was a very active child and required close supervision.

Music therapy goals with Christopher were as follows:

- To provide a restricted environment to prevent any further injuries. Items of interest were placed within Christopher's reach, such as music boxes, mobiles, and plastic blocks. Extra precautions were taken to lessen the risk of injuries and subsequent uncontrolled bleeding.

- To provide sensory stimulation. Two felt objects were placed in front of Christopher. The objects were felt drawings of a cat, dog, rooster, frog, and lizard. Christopher was instructed to find a specific animal as instructed in a song: "Can you find the puppy? The puppy, the puppy? Can you find the puppy? Can you find him now?" When Christopher chose the object called for, objects were switched around on the felt board and the song was repeated; this was done to see if Christopher really knew the correct answer. The felt animals were kept in his bed for him to play with when the music therapist was not present.

- To stimulate auditory and visual senses. Modeling and imitation was used. Christopher had a choice of hand bells, maracas, and a hand drum. As he played the instruments and moved around, he was imitated by the therapist. This became a game and as it progressed, Christopher began to do the imitating. Leadership was then passed back and forth between Christopher and the therapist.

- To provide a protected physical outlet and continuation of psychomotor development. Because Christopher was a very active child who enjoyed running, jumping, and kicking, music was used to provide him the opportunity to participate in these activities in a more controlled environment. He marched around the room to music and exercised to the song, "Head and shoulders, knees and toes" (Marley, 1982).

LEAD POISONING IN CHILDREN

Description

Lead poisoning is due to the gradual absorption and accumulation of lead within the blood and soft tissues of the body. Toxic effects of such poisoning to the central nervous system may result in permanent structural damage. Progressive lead poisoning can lead to cerebral edema, vascular damage, destruction of brain cells and disintegration of neuroglia. The condition can range from mild to severe and involves such symptoms as encephalitis, anemia, colic, peripheral neuritis, paresis, irritability, abdominal pain, vomiting, and insomnia. Studies reveal that half of the children and infants affected with lead poisoning exhibit encephalitic manifestations and of those who recover, one-half experience permanent neurologic or mental sequelae (Nelson et al., 1969).

Etiology

Lead can be absorbed into the body through the gastrointestinal tract, skin, and lungs. The major cause of lead poisoning in children is the ingestion of materials containing lead. Chewing on plaster or on utensils coated with lead-based paint is the most common manner in which children ingest lead. Newspapers, magazines, playing cards, and insecticides are other common sources of lead in the child's surroundings. Soil may contain lead from industrial waste discharged into the air. Many children place such objects into their mouths during the crawling stage as they explore the world around them. Moreover, poor diet or iron deficiency can lead to a condition called "pica" which compels the child to ingest inedible objects, such as plaster, sand, or paint from walls (Nelson et al., 1969).

Psychological Correlates

Encephalitis appears to be the primary cause of cognitive impairment from lead poisoning. Of those who have encephalitis, 25-50% suffer significant intellectual problems (Byers & Lord, 1943; Jenkins & Mellins, 1957; Lin-Fu, 1967; Novick, 1971). These problems can be in the form of mental retardation or specific learning disabilities. It is difficult to determine if lead poisoning is responsible for the intellectual difficulties, since children with lead poisoning tend to come from economically disadvantaged environments where the rate of learning disabilities and mental retardation is already high (Kappleman, Kaplan & Ganter, 1970).

Behavioral characterisitcs of children with lead poisoning include hyperactivity, lethargy, distractibility, emotional lability, and aggressiveness. In addition, these children tend to experience poor peer relations (Wright et al., 1979). They also tend to come from large, economically deprived families, characteristically including the absence of a father or an unemployed father, as well as maternal deprivation (Meigs, 1972).

Treatment

Goals for medical treatment include the reduction of lead concentrations in the blood and tissues. This is accomplished by means of preventing further lead absorption and by increasing the rate of excretion of lead, primarily in the urine. Therefore, all lead must be removed from the child's environment; in some cases, the child must be removed from the environment. Salts of ethylenediamine tetraacetic acid can be administered to decrease lead levels in the blood. These measures frequently reverse or prevent the damage caused by lead poisoning. If encephalitis is present, constant observation and care of the child is required. Furthermore, increased intracranial pressure due to cerebral edema may necessitate lumbar punctures to release small amounts of fluid (Nelson et al., 1969).

Parents of lead-poisoned children must be educated about the disease so they can aid in preventing progressive toxic effects. If cognitive problems are present, the child may require special education (Wright et al., 1979).

Music Therapy Intervention

The following is an example of a child with lead poisoning who was involved in music therapy. Carl was a 15-year-old black male who was being treated in a state residential program for emotionally disturbed children. Tests indicated that he had a significant amount of lead in his blood, justifying a medical diagnosis of lead poisoning. It was known that Carl had been locked in a closet by his mother as a young child and that he had eaten paint and plaster from the closet walls. He exhibited specific learning disabilities and experienced particular difficulty in learning to read. His behavioral characteristics included hyperactivity, problems related to concentration, and poor impulse control. Although often taking a leadership role with his peers, he compulsively insulted them verbally. Consequently, his peer relationships were poor.

Carl was referred for music therapy. As a part of his treatment plan, he was placed in a music therapy group with 15 peers. The group met in five one-hour sessions each week, led by two music therapists. Daily activities included structured rhythm games which required taking turns and individual participation. Additional activities included movement and creative dramatics. The adolescents in this group also wrote and performed musicals twice yearly. Initially, Carl was defensive and hostile. He was, however, highly motivated to sing and enjoyed acting out impromptu scenes; this positive aspect was used as a reward in a behavioral contract with Carl. He and his peers received a grade of A, B, C, D, or F at the end of each session, since the sessions were a part of the children's school program. The major goals in Carl's contract called for him to: (1) participate without interrupting others, (2) control his behavior by remaining in his seat, and (3) refrain from verbally insulting his peers. These were extremely difficult goals for Carl. Initially, his control was tenuous; he would act out and become angry when told that he had not met his goals.

After months of work, Carl began to take responsibility for his behavior, displaying increasingly significant improvement. He began to recognize the benefits of positive behavior and was able to make the choice to act out or to cooperate. Although he was not completely able to control his impulsivity, Carl was able to take lead roles in several musical productions, which necessitated remembering lines and behaving appropriately on stage (Schwankovsky, 1981).

CHILDREN WITH LEUKEMIA

Description

Leukemia is a family of diseases of unknown origin characterized by uncontrolled proliferation of white blood cells. Although rare, leukemia is the most common malignancy in children (Lansky, 1974; Lukens & Miles, 1970). Symptoms can be categorized into three pathological processes (Wright et al., 1979):

1. Hypermetabolism, the rapid growth and destruction of leukemia tissue causing fever, weight loss, physical weakness, and fatigue.

2. The replacement of fatty bone marrow by grayish-red leukemia marrow, accompanied by anemia, bleeding, bruising, and infections.

3. Enlargement of lymph glands and spleen process which result in bone pain, hematuria (blood in the urine), and general pain.

Leukemia is presently considered to be a fatal disease which can run an unpredictable course with remissions and relapses. During remission, the child may appear normal and healthy. However, symptoms such as low energy level and reduced physical endurance may be present even during this time. When leukemia has affected the central nervous system, symptomatology may include headaches, vomiting, increased intercranial pressure, and palsied cranial and peripheral nerves (Berry, 1974; Haghbin & Zuelzer, 1965; Thatcher, 1968).

Before 1947, there was no effective treatment for leukemia and the child usually died within a year of diagnosis. Between 1947 and 1963, new drugs were introduced which made it possible to prolong the life of a child with this disease. Since 1963, treatment interventions have been expanded, resulting in a post-diagnosis longevity of 3-4 years (Wright et al., 1979).

Etiology

The cause of leukemia is unknown; it is believed not to be genetic or contagious. Genetic predisposition, chromosomal instability, and possible viral involvements are among the areas being explored and researched in an attempt to discover the causes. The disease usually appears in children who are 3-4 years of age. Although leukemia is fatal, it does not normally cause sudden death (Richmond & Waisman, 1955).

Psychological Correlates

There are three major elements in leukemia which require adjustment from the child and family: (a) the diagnosis, (b) remissions and relapses, and (c) the terminal stage (Kaplan, Smith, Gobstein & Fischmann, 1973). The ability of the child and family to cope with the onset of leukemia often depends on the initial response of the family to the diagnosis. Most parents are stunned, refusing to believe that the diagnosis is accurate, thus using denial as a defense mechanism. During recurrence of symptoms, it becomes increasingly difficult for the parents to continue to deny the reality of their child's illness (Benoliel, 1972; Lansky, 1974). The use of denial as a defense mechanism is not prevalent during the periods of time when the symptoms of leukemia are in remission.

Once leukemia has been diagnosed, the parents experience various emotions that must be addressed. These include anxiety, grief, and helplessness. In addition, anticipatory mourning of the child's imminent death often begins at the time of diagnosis (Binger, Ablin, Feuerstein, Kushner, Zoger & Mikkelsen, 1969; Burgert, 1972; Knapp & Hansen, 1973). Related to the factor of anticipatory mourning is a unique pattern of parental and familial reactions when the child's health enters critical periods. As the parents and family prepare for the child's death, the child's health may improve and the symptoms enter a state of remission. The preparation for death, followed by the child's improved health, often causes the parents and other family members to experience emotional reactions of anger and guilt. Although this phenomenon is common, families may be unaware of the process and thus experience enormous guilt (Schoenberg, Carr, Kutscher, Peretz & Goldberg, 1974).

Due to the emotional reaction to their child's condition, parents often respond by being overly protective, remiss in providing discipline, and prone to giving special favors to the ill child (McCarthy, 1975). These responses may cause additional problems for the child as well as for other members of the family.

The child with leukemia has the difficult task of integrating limitations with potentialities for growth and development. Normally, behavior problems are few. There are, however, general problem areas:

1. Separation anxiety may cause the child to make increased demands for attention, indulgence, and physical contact (Futterman & Hoffman, 1970).

2. School problems may result because of absence during relapses. Other factors which may interfere with success in school are loss of hair, impaired peer relationships, and lack of self-confidence (McCarthy, 1975).

3. Children with leukemia may be a psychological threat to people around them because they symbolize human vulnerability and mortality (Kaplan, Smith & Grobstein, 1974).

4. In general, families of children with leukemia are a high risk for psychological difficulties because of the stress and possible length of time stress is endured (Hoffman & Futterman, 1971).

Treatment

Medical treatment of leukemia is based on the indication and maintenance of remissions and on the prevention of central nervous system (CNS) involvement (Thatcher, 1968). Remission-inducing drugs are used to bring about initial control of the disease. Besides their beneficial effects, these drugs also have toxic properties which cause side effects. Three drugs which are commonly used for inducing control of the disease are vincristine sulfate (side effects include loss of hair, constipation, and jaw pain), prednisone (causes weight gain), and l-asparaginase (causes depression). Remission-maintaining drugs are less toxic and include mercoptopuring which is toxic to liver tissue and may cause abdominal pain, hermaturia, and depression of normal bone marrow, and methotrexate which may cause pain and fracturing of bones (Wright et al., 1979). Preventive treatment of the CNS includes radiation therapy of the cranium or drugs administered intrathecally. However, prolonged chemotherapy results in the child being highly susceptible to infection, the condition requiring isolation to prevent bacterial or viral infection.

Education of the parents about the disease and the opportunity to participate in the care of the child are important factors in more successful adjustment of both the child and the family. The parents also need opportunities for open communication with physicians and for expression of hostility, grief, anger, and guilt (Orbach, Sutherland & Bozeman, 1955). Parent groups provide an important support system for these families.

The child with leukemia needs to lead as normal a life as possible. The fulfillment of several psychological needs may help to provide support and normalization for him:

1. The opportunity to know what is happening and to talk about it.

2. The opportunity to take part in decisions about his or her own death and dying.

3. The opportunity to express feeling bad rather than protecting adults by hiding feelings (Benoliel, 1972).

Music Therapy Intervention

The child with leukemia requires treatment in general areas of development as well as special attention to the effects of frequent hospitalization. Music therapy goals for the child also address several specific areas characteristic of the condition: (a) isolation, (b) physical consequences resulting from the illness, and (c) the terminal nature of the illness.

Children with leukemia are partially susceptible to respiratory infection and must occasionally be isolated which results in decreased social contact, lack of stimulation, and lack of physical activity. Emotional responses to isolation often include feelings of loneliness, depression, rejection, anger, and confusion (Rantz, 1979). The music therapist can provide activities which make isolation more tolerable for the child.

Physical results of the illness and treatment affect the child's self-concept. Physical changes which occur include loss of hair, yellowing of the skin, peeling of body skin, lumps, scars, and bruises. Music therapy can provide the child with an outlet for talking about and dealing with these changes. Group sessions give children the opportunity to interact with peers who are experiencing similar physical changes (Davis, 1980).

The terminal nature of the disease requires special attention from the music therapist. Understanding and acceptance of death and dying is a difficult and often delicate subject. The following activity was used by Davis (1980) at the New Orleans Children's Hospital to help children with the conceptualization and acceptance of death and dying:

> Gather the children into a group. Place a paper cup in the center of the group on the floor. Instruct them to "focus" on the cup and think of what it signifies or represents to them. Continue this for approximately five minutes in silence. Then, discuss the various feelings. After adequate discussion, physically destroy the cup by stepping on it or crushing it with your hands. Again discuss the various feelings, bring in how the cup is or is not what it used to be. Relate this to their lives. Music playing in the background often proves to be helpful in that it breaks the total silence and releases some of the group's tension or anxiety.

Music has been utilized as a medium for guided imagery work with terminally ill children. Guided imagery exercises can assist the child in processing his feelings, thoughts, and fears about death. In addition, guided imagery exercises may help to reduce the child's perception and experience of pain.

CHILDREN WITH NEPHRITIS

Description

Nephritis is a disturbance of the structure and function of the kidney and is manifested in several forms, including acute and chronic glomerulonephritis, hereditary nephritis, the hemolytic-uremic syndrome, and vascular nephritis (Nelson et al., 1969). Among them, only acute and chronic glomerulonephritis will be described in this section.

The most frequently diagnosed form of nephritis in children is acute glomerulonephritis. It usually occurs as a reaction to an infection in the body, for example, an upper respiratory tract infection. The kidneys become slightly enlarged. There is a wide range of other clinical symptoms and a wide variance in their severity. Symptoms can include high fever, headache, blood in the urine, hypertension, edema, and renal dysfunction. Mild cases last from 10 to 14 days, with a generally favorable prognosis. Severe cases may result in renal failure.

Chronic glomerulonephritis is less common in children than in adults. The kidneys become smaller in size resulting in a reduction in the blood supply. The symptoms can range from no apparent problem to severe renal failure and hypertension. The disease may be detected by routine urinalysis, revealing advanced functional deterioration of the kidneys. The general prognosis is for continued deterioration of renal function, ending in death within 5 to 10 years (Nelson et al., 1969).

Etiology

Acute glomerulonephritis may appear from 1 to 3 weeks after the onset of an infection, often streptococcal bacterial in the upper respiratory tract. The chronic form is more often a result of acute glomerulonephritis in adults than in children. The chronic form of nephritis can also be preceded by a nephrotic syndrome, nephritis of anaphylactoid purpura, or a hemolytic-uremic syndrome. Hereditary nephritis is also a common cause of this disease (Nelson et al., 1969).

Psychological Correlates

The course of nephritis in children can range from mild to severe. While some children may recover completely, others may suffer end-stage renal failure, requiring dialysis and perhaps a kidney transplant (Nelson et al., 1969). For children with progressive renal dysfunction, the disease is life threatening, a fact which remains constantly in the awareness of both the child and family. When disease becomes critical, the child may require dialysis up to 3 or 4 times per week and may experience intense psychological stress. Factors which contribute to such stress are:

1. Confrontation with the illness. The child has three alternatives: dialysis, kidney transplant, or death (Wright et al., 1979). This may result in feelings of uncertainty of survival and uncertainty of the quality of life.

2. Dependence-independence conflict. This results from the relationship the child has with the dialysis machine and attending staff (Abram, 1969; Anger, 1975). The child may experience a feeling of dehumanization due to the physiological dependency on the machine (Grushkin, Lewy, Cole, Holland, Lewy & Potter, 1974).

3. Physical and emotional responses to the condition. Children requiring dialysis often have feelings of fatigue, apathy, drowsiness, and general weakness (Anger, 1975).

4. Change in body image and self-concept. The dialysis process may result in the child fantasizing he is not all human. The flow of blood out of the body, through the machine, and back into the body can result in confusion of physical boundaries. In addition, the external A-V shunt serves as a constant reminder of the disease (Anger, 1975).

5. Adaptation to the treatment regime. In addition to the weekly treatment on the dialysis machine, other factors such as strict dietary restriction and restricted activity are required (Wright et al., 1979).

6. Interruption in school. Interrupted school attendance often results in academic and developmental lags as well as reduced peer contact (Wright et al., 1979).

If a kidney transplant is indicated, the search for a donor may have significant impact upon the family. The effects of pressure and guilt result from the process of determining which member of the family can and will be the kidney donor. Adolescent and pre-adolescent donors are more likely to experience positive benefits (Bernstein & Simmons, 1974). It is also important to realize that the donor must process feelings of stress and depression related to object loss (Kemph, 1971). Once the surgery has been completed, the child may suffer negative psychological reactions including feelings of separation, mutilation, and fear of death. According to Bernstein (1970), successful psychological adaptation is dependent upon three factors: (1) the child's developmental level, (2) the child's adaptive capacity, and (3) the parent-child relationship.

Treatment

Basic control of nephritis can be outlined as follows:

1. Prevention and control of acute infections;
2. Establishment of good nutrition;
3. Readjustment of disturbed metabolic processes;
4. Control of edema;
5. Control of progression of renal lesion;
6. Establishment of good mental hygiene (Nelson et al., 1969).

Hemodialysis, the purification of the blood by an artificial kidney machine, may be indicated, either for those patients waiting for a kidney transplant or for those who have no prospect for such a transplant. Dialysis is usually required twice weekly for 7 to 15 hours. During this time, the child's blood is cycled through the machine, purified of toxic waste, and returned to the child's body.

The child with kidney disease needs family support in dealing with the physical and psychological problems caused by the chronic course of the illness. If the condition becomes severe and life threatening, the child will need assistance in coping with the additional emotional stress. Such stress can be induced and exacerbated by such factors as friction with nurses, absent doctors, dietary restrictions, setbacks, death of another patient, and denial of home visit privileges (Ferris, 1969).

Music Therapy Intervention

The music therapist may provide treatment for the child with renal failure in the hospital, home, or school setting. Goals addressed by the music therapist include:

*   Remediation of developmental lags and maintenance of developmental level.
*   Provide distraction, relaxation, and support during dialysis.
*   Provide the opportunity for expression of feelings related to the condition verbally and nonverbally.
*   Provide the opportunity for peer interaction in small and large group music therapy sessions.
*   Enhance self-concept by involving the child in musical activities focusing on success, mastery, and creativity.

The following is an example of a child with nephritis who took part in music therapy sessions. Billy was an 8-year-old boy with an extensive and complex medical history. He was cyanotic at birth, requiring 100% oxygen and a respirator for assistance in breathing. He encountered chronic renal failure, secondary to congenital bilateral kidney dysplasia, and renal rickets which necessitated leg braces. His medical condition resulted in frequent hospitalization, including dialysis three times per week. Billy was currently awaiting a transplant donor. Prior to wearing braces, Billy walked on his ankles. Other development was within normal limits. Intellectual functioning fell within the borderline-to-average range. His language skills were appropriate for his age, as were his receptive vocabulary skills. He demonstrated problems of impulsivity and lack of internal controls; his medical condition resulted in frequent absences from school.

Billy was evaluated for music therapy services and his strengths and needs were noted. Because he experienced delays in all academic areas, a program of developmental activities was recommended. It also was noted that a behavioral approach of ignoring immature behaviors was effective in lengthening attention span and maintaining on-task behavior.

A program of small-group music therapy activities was implemented. Billy responded well to the group situation and to structured music activities, demonstrating significant progress in the areas of impulse control and on-task behavior. Because most of his classroom work was carried out on an individual basis, the group experience assisted him in reducing manipulative behaviors and attention-seeking devices. Music activities were designed to remediate academic lags by emphasizing concepts of directionality, relationships, spatial awareness, numbers, and colors. Rhythm instrument playing and other music activities requiring fine motor movements were implemented.

Billy responded well to the music therapy interventions. He continued in treatment while taking part in his home and hospital educational program (Johnson, 1981).

CHILDREN WITH SICKLE CELL ANEMIA

Description

Sickle cell anemia is a severe, chronic anemia resulting from a genetically determined change in the amino acid make-up of the hemoglobin molecule. The abnormal red blood cell is referred to as HbS. Normal red blood cells live approximately 120 days, whereas sickle cell is characterized by its sickle shape, short survival time, and an unusual fragility (Brown, Merkow, Weiner & Khajezadeh, 1972).

The red blood cells are the oxygen carriers of the body. A decrease in the ability of the blood to carry oxygen, which occurs in sickle cell anemia, results in severe negative consequences. Physical symptoms include anemia, reduced growth, neurological impairment, gall bladder disease, heart disease, eye pathology and blindness, leg ulcers, and painful acute crises (Wright et al., 1979). There are two types of acute crises which can occur (Johnson & Hatcher, 1974; Pearson & Diamond, 1971; Scott & Kessler, 1971):

1. *Hemolytic crisis* is an imbalance between blood formation and destruction, which is brought on by infection, nutritional deficiency, dehydration and drugs. This type of crisis can result in death due either to severe anemia or heart failure. There are three sub-types of hemolytic crises: the aplastic crisis caused by viral infection, hyper-hemolytic crisis which results from acute infection or toxicity from certain drugs, and splenic sequestration crisis, in which the spleen accumulates a large quantity of blood.

2. *Vaso-occlusive crisis,* the most common and painful, is caused by the grouping of sickle cells in blood vessels, blocking circulation. The blockage can occur anywhere in the body. In infants, the symptoms of this crisis are fever, paleness, irritability, loss of appetite, enlargement of internal organs, and painful swelling of the soft tissues of the hands and feet (the hand-and-foot syndrome). The condition is not as apparent in young children but results, nevertheless, in permanent damage such as heart murmurs, gall bladder disease, progressive liver damage, and abnormal kidney function.

Mortality rates for children with sickle cell anemia are generally not known. A study by Scott (1970), however, concluded that 50% of affected children die before age 20, and most before age 40.

Etiology

Sickle cell anemia is genetically transmitted and is probably the most prevalent genetic disease in the world. It is found in Blacks, some American Indian tribes, as well as in populations from the Mediterranean area, Middle East, South India, and Caribbean. The disease appears to have originated in Africa. Persons carrying the sickle cell trait are immune to malaria, which suggests a biological mechanism in its development. Researchers agree that approximately 10% of American Blacks have the sickle cell trait (Cecil & Loeb, 1963; Pochedly, 1971; Scott & Kessler, 1971; Standard, 1972).

Psychological Correlates

Sickle cell anemia is one of the most neglected public health problems in the United States. As a result, little is known about the intellectual, academic, behavioral, emotional, and social functioning of affected children and families (Wright et al., 1979). This lack of information may be attributable to the fact that the major affected population in the United States, Blacks, are desirous of receiving medical services but less agreeable to submitting themselves to research studies (Whitten & Fischoff, 1974).

In spite of the minimal amount of information available, there is indication that the disease does not appear to affect intelligence (Chodorkoff & Whitten, 1963; Duckett, 1971). The disease can, however, cause academic problems. Diggs and Flowers (1971) found that, of 177 children ages 2-13 years, the number of crisis averaged 3.9 per year per child. The anemic children missed an average of 14 school days per year because of disease-related illness. Such absenteeism easily may result in the children dropping back in school or dropping out of school, even at the elementary level (Whitten & Fischoff, 1974).

A child with sickle cell anemia struggles with problems which can cause emotional stress and developmental lags. Interruption of normal day-to-day experiences, for example, contributes to such developmental lag (Duckett, 1971; Whitten & Fischoff, 1974). In addition, dependency on adults can inhibit normal development of independence during formative years. Because of the unpredictable nature of this disease, the child obtains no sense of mastery over the illness. Disease-related problems can have a negative effect on the development of peer relationships; for example, weakness, chronic fatigue, and absence from school create difficulties for the child in competing with peers (Duckett, 1971). Growth reduction and delayed puberty may encourage teasing by peers (Johnson & Hatcher, 1974).

The child's illness affects the parents emotionally, as well as the child. Parents often experience feelings of distress, shame, and guilt when they realize that they are carriers of the disease (Heimler & Chabot, 1974). Parents may also have feelings of resentment and anger toward the child as well as concern for the child's quality of life. In addition, parents experience a range of felt anxiety due to the possibility of the child's early death.

Treatment

At present, there are no known cures for sickle cell anemia. The major factor preventing development of a cure is a lack of a method for correcting the molecular defect of HbS (Duckett, 1971; Fleming 1965). The only known means of prevention of the disease, at this time, is genetic counseling (Diggs & Flowers, 1971; Johnson & Hatcher, 1974; Scott, 1970; Scott & Kessler, 1971).

The goal of medical treatment is to reduce the number of crises. The treatment for anemia and hemolytic crises is prompt blood transfusion; these types of crises seem to decline in frequency during adolescence (Johnson & Hatcher, 1974; Scott & Kessler, 1971; Whitten, 1961). The treatment approach for vaso-occlusive crisis is to prevent conditions that cause the sickling of cells and their aggregation. This is done by protecting the child from infection, in some cases by administering antibiotics and by avoiding fatigue.

Nonmedical intervention includes addressing factors that affect a child. The child should be assisted in living as normal a life as possible. Academic intervention can remediate educational deficits due to absenteeism (Duckett, 1971; Whitten & Fischoff, 1974). Since a majority of children with sickle cell anemia live in economically disadvantaged areas, public health intervention can address nutrition and hygienic living conditions. The child's needs for peer-related recreation can be met by participation in activities such as community drama clubs, bowling, arts and crafts, swimming, or related activities (Tetrault & Scott, 1974).

Music Therapy Intervention

The following is an example of a child with sickle cell anemia who underwent music therapy. Michael, age 13, had a medical diagnosis of sickle cell disease and right hemiplegia which was a result of a crisis-induced stroke at age 3½. Diagnosis of sickle cell anemia was made at age 6 months, when Michael experienced pain in his stomach and legs. Until the crisis, developmental milestones were normal. Michael attended regular school for one year but continued to experience stroke-related problems He was then enrolled in a school for the physically handicapped. He enjoyed this school experience, especially math, swimming, and music. Since age 3, Michael was hospitalized many times for disease-related pain, scarlet fever, and for additional episodes of vaso-occulsive crisis.

Michael was an independent ambulator on all surfaces and was independent in self-care activities. He had increased muscle tone on the right side, decreased weight bearing on the right arm and leg and, decreased balance reactions on the right side. He functioned within the borderline-to-low-average range of intelligence. His use of vocabulary, grammar, and information in spontaneous conversation suggested better intellectual potential than was measured.

Michael was eventually identified as a candidate for a transitional classroom, and at age 10, moved with some classmates and a teacher from an orthopedic school to a regular school environment. Michael's academic progress was slow in this climate, and reading progress seemed to stop. He continued to have good auditory comprehension but poor visual reading ability.

Michael was referred for a music therapy assessment and the following needs and strengths were noted. He demonstrated good auditory skills in the area of rhythmic discrimination but displayed poor auditory memory in repeating rhythm patterns. His auditory skills improved during testing when stimuli were combined with other sensory experiences. Consequently, auditory association activities were implemented. Recommendations included opportunities for decision-making and for taking age-appropriate responsibility, as well as intervention addressing his denial of his right side for bilateral and fine motor tasks.

When Michael was placed in the "transition class," he received music therapy services on an outpatient basis at the orthopedic school. He worked weekly on a drum set, adjusting to the bilateral activity inherent in playing the set, learning variations in style (i.e., creating "endings" for songs), and repeating rhythm patterns of progressively increasing length. Michael responded to all aspects of the drum format including setting up the drums and putting away his playing equipment. He made progress in all the stated goal areas, becoming able to accompany solo or group activities on the drums. At age 12, he began to learn basic rhythmic notation. Further recommendations for music therapy included a continuation of service on an outpatient basis, increased involvement in more difficult sensorimotor experiences using the drum set, increased use of visual/auditory association activities, and opportunities for peer- and self-acceptance in a normal social environment (Johnson, 1981).

CONCLUDING REMARKS

The intent of this monograph has been to explore the primary needs of health impaired children and the role of music therapy in the treatment of those needs. In reviewing the literature, it is apparent that medical and psychological factors are interrelated in the care and treatment of these children. A wide variety of physical and medical conditions are included in this category of health impaired children as shown in the discussion of 11 chronic childhood diseases. The common denominator for these children is the area of psychological needs which include:

1. Adaptation to the illness and the limitations it imposes.
2. Adjustment of the family to the illness.
3. Dealing with hospitalization.
4. Learning and use of age-appropriate defense mechanisms.
5. Resolving fear-provoking fantasies.
6. Need for a normalized environment.
7. Continuation of school and social development.
8. Prevention and remediation of developmental delays.
9. Normalization of physical activity.
10. Facing issues of death and dying.

Music therapy is presented as an effective element in the treatment of health impaired children. This is demonstrated by the inclusion of related studies and reports from music therapists presently involved in clinical work. Examples of music therapy intervention with health impaired children illustrate the use of music in the treatment of medical and psychological needs. Of particular significance is the role of music therapy in hospitalization and the process of death and dying.

REFERENCES

Abbott Laboratories, *Epilepsy Pamphlet* (#97-2154). Chicago: Abbott Laboratories, n.d.

Abram, H. The psychiatrist, the treatment of chronic renal failure and the prolongation of life: II. *The American Journal of Psychiatry,* 1969, *126*(2), 157-167.

Adams, F. H. & Moss, A. J. Physical activity of children with congenital heart disease. *The American Journal of Cardiology,* 1969, *24,* 605-606.

Agle, D. Psychiatric studies of patients with hemophilia and related states. *Archives of Internal Medicine,* 1964, *114,* 76-82.

Agle, D. & Mattsson, D. Psychiatric and social care of patients with hereditary°hemorrhagic disease. *Modern Treatment,* 1968, *5,* 11-124.

Ajemian, I. & Mount, B. (Eds.). *The Royal Victoria Hospital Manual on palliative/hospice care.* New York: Arno Press, 1980.

American Heart Association. *If your child has congenital heart defect,* 1970.

American Public Health Association. *Services for children with heart disease and rheumatic fever.* New York: Committee on Child Health, 1960.

Anger, D. The psychologic stress of chronic renal failure and long-term hemodialysis. In M. O'Neill (Ed.), *The nursing clinics of North America.* Philadelphia: W. B. Saunders, 1975.

Bauer, I. L. Attitudes of children with rheumatic fever. *Journal for Pediatrics,* 1952, *40,* 796-806.

Becker, R. D. Therapeutic approaches to psychopathologic reactions to hospitalization. *International Journal of Child Psychotherapy,* 1972, *1,* 65-97.

Belmont, H. S. Hospitalization and its effect upon the total child. *Clinical Pediatrics,* 1970, *9,* 472-483.

Benoliel, J. Q. The concept of care for a child with leukemia. *Nursing Forum,* 1972, *11,* 194-204.

Bernstein, D. M. Emotional reactions of children and adolescents to renal transplantation. *Child Psychiatry and Human Development,* 1970, *1,* 102-111.

Bernstein, D. M. & Simmons, R. G. The adolescent kidney donor: The right to give. *American Journal of Psychiatry,* 1974, *131,* 1338-1343.

Berry, D. H. The child with acute leukemia. *American Family Physician,* 1974, *10,* 129-135.

Betts, T. A. Psychosomatic aspects of epilepsy. *Psychosomatic Medicine,* 1972, *209,* 574-582.

Billington, G. F. Play program reduces children's anxiety, speeds recoveries. *Modern Hospital,* 1972, *118,* 90-92.

Binger, C. M., Albin, A. R., Feuerstein, J. H., Kushner, J. H., Zoger, S. & Mikkelsen, C. Childhood leukemia: Emotional impact on patient and family. *New England Journal of Medicine,* 1969, *280,* 411-418.

Bluebond-Langner, M. I know, do you? A study of awareness, communication, and coping in terminally ill children. In B. Schoenberg, A. C. Carr, A. H. Kitscher, D. Peretz & I. K. Goldberg (Eds.). *Anticipating Grief.* New York: Columbia University Press, 1974.

Bonny, H. *Facilitating guided imagery & music sessions.* Baltimore: ICM Publishing, 1978.

Boon, A. R. Tetralogy of fallout: Effect on the family. *British Journal of Preventive & Social Medicine,* 1972, *26,* 263-268.

Boon, R. A. & Roberts, D. F. The social impact of hemophilia. *Journal of Biosocial Science,* 1970, *2,* 237-264.

Boxberger, R. History of the National Association for Music Therapy, Inc. In E. H. Schneider (Ed.), *Music therapy 1962: Proceedings of the National Association of Music Therapy.* Lawrence, KS: National Association for Music Therapy, 1963.

Brown, S., Merkow, A., Weiner, M. & Kahjezadeh, J. Low birth weight in babies born to mothers with sickle cell trait. *Journal of the American Medical Association,* 1972, *221,* 1404-1405.

Buhrmann, M. V. The dying child. *South African Medical Journal,* 1973, *47,* 1114-1116.

Burgert, E. O. Emotional impact of childhood acute leukemia. *Mayo Clinic Proceedings,* 1972, *47,* 273-327.

Burling, K. A. & Collipp, P. J. Emotional responses of hospitalized children. Results of a pulse-monitor study. *Clinical Pediatrics,* 1969, *8,* 641-646.

Byers, R, K. & Lord, S. E. Late effects of lead poisoning on mental development. *American Journal of Disease of Children,* 1943, *66,* 471-494.

Cassell, S. & Paul, M. H. The role of puppet therapy on the emotional responses of children hospitalized for cardiac catheterization. *Journal of Pediatrics,* 1967, *71,* 233-239.

Cecil, R. L. & Loeb, R. F. *A textbook of medicine.* Philadelphia: W. B. Saunders, 1963.

Chetta, H. D. The effect of music and desensitization on pre-operative anxiety in children. *Journal of Music Therapy,* 1981, *18,* 74-87.

Chodorkoff, J. & Whitten, C. F. Intellectual status of children with sickle cell anemia. *Journal of Pediatrics,* 1963, *63,* 29-35.

Connor, F. P. The hemophiliac child in school. *Annals of the New York Academy of Sciences,* 1975, *240,* 238-245.

Cytryn, L., Moore, P., Van, P. & Robinson, M. E. Psychological adjustment of children with cystic fibrosis. In E. J. Anthony & C. Koupernik (Eds.), *The child in his family: The impact of disease and death.* New York: John Wiley, 1973.

Davenport, H. T. & Werry, J. S. The effect of general anesthesia, surgery and hospitalization upon the behavior of children. *American Journal of Orthopsychiatry,* 1970, *40,* 806-824.

Davis, L. *Leukemia: Implications for music therapy.* Unpublished manuscript, Children's Hospital of New Orleans, 1980.

Densmore, F. The use of music in the treatment of the sick by American Indians. In D. I. Schullian & M. Schoen (Eds.), *Music in medicine.* Freeport, NY: Books for Libraries Press, 1948.

Diggs, L. W. & Flowers, E. Sickle cell anemia in the home environment. *Clinical Pediatrics,* 1971, *10,* 697-700.

Diserens, C. & Fine, H. *A psychology of music: The influence of music on behavior.* Princeton, NJ: Princeton University Press, 1969.

Dombro, R. H. & Haas, B. S. The chronically ill child and his family in the hospital. In M. Debruskey (Ed.), *The chronically ill child and his family.* Springfield, IL: Charles C Thomas, 1970.

Drash, A. Obesity and diabetes in childhood. *Journal of the Florida Medical Association,* 1971, *58,* 38-40.

Duckett, C. L. Caring for children with sickle cell anemia. *Children,* May, 1971.

Edwards, D. *Four season's workshop.* Workshop presentation in Chicago, May, 1977.

Engle, M. A., Adams, F. H., Betson, C., DuShane, J., Elliot, L., McNamara, D. G., Rashkind, W. J. & Talner, N. S. Primary prevention of congenital heart disease. *Circulation,* 1970, *41,* A25-A28.

Erickson, F. Stress in the pediatric ward. *Maternal-Child Nursing Journal,* 1972, *1,* 113-116.

Ericksson-Lihr, Z. Special features in allergy in children. *Acta Allergologica,* 1955, *8,* 289-313.

Favre-Gilly, J. Medicosocial aspects of hemophilia. In K. M. Brinkhous (Ed.), *Hemophilia and hemophiloid diseases.* Chapel Hill: University of North Carolina Press, 1957.

Federal Register, August 23, 1977.

Ferris, G. N. Psychiatric considerations in patients receiving cadaveric renal transplants. *Southern Medical Journal,* 1969, *62,* 1482-1484.

Fuery, J. *Case study on music therapy and epilepsy.* Unpublished manuscript, 1981.

Fleming, J. W. The child with sickle cell disease. *American Journal of Nursing,* 1965, *65,* 88-91.

Futterman, E. H. & Hoffman, I. Transient school phobia in a leukemic child. *Journal of the American Academy of Child Psychologists,* 1970, *9,* 477-494.

Gardner, J. E. Behavior therapy treatment approach to a psychogenic seizure case. *Journal of Consulting Psychology,* 1967, *31,* 209-212.

Gardner, W., Licklider, J. C. R. & Weisz, A. Z. Suppression of pain by sound. *Science,* 1960, *132,* 32-33.

Gilbert, J. Music therapy perspectives on death and dying. *Journal of Music Therapy,* 1977, *14*(4), 165-171.

Glaser, H. Psychological aspects of heart disease. In R. Pryor (Ed.), *Heart disease in children* (Public Health Service, Publication No. 1374). Washington: U.S. Government Printing Office, 1966.

Glaser, H. H., Harrison, G. S. & Lynn, D. B. Emotional implications of congenital heart disease in children. *Pediatrics,* 1964, *33,* 367-379.

Goldy, F. B. & Katz, A. H. Social adaptation in hemophilia. *Children,* 1963, *10,* 189-193.

Griffith, E. *Case study on music therapy and diabetes.* Unpublished manuscript, 1981.

Grushkin, C., Lewy, J. E., Cole, E., Holland, N., Lewy, P. & Potter, D. Hemodialysis and renal transplantation in children: The role of the pediatric nephrology team. *Pediatrics,* 1974, *53,* 864-866.

Gyulay, J. *The dying child.* New York: McGraw-Hill, 1978.

Haghbin, M. & Zuelzer, W. W. A. long-term study of cerebrospinal leukemia. *Journal of Pediatrics,* 1965, *67,* 23-28.

Harper, B. C. *Death: The coping mechanism of the health professional.* Southeastern University Press, 1977.

Heimler, A. & Chabot, A. Sickle cell counseling: A children & youth project. *American Journal of Public Health,* 1974, *64,* 995-997.

Heinicke, C. M. & Westheimer, I. *Brief separations.* New York: International University Press, 1965.

Hill, L. F. The child with rheumatic fever. In E. E. Martner (Ed.), *The child with a handicap.* Springfield, IL: Charles C Thomas, 1959.

Hodges, D. A. Appendix A: Physiological responses to music. In D. A. Hodges (Ed.), *Handbook of music psychology.* Lawrence, KS: National Association for Music Therapy, 1980.

Hoffman, I. & Futterman, E. H. Coping with waiting: Psychiatric intervention and study in the waiting room of a pediatric oncology clinic. *Comprehensive Psychiatry,* 1971, *12,* 67-81.

Hoffmann, A. D., Becker, R. D. & Gabriel, H. P. *The hospitalized adolescent.* New York: Free Press, 1967.

Hunt, V. V. *Recreation for handicapped.* Englewood Cliffs, NJ: Prentice-Hall, 1955.

Jenkins, D. & Mellins, R. B. Lead poisoning in children. *Archives of Neuropsychiatry,* 1957, *77,* 70-78.

Johnson, F. *Case study on music therapy with congenital heart disease, nephritis and sickle cell anemia.* Unpublished manuscript, 1981.

Johnson, F. P. & Hatcher, W. The patient with sickle cell disease. *Nursing Forum,* 1974, *13,* 259-288.

Kaplan, D. M., Smith, A. & Grobstein, R. School management of the seriously ill child. *Journal of School Health,* 1974, *44,* 250-254.

Kaplan, D. M., Smith, A., Gobstein, R. & Fischmann, S. E. Family mediation of stress. *Social Work,* 1973, *18,* 60-69.

Kappleman, M. K., Kaplan, E. & Ganter, R. L. A study of learning disorders in disadvantaged children. In S. Chess & A. Thomas (Eds.), *Annual progress in child psychiatry and child development.* New York: Brunner/Mazel, 1970.

Kavanaugh, R. *Facing death.* Los Angeles: Nash Publishing, 1972.

Keating, L. M. A review of the literature on the relationship of epilepsy and intelligence in school children. *Journal of Mental Science,* 1960, *106,* 1042-1059.

Kemph, J. P. Psychotherapy with donors and recipients of kidney transplants. *Seminars in Psychiatry,* 1971, *3,* 145-158.

Kenny, C. B. *The mythic artery: The magic of music therapy.* Atascdero, CA: Ridgeview Publishing, 1982.

Kenny, T. J. The hospitalized child. *Pediatric clinics of North America,* 1975, *22,* 583-593.

Knapp, V. S. & Hansen, H. Helping the parents of children with leukemia. *Social Work,* 1973, *18,* 70-75.

Koch, M. F. & Molnar, G. D. Psychiatric aspects of patients with unstable diabetes mellitus. *Psychosomatic Medicine,* 1974, *36,* 57-68.

Kubler-Ross, E. *On death and dying.* New York: MacMillan, 1969.

Landtman, B. & Valanne, C. Psychosomatic studies of children with congenital heart disease. *Acta Paediatrica,* 1958, *118,* 113-154.

Langford, W. S. The child in the pediatric hospital: Adaptation to illness and hospitalization. *American Journal of Orthopsychiatry,* 1961, *31,* 667-684.

Langford, W. S. Children's reactions to illness and hospitalization. *Feelings and Their Medical Significance,* 1966, April, 3-4.

Lansky, S. B. Childhood leukemia. The child psychiatrist as a member of the oncology team. *Journal of the American Academy of Child Psychiatry.* 1974, *13,* 499-508.

Lascari, A. D. The family and the dying child: A compassionate approach. *Medical Times,* 1969, *97,* 207-215.

Lathom, W. Personal communication, 1982.

Lavine, R., Buchsbaum, M. & Poncy, M. Auditory analgesia: Somato-sensory evoked response and subjective pain rating. *Psychophysiology,* 1976, *13*(2), 140-148.

Leonard, G. *The silent pulse.* New York: E. P. Dutton, 1978.

Licht, S. *Music in medicine,* Boston: New England Conservatory of Music, 1946.

Linde, L. M., Rasof, B., Dunn, O. J. & Rabb, E. Attitudinal factors in congenital heart disease, *Pediatrics,* 1966, *38,* 92-101.

Lin-Fu, J. S. *Lead poisoning in children.* (Children's Bureau Publication No. 452-1967). Washington: U.S. Government Printing Office, 1967.

Livingston, S. & Pauli, L. L. Medical treatment of epilepsy, *Pediatric Annals,* 1973, *2,* 1178-1184.

Locsin, R. The effect of music on the pain of selected post-operative patients. *Journal of Advanced Nursing,* 1981, *6,* 19-25.

Lukens, J. N. & Miles, M. R. Childhood leukemia. Meeting the needs of patient and family. *Missouri Medicine,* 1970, *67,* 236-241.

MacClelland, D. Music in the operating room. *AORN Journal,* 1979, *29,* 252-260.

Marley, L. Case study on music therapy with asthma and hemophilia. Unpublished manuscript, 1982.

Mason, E. A. The hospitalized child: His emotional needs. *The New England Journal of Medicine,* 1965, *272,* 406-414.

Mattsson, A. & Gross S. Adaptation and defensive behavior in young hemophiliacs and their parents. *American Journal of Psychiatry,* 1966, *122,* 1349-1356.

McCarthy, M. Social aspects of treatment in childhood leukemia. *Social Science and Medicine,* 1975, *9,* 263-269.

McCarthy, T. *Asthma: Implications for music therapy.* Unpublished manuscript, Children's Hospital of New Orleans, 1980.

Meigs, J. W. Can occupational health concepts help us deal with childhood lead poisoning? *American Journal of Public Health,* 1972, *62,* 1483-1485.

Melzack, R., Weisz, A. Z. & Sprague, L. T. Stratagems for controlling pain: Contributions of auditory stimulation and suggestion. *Experimental Neurology,* 1963, *8,* 239-247.

Merritt, A. D. Population genetics and hemophilia: Implications of mutation and carrier recognition. *Annals of the New York Academy of Sciences,* 1975, *240,* 121-131.

Munro, S. & Mount, B. Music therapy in palliative care. In I. Ajemain & B. Mount (Eds.), *Royal Victoria Hospital manual on palliative/hospice care.* New York: Arno Press, 1980.

Nagy, M. H. The child's view of death. In H. Feifel (Ed.), *The meaning of death.* New York: McGraw-Hill, 1959.

National Cystic Fibrosis Research Foundation. *Your child and cystic fibrosis.* New York: National Cystic Fibrosis Research Foundation n.d..

Nelson, W. E., Vaughan, V. C. & McKay, R. J. (Eds.). *Textbook of pediatrics.* Philadelphia: W. B. Saunders, 1969.

Novick, R. E. The control of childhood lead poisoning. *U.S. Department of Health, Education & Welfare—Programs for the Handicapped,* 1971, *8,* 1-8.

Olch, D. Effects of hemophilia upon intellectual growth and academic achievement. *Journal of Genetic Psychology,* 1971, *119,* 63-74. (a)

Olch, D. Personality characteristics of hemophiliacs. *Journal of Personality Assessment,* 1971, 35, 72-79. (b)

Orbach, C. E., Sutherland, A. M. & Bozeman, M. F. Psychological impact of cancer and its treatment, III. The adaptation of mothers to the threatened loss of their children through leukemia: Part II. *Cancer,* 1955, *8,* 20-33.

Oswald, N. C., Waller, R. E. & Drinkwater, J. Relationship between breathlessness and anxiety in asthma and bronchitis: A comparative study. *British Medical Journal,* 1970, *2,* 14-17.

Pearson, J. A. & Diamond, L. K. The critically ill child: Sickle cell disease crises and their management. *Pediatrics,* 1971, 629-635.

Petrillo, M. & Sanger, S. *Emotional care of hospitalized children: An environmental approach.* Philadelphia: J. B. Lippincott, 1980.

Pochedly, C. Sickle cell anemia: Recognition and management. *American Journal of Nursing,* 1971, *71,* 1948-1951.

Poinsard, P. J. Psychiatric aspects of hemophilia. In K. M. Brinkhaus (Ed.), *Hemophilia and hemophiloid diseases.* Chapel Hill: University of North Carolina Press, 1957.

Radocy, R. & Boyle, J. D. *Psychological Foundations of Musical Behavior.* Springfield, IL: Charles C Thomas, 1979.

Rantz, J. *Music therapy with terminally ill children: A pilot project.* Presentation at National Conference of the National Association for Music Therapy, Dallas, October 1979.

Reynolds, M. C. & Birch, J. *Teaching exceptional children in all America's schools. A first course for teachers and principals.* Reston, VA: The Council for Exceptional Children, 1977.

Richmond, J. B. & Waisman, H. A. Psychological aspects of management of children with malignant disease. *American Journal of Diseases of Children,* 1955, *89,* 42-47.

Robertson, J. *Hospitals and children: A parent's eye-view. A review of letters from parents to the observer and the B.B.C.* New York: International Universities Press, 1962.

Robinson, S. J. & Gasul, B. M. The child with a congenital heart defect. In E. E. Martner (Ed.), *The child with a handicap.* Springfield, IL: Charles C Thomas, 1959.

Salk, L. Emotional factors in pediatric practice. *Pediatric Annals,* 1974, *3,* 97-98.

Salk, L., Hilgartner, M. & Granich, B. The psychosocial impact of hemophilia on the patient and his family. *Social Science and Medicine,* 1972, *6,* 491-505.

Scarr-Salopatek, S. & Williams, M. L. The effects of early stimulation of low birth weight infants. *Child Development,* 1973, *44*(1), 97-101.

Schiffer, C. G. & Hunt, E. P. *Illness in children.* Data from the National Health Survey. Washington: U.S. Government Printing Office, 1963.

Schoenberg, B., Carr, A. C., Kutscher, A. H., Peretz, D. & Goldberg, I. K. *Anticipatory grief.* New York: Columbia University Press, 1974.

Schowalter, J. E. The child's reaction to his own terminal illness. In B. Schoenberg, A. C. Carr, D. Peretz & A. H. Kutscher (Eds.), *Loss and grief: Psychological management in medical practice.* New York: Columbia University Press, 1970.

Schullian, D. & Schoen, M. (Eds.). *Music and medicine.* Freeport, NY: Books for Libraries Press, 1948.

Schwankovsky, L. *Music therapy in lead poisoning.* Unpublished manuscript, 1981.

Scott, R. B. Health care priority and sickle cell anemia. *Journal of the American Medical Association,* 1970, *214,* 731-734.

Scott, R. B. & Kessler, A. D. *Sickle cell anemia and your child. Questions and answers on sickle cell anemia for parents.* Washington: Howard University College of Medicine, 1971.

Segerberg, O. *Living with death,* New York: E. P. Dutton, 1976.

Shirley, H. F. Meeting the emotional and social needs of children with rheumatic heart disease. *Quarterly Journal of Child Behavior,* 1952, *4,* 289-298.

Shore, M. F., Geiser, R. L. & Wolman, H. M. Constructive uses of a hospital experience. *Children,* 1965, *12,* 3-8.

Smith, J. M. A five-year prospective survey of rural children with asthma and hay fever. *Journal of Allergy,* 1961, *47,* 23-30. (a)

Smith, J. M. Prevalence and natural history of asthma in school children. *British Medical Journal,* 1961, *5227,* 711-713. (b)

Solnit, A. J. Who mourns when a child dies? In E. J. Anthony & C. Koupernik (Eds.), *The child in his family.* New York: John Wiley, 1973.

Spencer, R. F. Psychiatric impairment versus adjustment in hemophilia: Review and five case studies. *Psychiatry in Medicine,* 1971, *2,* 1-12.

Spencer, R. F. & Behar, L. Adaptation in hemophiliac adolescents. *Psychosomatics,* 1969, *10,* 304-309.

Standard, R. L. Sickle cell anemia. A public health problem in the District of Columbia. *Medical Annals of the District of Columbia,* 1972, *41,* 304-305.

Sterky, G. Diabetic school children. *Acta Paediatrica Scandinavica,* 1963, Supplement 144.

Strawczynski, H., Stachewitsch, A., Morgenstern, G. & Shaw, M. E. Delivery of care to hemophiliac children: Home care versus hospitalization. *Pediatrics,* 1973, *51,* 986-991.

Taylor, D. B. Music in general hospital treatment from 1900 to 1950. *Journal of Music Therapy,* 1981, *18*(2), 62-73.

Tetrault, S. M. & Scott, R. B. Recreation and hobbies and developmental supports for a child with sickle cell anemia, *Clinical Pediatrics,* 1974, *13,* 496-497.

Thatcher, L. G. Treatment of acute leukemia in children. *Wisconsin Medical Journal,* 1968, *67,* 530-533.

Thomas, L. A., Milman, D. H. & Rodriques-Torres, R. Anxiety in children with rheumatic fever. Relation to route of prophylaxis. *Journal of the American Medical Association,* 1970, *212,* 2080-2085.

Thompson, R. H. & Stanford, C. *Child life in hospitals, theory and practice.* Springfield, IL: Charles C Thomas, 1981.

Tropauer, A., Franz, M. N. & Dilgard, V. W. Psychological aspects of the care of children with cystic fibrosis. *American Journal of Diseases of Children,* 1970, *119,* 424-432.

Turk, J. Impact of cystic fibrosis on family functioning. *Pediatrics,* 1964, *34,* 67-71.

Vernick, J. & Karon, M. Who'a afraid of death on a leukemia ward? *American Journal of Diseases of Children,* 1965, *109,* 393-397.

Vernon, D. T. A., Foley, J. M., Sipowicz, R. R. & Schulman, J. L. *The psychological responses of children to hospitalization and illness.* Springfield, IL: Charles C Thomas, 1965.

Waechter, E. H. Children's awareness of fatal illness. *American Journal of Nursing*, 1971, *71*, 1168-1172.

White, D. W. Living with hemophilia. *Nursing Outlook*, 1964, *12*, 36-39.

Whitten, C. F. Growth status of children with sickle cell anemia. *American Journal of Diseases of Children*, 1961, *102*, 355-364.

Whitten, C. F. & Fischoff, J. Psychosocial effects of sickle cell disease. *Archives of Internal Medicine*, 1974, *133*, 681-689.

Wilson, G. F. Asthma in school children. *Royal Society of Health Journal*, 1958, *78*, 274-280.

Wolfe, D. Pain rehabilitation and music therapy. *Journal of Music Therapy*, 1978, *5*(4), 162-178.

Wolters, W. H. G. The dying child in the hospital. In E. J. Anthony & C. Koupernik (Eds.), *The child in his family*. New York: John Wiley, 1973.

Wright, L., Schaefer, A. B. & Solomons, G. *Encyclopedia of pediatric psychology*. Baltimore: University Park Press, 1979.

Zander, C. *Cystic fibrosis: Implications for music therapy*. Unpublished manuscript, Children's Hospital of New Orleans, 1980.

Zelig, R. *Children's experience with death*. Springfield, IL: Charles C Thomas, 1974.